AF817550

India and the World

Sanjaya Baru is one of India's most respected economic and political analysts. He has been Chief Editor of major financial newspapers, a media advisor and spokesman of a Prime Minister of India; a professor at important universities and think tanks in New Delhi and Singapore, author of best-selling books, including *Strategic Consequences of India's Economic Performance* (Academic Foundation, 2006) and *The Accidental Prime Minister* (Penguin Viking, 2014). He was till recently Director for Geo-economics and Strategy, International Institute for Strategic Studies, London. He was a member of India's National Security Advisory Board.

India and the World

Essays on Geoeconomics and Foreign Policy

SANJAYA BARU

ACADEMIC FOUNDATION
NEW DELHI

www.academicfoundation.org

First published in 2016
by

ACADEMIC FOUNDATION
4772-73 / 23 Bharat Ram Road, (23 Ansari Road),
Darya Ganj, New Delhi - 110 002 (India).
Phones : 23245001 / 02 / 03 / 04.
Fax : +91-11-23245005.
E-mail : books@academicfoundation.com
www.academicfoundation.org

Disclaimer:
The findings/views/opinions expressed in this book are solely those of the author and do not necessarily reflect the views of the publisher.

© 2016. Sanjaya Baru.

ALL RIGHTS RESERVED.
No part of this book shall be reproduced, stored in a retrieval system, or transmitted by any means, electronic, mechanical, photocopying, recording, or otherwise, without the prior written permission of the copyright holder(s) and/or the publishers.

Cataloging in Publication Data--DK
Courtesy: D.K. Agencies (P) Ltd. <docinfo@dkagencies.com>

India and the world : essays on geoeconomics and foreign policy/
editor, Sanjaya Baru.
pages cm
ISBN 9789332703797

1. India--Foreign economic relations. 2. International economic relations. I. Baru, Sanjaya, editor.

HF1589.I53 2016 DDC 337.54 23

Typeset, printed and bound by The Book Mint, New Delhi.
www.thebookmint.in

CONTENTS

Introduction 9

1. **Shifts and Shocks: Understanding Geoeconomics and Strategy** 13

Post-Cold War Geoeconomics

The Geoeconomics of the Asian Financial Crisis

Geoeconomics of the Trans-Atlantic Financial Crisis

India, G-20 and the G-4

2. **The Geoeconomics of a Multipolar World** 27

The Next, Apart from China

From Geoeconomics to Geopolitics

Structural Shifts and Economic Shocks: Drivers of Strategic Change

Knowledge Power and Demographics

Fiscal Capability of the State

Global Economic Competitiveness

Access to Markets and Natural Resources

3. **India and the Geoeconomics of the Trans-Atlantic Financial Crisis** 45

Policy Impact of the Triple Crises of the 1990s

Closing the Two Gaps

Banking and Finance

Fiscal Policy
India and the Global Slowdown: New Vulnerabilities
Globalisation, Geopolitics and India's Grand Strategy
The Re-hyphenation with Pakistan
The G-2 Challenge
Crisis Management, Regional Stability and Implications for India-US Relations

4. The Economic Imperative to Indian Foreign Policy 81

Planning and Foreign Relations
Non-Alignment and Mixed Economy
The Post-Cold War–Post-Liberalisation Era
Economic Inter-dependence and International Relations
Conclusion

5. The Political Economy of Post Cold War Indian Foreign Policy 99

Impact of Successful External Liberalisation
The United States and Major Powers
India and Immediate Neighbours
Asymmetric Trade Liberalisation
India and Wider Asian Neighbourhood: East Asian Community
South-South Cooperation
New Thinking on Globalisation
Inclusive Globalisation
Challenges to the Manmohan Singh Doctrine

6. Realism in India's Economic Multilateralism. 129

'Realistic Restructuring' of the Bretton Woods Institutions
Hedging its Bets on the Multilateral Trade Regime
The China Syndrome

7. The Influence of Business and Media on Indian Foreign Policy 151

The Influence of Business in Foreign Policy
Track Two Diplomacy
The Influence of Media in Foreign Policy
Conclusion

8. India's Economic Rise and South Asian Integration . . . 173

Indian Sub-continent as an Integrated Economic System
Regional Cooperation and Institution Building in South Asia: P2P, B2B and G2G
SAARC as G2G: Institutions and Iconic Projects/Programmes
Building Blocks of B2B and P2P Cooperation
India as an Opportunity
A Summing Up

9. China and India: Bilateral Economic Relations and the Global Economy 197

Historical Background
From Inward to Outward Orientation
The New Bilateral Economic Relationship
Trade Deficit and Trust Deficit
Managing Competition and Cooperation
Opportunities for Regional Cooperation
The Multilateral System
Conclusion

10. The Geoeconomics of the GCC and Asia 219

The Changing Global Economy
The Gulf and Asia
Gulf Regional and Maritime Security: Role of Asian Powers

Introduction

My interest in the interrelationship between India's economic and foreign policy was stimulated during my tenure at *The Economic Times* and the *Times of India* during the 1990s. In 1998 I was invited by Prime Minister Atal Behari Vajpayee to be a member of a newly created policy advisory group of non-officials and retired officials, the National Security Advisory Board (NSAB). The NSAB was chaired by the guru of Indian grand strategists, the late K. Subrahmanyam, who tasked me to write the chapter on 'economic security' for the first ever *Strategic Defence Review* (SDR) that the NSAB presented the government of the day in 2000. Many of the essays and columns I wrote during that period, and till I joined the government in 2004, were published in my book *Strategic Consequences of India's Economic Performance* (Academic Foundation, 2006).

In his Foreword to that volume, Subrahmanyam drew attention to the book's attempt to present a holistic view of what he dubbed as "the symbiotic relationship between international economics and international strategic developments." Geo-economics is the study of such relationships. A globalised economy, observed Subrahmanyam, "with this degree of interdependence among nations, and in a balance of power strategic system, has not existed before; at least not in the industrial age..... Nor have we a precedent to a world where knowledge will be the currency of power".

The book, *Strategic Consequences of India's Economic Performance*, recorded in detail how India's improving economic performance had become a 'strategic differentiator'; how 'new relations of interdependence' between India and various parts of the world, especially the East and the South-east Asia and the trans-Atlantic economies, had altered India's global strategic environment; and, how India had to complete the unfinished task of investing in the capabilities of its people to be able to realise its full potential as one of the great powers of the world. That book was an essay in geo-economics.

My time in the office of Prime Minister Manmohan Singh as one of his advisors, from 2004 to 2008, enabled me to acquire a more intimate understanding of the inter-relationship between economic and strategic aspects of Indian policy. In my book *The Accidental Prime Minister* (Penguin Viking, 2014), I devoted 4 of its 13 chapters to a discussion of Singh's foreign policy and the underlying economic interests shaping it. Chapter 6 in this volume on the political economy of Indian foreign policy elaborates that theme.

I left the government on the eve of what I call the 'Trans-Atlantic Financial Crisis' of 2008, which has since opened a new era in international power relations. Months after the collapse of Lehman Brothers, in September 2008, I wrote an essay on the likely geopolitical consequences of the financial crisis, drawing attention to increased economic interdependence between China and the US and the geopolitical implications of China's economic rise. Over the past eight years I have had the opportunity to explore many of these ideas in greater depth. My tenure as the director for geoeconomics and strategy at the International Institute for Strategic Studies (London), gave me opportunities to discuss these ideas relating to economic performance and shifts in global balance of power with a wide range of scholars, practitioners and business leaders. Many of the essays in this volume have been presented at various conferences and published in various edited volumes.

The first chapter offers a summary view of the early writing on geoeconomics and what constitutes its terrain today. In chapter 2 we discuss how economic performance of nations is shaping the geoeconomic and geopolitical balance of power in the post-Cold War era. Chapter 3 was written in the immediate aftermath of the trans-Atlantic financial crisis and considers its geopolitical implications. Chapters 4 and 5 offer an analysis of Indian foreign policy from a geoeconomics perspective. Chapter 6 draws attention to the differing perspectives within India on multilateralism, while chapter 7 analyses the role of business and media in shaping Indian foreign policy. Chapters 8 and 9 discuss in some detail India's economic relations with her immediate neighbours. Chapter 10 focuses on the changing geoeconomics of the GCC and Asia. The reader will find some repetition among chapters since these essays were written as stand alone papers for different audiences. I have not deleted the repetition so that each chapter can in fact be read as a stand alone essay.

By bringing these essays together I hope to offer the reader a better understanding of the geoeconomics of the post-Cold War period and its relevance for Indian foreign policy. It is now commonplace for geopolitical analysts to describe the evolving balance of power system as one characterised by 'multi-polarity'—several centres of power—as opposed to the 'bipolarity' of the Cold War era and the 'unipolar' moment that followed the collapse of the Soviet Union. I believe the foundation of the emerging multipolar world is constituted by the differential economic performance of various nations. The relative economic decline of the West and the 'Rise of the Rest', especially the newly industrialising economies of the east Asia and the Indo-Pacific region, including Japan, China, South Korea, Taiwan, the Association of South East Asian Nations (ASEAN), and India, has enabled 'rising economies' to become 'rising powers' because their newly acquired economic and fiscal capacity is allowing them to invest in the infrastructure of 'hard power'.

While conflict today continues to be caused by a variety of historical and longstanding issues and grievances, the balance of power between nations will, in the final analysis, be determined by the investment nations make in the acquisition and deployment of knowledge, economic capacity and human capability. These essays seek to reinforce that point.

1

Shifts and Shocks

Understanding Geoeconomics and Strategy

Geoeconomics may be defined in two different ways: as the relationship between economic policy and change and national power and geopolitics, or, as the economic consequence of geopolitical trends and national power. Both the notion of "trade follows the flag"—that there are economic consequences of the projection of national power—and 'the flag follows trade'—that there are geopolitical consequences of essentially economic phenomenon—would constitute the subject matter of geoeconomics.

Either way, the intellectual roots of geoeconomics are embedded in the 17th century European, largely French, 'mercantilism'. The military pursuit of markets, resources and bullion for a country to be able to 'export more and import less', 'buy cheap and sell dear' preceded the advent of modern economics based on ideas of free trade and laissez-faire. While the 19th century was dominated by these ideas of 'classical political economy', mercantilism was never buried and has repeatedly raised its head, in inter-war Europe of the 1920s and the 1930s and most recently in China.[1] In the 1980s, the rise of Japan elicited mercantilist responses from Europe and the United States based on fears that Japan had in fact risen on the back of mercantilism. More recently, the crises in Europe and North America have revived latent mercantilism, with many accusing Germany and the US of pursuing a mercantilist agenda.

In the post-war era, from 1950 to 1990, international economics and politics were marked by a conflict between the ideas of free trade and liberal democracy, on the one hand, and those of *etatism* and

1. For a discussion on mercantilism and geopolitics see Findlay and O'Rourke, 2007.

authoritarianism on the other, with a few countries experimenting a mix of the two; some mixing liberal democracy with state capitalism (like India) and others mixing free enterprise with military or one-party rule (like the 'Asian Tigers' and many Latin American countries).

However, the dominant paradigm in this period, the Cold War era, was one in which politics remained in command and geopolitics was driven by ideological rather than purely economic factors. It is, therefore, not a coincidence that the three most important ideas defining contemporary geoeconomics were all articulated at the time when the Cold War was on the verge of ending or had just ended and a new era of economic rivalry between nations was inaugurated.

The first important articulation of the contemporary geopolitical consequences of post-War economic trends was Paul Kennedy's study of *The rise and fall of Great Powers* (1987) that put forward the thesis of imperial overstretch, drawing attention to the fiscal and other economic limits on national power and its projection. Its prescient character is under scored by the fact that it was written at a time when the Cold War had not yet formally ended. As Kennedy put it:

> ...all of the major shifts in the world's *military-power* balances have followed alterations in the productive balances; and further, that the rising and falling of the various empires and states in the international system has been confirmed by the outcomes of the major Great Power wars, where **victory has always gone to the side with the greatest material resources.** (*italics in the original, bold ours.*)

The second important articulation of the idea of 'geoeconomics' was the 1990 essay of Edward Luttwak, "From Geopolitics to Geoeconomics: Logic of Conflict, Grammar of Commerce". Observed Luttwak:

> Everyone, it appears, now agrees that the methods of commerce are displacing military methods—with disposable capital in lieu of firepower, civilian innovation in lieu of military-technical advancement, and market penetration in lieu of garrisons and bases. States, as spatial entities structured to jealously delimit their own territories, will not disappear but reorient themselves toward

> geoeconomics in order to compensate for their decaying geopolitical roles. ......'geoeconomics' is the best term I can think of to describe the admixture of the logic of conflict with the methods of commerce.

It was an argument that drew attention to the nascent neo-mercantilism of the Cold War era, especially on the part of Japan and the architects of the European Common Market (ECM) that began to worry the United States. The 'logic of conflict' in the 'methods of commerce' was not visible in the statecraft of either the decaying Soviet Union or the as yet dormant China. Rather, it was seen in the aggressive export-led growth models of Japan and the Asian Tigers, and in the creation of the ECM.

A more forthright articulation of this view was made by the third intervention in 1993 of Samuel Huntington. His essay, "Why International Primacy Matters", extending Daniel Bell's (1990) assertion that "economics is the continuation of war by other means," set out a bold hypothesis:

> In the coming years, the principal conflict of interests involving the United States and the major powers are likely to be over economic issues. US economic primacy is now being challenged by Japan and is likely to be challenged in the future by Europe. Obviously the United States, Japan and Europe have common interests in promoting economic development and international trade. They also, however, have deeply conflicting interests over the distribution of the benefits and costs of economic growth and the distribution of the costs of economic stagnation or decline. The idea that economics is primarily a non-zero sum game is a favourite conceit of tenured academics. ..... Economists are blind to the fact that economic activity is a source of power, as well as well being. It is, indeed, probably the most important source of power and in a world in which military conflict between major states is unlikely economic power will be increasingly important in determining the primacy or subordination of states.
>
> In the realm of military competition, the instruments of power are missiles, planes, warships, bombs, tanks and divisions. In the realm of economic competition, the instruments of power are productive efficiency, market control, trade surplus, strong currency, foreign exchange reserves, ownership of foreign companies, factories and technology.

The end of the Cold War coinciding with the rise of a new Japan shaped the view that a new era of geoeconomics was upon us.[2]

Post-Cold War Geoeconomics

The implosion of the Soviet Union was in itself the most important 'geoeconomic' phenomenon of the post-War period. Long before the Soviet Union actually dissolved itself the economic basis for its dissolution was laid as the Russian economy began to falter. Few analysts actually predicted the dissolution of the Soviet Union, and even as late as 1987 Kennedy summed up his analysis of the paradox of Soviet economic decline and military build up thus:

> This does *not* mean that the USSR is close to collapse, any more than it should be viewed as a country of almost supernatural strength. It *does* mean that it is facing awkward choices .... It is to be expected that the efforts and exhortations to improve the Russian economy will intensify. But since it is highly unlikely that even an energetic regime in Moscow would either abandon 'scientific socialism' in order to boost the economy or drastically cut the burdens of defense expenditures and thereby affect the military core of the Soviet state, the prospects of an escape from the contradictions which the USSR faces are not good.[3] (italics in original.)

While few appreciated the inevitable geopolitical consequences of Russian economic decline, political fears related to Japan's economic rise now appear exaggerated. Huntington in fact theorised on what he called the "Japanese strategy of economic power maximisation", identifying five sources of such power: (i) producer dominance—opting for economic power over well-being; (ii) industry targeting —building manufacturing capability and capacity both for a home and an export market, with a focus on strategic, high-technology and high value-added industries; (iii) market shares over profits —a deliberate strategy to invest in losses for the sake of ultimate domination of an industry'; (iv) import restriction—placing curbs on imports and inward foreign direct investment; and, (v) sustained

2. See, for example, Thirlwell, 2010 (accessed at: *http://www.lowyinstitute.org/Publication.asp?pid=1388);* Soilen, 2010; Ward and Hoff, 2007.
3. Kennedy (1987: 513).

surplus—building foreign exchange reserves through sustained trade surplus and by intervening in currency markets with the intention of maintaining a strong currency.

Given his pre-occupation with culture and the 'conflict' between 'civilisations' it was not surprising that Huntington took a dim and worrisome view of Japan's rise. Huntington quotes Sony's co-founder Akio Morita as saying, "We are going to have totally new configuration in the balance of power in the world. The time will never again come when America will regain its strength in industry." Japan was seen in the late 1980s as China has come to be in the late 2000s—the 'neo-mercantilist' and 'geoeconomic' power of the day.

Europe responded to Japan's 'geoeconomic' challenge with the creation of the European 'Single Market'. Paollo Cecchini's (1988) report on the "Costs of Non-Europe" was written against the background of Japan's growing competitiveness and the European fear of losing global market shares to Japanese and US firms.

Interestingly, notwithstanding its rise as a major economic power, the world's second largest economy, Japan did not emerge as a 'geoeconomic' power, having failed to convert its new economic clout into military and political power. Thus, a Japanese initiative to stitch together a new regional grouping, the East Asian Economic Group (EAEG), canvassed vigorously by Malaysia on behalf of Japan, failed to take off. In 1995 Japan made a concerted bid to secure the leadership of the International Monetary Fund (IMF), sponsoring the candidature of the governor of the bank of Japan, Toyoo Gyohten and failed. It followed this up with the idea of creating an Asian Monetary Fund (AMF) and that too was rebuffed.

While in 1988-1990 Japan was viewed as a new challenger to Europe and the US, by the mid-1990s it was clear that Japan was still unable to convert its economic power into geopolitical power. As Thirlwell (2010: 10) put it, "Japan's challenge was fading fast. And as the supposed competitive threat from Japan started to recede, so did the attractions of geoeconomics".

German reunification, also a consequence of the end of the Cold War, had geoeconomic consequences in terms of the expansion of the European Union and a surge towards greater economic and monetary integration within the EU. However, because of Germany's preoccupation with the management of that reunification, there were limited geopolitical consequences as far as Germany itself was concerned. Rather, the focus was on EU's geoeconomic and geopolitical role in world affairs. This contrasts with what is happening now, with Europe's fiscal crisis offering Germany greater geopolitical space. We return to this idea later.

The Geoeconomics of the Asian Financial Crisis

The really important geoeconomic event of the post- Cold war period was the 'Asian financial crisis' of 1997-98. That crisis began in Thailand in the summer of 1997 with speculative attacks on the Thai Baht. Within months it engulfed several South-east Asian and East Asian economies including Indonesia and South Korea. While the IMF responded in a predictable manner, as it did in Latin America, Russia and India in the early 1990s, China stepped in to offer support and subsequently leverage its geoeconomic power. Thus, China's first step was to extend a line of credit to Thailand to enable it to defend the Thai Baht. After an overnight offer of a billion dollars to Thailand, China provided an additional US$3.5 through the IMF to other Asian economies. In following months China ensured that the Renminbi remained a rock solid currency, with no change in exchange rate even as almost all other Asian currencies devalued.

Summing up China's actions during the crisis, the Chinese foreign ministry claimed:

> To ease off the financial crisis, the Chinese Government adopted a series of pro-active policies. They included: It actively participated in the IMF-organized aid projects for some Asian countries. In the wake of the financial crisis in 1997, the Chinese Government provided Thailand and other Asian countries with over 4 billion US dollars in aid, within the framework of IMF or through bilateral channels. It offered Indonesia and other countries export credit and emergency medicine given gratis. The Chinese Government, with a high sense of responsibility, decided not to devaluate its Renminbi in the overall interest of maintaining stability and development in the region. It did so under huge pressure and at a big price. But it contributed

considerably to the financial and economic stability and to the development in Asia in particular and the world at large.

While sticking to its non-devaluation policy, the Chinese Government adopted the policy of boosting domestic demand and stimulating economic growth. This policy played an important role in ensuring a healthy and stable economic growth at home, easing the pressure on the Asian economy and leading it into recovery. China actively participated in and encouraged regional and international financial cooperation together with the relevant parties.[4]

A payments crisis was followed by a banking and financial crisis that was in turn followed by an economic slowdown that had internal political consequences for the countries involved and geo-political consequences for Asia as a whole.[5] China emerged as a major exporting power with the 'rest of the world' but as an 'importing power' in Asia. Altering the so-called "Flying Geese" pattern of export led industrialisation in Asia, China became an exporter to the West, North America and Europe, and an importer within Asia—of goods, resources, technology and capital.[6]

By the time China entered the World Trade Organization (WTO) in 2001, with US support, it had already become a major trading nation and a geoeconomic power. The subsequent decade has seen China emerging as a resources guzzler with its own geopolitical consequences.[7] The Asian financial crisis, therefore, contributed to China's rise as the original 'Asian tigers' faltered and the region's laggard economies became increasingly dependent on the Chinese economy both for their exports and imports, as well as for external financial assistance.

---

4. Ministry of Foreign Affairs (2000).
5. For a detailed discussion of the geoeconomics and geo-politics of the Asian financial crisis see Chapter 30, "The Asian Economic Crisis and India's External Economic Relations", in Baru, 2007.
6. For a discussion of China's rising profile as a trading power in its neighbourhood see Chapter 38, "India, China and the Asian Neighbourhood: Issues in External Trade and Foreign Policy" in Baru (2007).
7. For a discussion of the geoeconomics of China's resources strategy in Africa see Raine, 2009.

Geoeconomics of the Trans-Atlantic Financial Crisis

While the Asian financial crisis consolidated China's power in Asia, the trans-Atlantic financial crisis has had the effect of consolidating Chinese power globally, though it has not led to a new bipolarity referred to as G-2.[8] The restructuring of the share-holding of multilateral financial institutions, especially the IMF, the creation of a new regional architecture in Asia through the Chiang Mai Initiative Multilateration (CMIM) and the creation of an Asian bond market, all have enhanced China's economic power globally.

If China was the geopolitical beneficiary of the Asian financial crisis, Germany has emerged as the geopolitical beneficiary of the European debt crisis. Germany has deployed its economic and financial power in Europe to acquire political power there of a kind that it has not enjoyed in a long time. Kundnani (2001) summed it up succinctly:

> The concept of geoeconomics now seems particularly helpful as a way of describing the foreign policy of Germany, which has become more willing to impose its economic preferences on others within the European Union in the context of a discourse of zero—sum competition between the fiscally responsible and the fiscally irresponsible. For example, instead of accepting a moderate increase in inflation, which could harm the global competitiveness of its exports, Germany has insisted on austerity throughout the eurozone, even though this undermines the ability of states on the periphery to grow and threatens the overall cohesion of the European Union. In Luttwak's terms, Germany is applying the methods of commerce within a logic of conflict.

While some may dispute this view of German policy in the Eurozone, both China and Germany have deployed exchange rate policy as a means to enhance their geoeconomic power. China's consistent undervaluation of the Yuan, which has been widely viewed as a mercantilist intervention, is not very different in its impact on the competitiveness of its trade partners in Asia than that of German policy on the Euro. Implicit in China's and Germany's exchange rate

8. Baru (2009).

policy is a 'beggar-my-neighbour' strategy that has helped both the countries generate high current account surplus, while shifting the burden of adjustment to neighbouring economies.

Both China and Germany appear to have succeeded where Japan failed, namely, convert their economic clout into regional political influence, if not as yet global influence. Both have made good use of a regional financial and economic crisis to shift the regional balance of power in their favour. In doing so, they have also shifted the global balance of power in their favour. They are the geoeconomic powers of our times.

India, G-20 and G-4

In the new world of multiple partnerships new clubs of the willing can, however, prevent any one power, or even two, acquire hegemonic status. The facile view that while Britain was the hegemonic power of the 19th century and the US of the 20th, China would acquire that status in the 21st is blind to the geoeconomics of multi polarity. The post-2008 view that the global unipolar moment of the post-Cold War period would now be replaced by a new G-2 condominium between the US and China was a premature assessment of changing power equations both within the Rest and in the West.[9]

Even as the US grapples with a sullen Russia and a rising China, the coming together of Brazil, Germany, India and Japan to form a G-4, seeking membership of the United Nations Security Council (UNSC) opens new alliance possibilities in regions such as the Indo-Pacific (India and Japan) and the Indo-Atlantic (Brazil, India and EU). The G-4 may not yet achieve their immediate objective of securing permanent membership of UNSC, but there is much that they can do to underscore the urgency of reforming an outdated, antediluvian global governance system.

Each of the four countries have a global profile and are corner stones of regional security in their respective regions. They play an important role in other multilateral forums and organisations, and

9. Bergsten (2008).

have contributed more to global and regional peace, security and development than some of the existing permanent members, the P-5.

Whatever the reasons for the G-4 initiative to have lost steam since its first launch over a decade ago, each of the four countries have new reasons to come together and assert their global relevance. Germany has been embattled within Europe since 2009, Japan has been under Chinese pressure, Brazil's economy has lost momentum just before it *hosts* the Olympic Games and India is seeking to regain momentum both economically and geopolitically after the wasted second term of the Manmohan Singh government.

The case for G-4 is easily made. There is no reason at all why the so-called victors of the Second World War—(*'so-called' because the contribution of Gaullist France* and *Communist China to the defeat of fascism is a bit overstated*) should retain veto powers in the organisation of global security in a world so changed. That point can be and has been made by several countries and many of them seek membership of the UNSC with equal vehemence. If the G-4 have chosen to come together and make their case, how can anyone object?

Will they succeed? No harm trying. Does India weaken its case by aligning with the G-4? Nonsense. China's argument that it would support India if it were to break ranks with Japan; and, the US argument that it has no problem with India's candidature but remains conflicted on Germany over Italy and on Brazil over Mexico, are all 'divide-and-rule' tactics and have to be exposed as such. None of the P-5 have given cast iron guarantees to India that they would get India into the UNSC if it abandons the G-4. So, the argument that the G-4 route weakens India's case is a red herring.

The G-4 ought to include an African nation and, it could be argued, also an Islamic nation. The case for an African nation is easily made and the African group at the United Nations (UN) has sought timeout till the group comes to a consensus on which country it wishes to support. South Africa has weakened its case under its present leadership and both Nigeria and Egypt have an equally strong case. Egypt is also an Islamic nation and one of the founder-leaders of the non-aligned movement.

In considering the utility of G-4 for India one must, however, look beyond the UNSC. The post-Cold War 21st century world is increasingly defined by multiple partnerships between major and medium powers. Moreover, individual major powers have not hesitated to form like-minded groups and 'coalitions of the willing', primarily in pursuit of their own interests and, secondarily, the interests of the group. Consider some examples.

Russia took the initiative to create an association of countries—Brazil, Russia, India, China (BRIC) and China invited South Africa to form BRICS. Both Russia and China have used BRICS to leverage their own geopolitical and geoeconomic interests in partnership with emerging economies Brazil, India and South Africa. One negative consequence of BRICS has been that Brazil and South Africa have not found time for the forum of the countries—India, Brazil, South Africa (IBSA)—the alliance of the third world democracies.

On its part, China created the Shanghai Cooperation Organisation (SCO) to pursue its own geopolitical and geoeconomic interests in Eurasia. The United States has not hesitated to created mega-regional trade groups, the Trans-Pacific Partnership (TPP) and the Trans-Atlantic Trade and Investment Partnership (TTIP) to deal with the trade threat from China. Diplomats and analysts will debate forever on the usefulness of these and other such associations, groups, alliances and partnerships. Some succeed in attaining their objectives, many fail. Yet, more are getting created.

The world of many Gs may run the risk of becoming a world of G-Zero, 'a leaderless world', to use a phrase coined by strategic affairs analyst Ian Bremmer (2011). But why should India, excluded from the board rooms, so to speak, of so many post-war multilateral institutions worry?

For India, G-4 also has another relevance. As a resources-deficient, capital deficit and technology importing economy, India can gain from closer relations with Japan, Germany and Brazil. It may serve India well to engage them on a wider set of issues including trade, climate change, migration, intellectual property rights and technology transfer, regional security, terrorism and so on and so forth, even if to keep the pot boiling.

References

Baru, Sanjaya (2007). "The Asian Economic Crisis and India's External Economic Relations', in *Strategic Consequences of India's Economic Performance*. New Delhi: Academic Foundation and London: Routledge.

———. (2009). "India: Rising through the Slowdown", in Ashley J. Tellis, Andrew Marble and Travis Tanner (eds.), *Strategic Asia 2009–10: Economic Meltdown and Geopolitical Stability*. Seattle, US: National Bureau of Asian Research. Accessed at: *http://www.nbr.org/publications/issue.aspx?id=186*Bell, Daniel (1990) 'Germany: The Enduring Fear,' Dissent, Vol. 37 (Fall).

Bergsten, Fred (1999). *Do Sanctions Work?*". Text of Lecture at the Indian Council for Research on International Economic Relations (ICRIER), 11 March. Available at *www.icrier.org*

———. (2008). "A Partnership of Equals", *Foreign Affairs*, July-August. Accessed at: *https://www.foreignaffairs.com/articles/asia/2008-06-01/partnership-equals*

Bremmer, Ian (2011). "A G Zero World", *Foreign Affairs*, March-April. Accessed at: *https://www.foreignaffairs.com/articles/2011-01-31/g-zero-world*

Cecchini, Paolo (1998). *The European Challenge, 1992: The Benefits of the Single Market*. Wildwood House.

Ferguson, Niall (2001). *The Cash Nexus: Money and Power in the Modern World, 1700-2000*. Allen Lane and The Penguin Press.

Findlay, Ronald and Kevin H. O'Rourke (2007). *Power and Plenty: Trade, War and the World Economy in the Second Millennium*. Princeton: Princeton University Press.

Gagné, Jean-François (2007). "Geopolitics in a Post-Cold War Context: From Geo-Strategic to Geoeconomic Considerations?", *Occasional Paper* No 15. Raoul Dandurand Chair of Strategic and Diplomatic Studies, University of Québe.

Garten, Jeffrey E. (1993). *A Cold Peace: America, Japan, Germany, and the Struggle for Supremacy*. United States: The Twentieth Century Fund.

Hamilton, Alexander (1928). *Industrial and Commercial Correspondence of Alexander Hamilton: Anticipating His Report on Manufactures*. Chicago: A. W. Shaw Company.

Huntington, Samuel P. (1993). "Why International Primacy Matters", *International Security* 18(4).

Inan, Sukru (2005). "Geoeconomic Policies for Regional Development: Turkey as a Catalyst for Eastern Europe", *Ekonomika*. Available at: *http://www.leidykla.vu.lt/fileadmin/Ekonomika/2005_69/30-45.pdf*

Kapstein, Ethan B. and Michael Mastanduno (eds.) (1999). *Unipolar Politics: Realism and State Strategies after the Cold War*. New York: Columbia University Press.

Kennedy, Paul (1987). *The Rise and Fall of the Great Powers: Economic Change and Military Conflict From 1500 to 2000*. New York: Random House. p.439.

Kindleberger, Charles P. (1996) *World Economic Primacy*. New York: Oxford University Press.

Krasner, Stephen D. (1991). "State Power and the Structure of International Trade", in Jeffrey A. Frieden and David A. Lake (eds.), *International Political Economy*. New York: St. Martin's Press.

Kundnani, Hans (2001). "Germany as a Geoeconomic Power", *The Washington Quarterly* (Summer): 41. Accessed at: *http://www.twq.com/11summer/docs/11summer_Kundnani.pdf*

List, Friedrich (1904). *The National System of Political Economy*. London, New York, Bombay: Longmans & Green.

Luttwak, Edward (1990). "From Geopolitical to Geoeconomics, Logic of Conflict, Grammar of Commerce", *The National Interest* 20: 17-24.

———. (1993). "The Coming Global War for Economic Power: There are No Nice Guys on the Battlefield of Geoeconomics", *The International Economy* 7(5).

———. (2012). *The Rise of China vs. the Logic of Strategy.* Belknap Press.

Ministry of Foreign Affairs (2000). "Pro-Active Policies by China in Response to Asian Financial Crisis", 17 November. Beijing. Accessed at: *http://www.fmprc.gov.cn/eng/ziliao/3602/3604/t18037.htm*

O'Loughlin, John and Luc Anselin (1996). "Geoeconomic Competition and Trade Bloc Formation: United States, German, and Japanese Exports 1968-1992", *Economic Geography* 72(2) (April): 131-60.

Raine, Sarah (2009). *China's African Challenges.* IISS Adelphi paper. Routledge.

Soilen, Klaus Solberg (2010). *The Shift from Geopolitics to Geoeconomics and the Failure of our Modern Social Sciences*, Electronic Research Archive of Blekinge Institute of Technology. *http://www.bth.se/fou/*

Sparke, Matthew (2007) "Geopolitical Fear, Geoeconomic Hope and the Responsibilities of Geography", *Annals of the Association of American Geographers* 97(2): 338-49.

Thirlwell, Mark P. (2010) *The Return of Geoeconomics: Globalisation and National Security.* Lowy Institute for International Policy, September.

Waltz, Kenneth N. (1993). "The Emerging Structure of International Politics", *International Security* 18(2) (Fall): 75-76.

Ward, Michael D. and Peter D. Hoff (2008). "Analyzing Dependencies in Geoeconomics and Geopolitics", in Jacques Fontanel and Manas Chatterji (eds.), *War, Peace and Security* (Contributions to Conflict Management, Peace Economics and Development, Volume 6). Emerald Group Publishing Limited. pp.133-60

World Economic Forum (2012). *Global Risks 2012.* Geneva.

2

The Geoeconomics of a Multipolar World

Since the turn of the century, the attention of geoeconomists and geopolitical analysts has been riveted on China's spectacular economic rise. In the shadow of the 2008-09 trans-Atlantic financial crisis and against the backdrop of the 'global imbalance' (that the United States-China relationship came to represent), analysts even entertained the possibility of a G-2 condominium between the US and China, both jointly managing world affairs.[1] More recently it has been suggested, by economist Joseph Stiglitz (2015) and perhaps appropriately in *Vanity Fair*, that just as the 19th century was Great Britain's and the 20th of the US, the 21st would be a Chinese Century.

In their understandable focus on China's economic rise geopolitical analysts often miss the wider process of the rise of several nations across Asia and Latin America. While the game at present may appear as a race between the West and China, the fact is that the West has for some time now been dealing with the challenge of "*The Rise of the Rest*". That was Alice Amsden's (2001) thesis in a classic written at the turn of the century in which she examined the more generalised rise of a group of 'emerging economies'. Amsden's chosen dozen 'non-western' economies that were rising through industrialisation included—Argentina, Brazil, Chile, China, India, Indonesia, Malaysia, Mexico, South Korea, Taiwan, Thailand and Turkey.

Given this list it is understandable that China became the cynosure of all geopolitical eyes not only because the Latin American countries listed here failed to meet the expectations they generated

1. Bergstein (2008).

in the 1970s and 1980s, but also because China dwarfed all other Asian economies after the Asian financial crisis of 1997-98. The question still arises: whether China's more recent spurt can be taken as evidence of the entire century being China's? While capturing the impressiveness of China's rapid rise, this view of understanding the global order misses the fact, that the 19th Century was Britain's because it managed to build and run a global empire on which the sun never set, and, the US emerged a global power through the 20th century by building military alliances with powerful nations around the world including the ones it defeated, Japan and Germany. China has neither an empire nor such powerful military allies and, as of now, does not appear anywhere near acquiring either. Hence, it is premature to refer to the 21st century as China's. What it seems destined to be, however, is Asia's.

The Next, Apart from China

In the 1970s the 'economies of the future', so to speak, were assumed to be the rapidly rising economies of Latin America, especially Argentina and Brazil. In the 1980s, the West's attention was focused on 'the threat from Japan' in response to which Europe embarked on the Single Market project.[2] With Latin American economies being overtaken by East Asian economies and with Japan slowing down, Amsden's 'Rest' narrowed down to mainly Asian economies, especially China.

However, given that many of the 'Rest' continued to pursue industrialisation and have sought to 'catch up' with the West, they have found themselves in competition with China. The newly industrialising economies of Asia, Africa and Latin America see in China's rise as 'the factory of the world' a new challenge to their own 'catch up' process.

Amsden's message, that there are many other nations on the rise, has been echoed recently in Deepak Nayyar's (2013) important study of this 'catch up' phenomenon and global development. Nayyar's central thesis is that several developing economies are contributing

2. Cecchini et al (1988).

to a convergence in the levels of development between the West and the Rest by pursuing a set of policies aimed at promoting local industrialisation. In doing so they are all seeking a share of the global space for industrial growth.

Nayyar's *catch up* is a hopeful account of the vanguard role of 14 developing economies—The Next 14 or 'The Nayyar 14'—contributing to a "dramatic transformation" in the structure of world output within a span of four decades, 1970–2010.[3] The 'Nayyar 14' are Argentina, Brazil, Chile, Mexico (in Latin America), China (including Hong Kong), India, Indonesia, Malaysia, South Korea, Taiwan, Thailand and Turkey in Asia and Egypt and South Africa in Africa, marginally different from Amsden's 'Next 12'. Nayyar offers detailed data on structural shifts in industrial production and world trade to make three basic points: first, the shift of the global economic balance towards the 'Rest' is now irreversible; second, most of the growth of the 'Rest' is centred in Asia, running eastwards from India to the Pacific, with China at the core; third, the decline of the West is largely on account of Europe's loss of competitiveness.

There are few shared attributes between the 'Nayyar 14'. Some are democracies, some autocracies, some one-party states. Some have followed inward-oriented import-substituting industrialisation, others have pursued export-oriented growth. Some have become heavily dependent on state-financed industrialisation, while some others have opted for private sector and even foreign-funded industrial development. While the differences are many what is common to all of them, especially in the last quarter of the 20th Century, is their focused pursuit of industrialisation and foreign trade, albeit with varying degrees of success.

Nayyar cautions us that the 'Next 14' are mainly in Asia and that it is really the rise of East Asia, and subsequently South-east Asia and India. This has shaped Amsden's view of an East-West structural shift in the locus of global economic activity. The process, however, is nascent. Even China has some distance to go and the others have even longer journeys ahead. Economic growth and

3. Nayyar (2013: 124).

increased competitiveness of their manufacturing sectors has to get translated into human development and ecologically and socially sustainable development. However, for any real shift in the global balance of power from the West to the 'Rest', so to speak, the shift in the weight of economic activity has to be followed by a similar shift in defence spending and military capability. It is the translation of economic power into military power that would convert multipolar geoeconomics into multipolar geopolitics.

From Geoeconomics to Geopolitics

The long-term nature of China's rise was historically contextualised by the seminal statistical work of historian Angus Maddison on structural changes in the world economy.[4] Based on time series data spanning a millennium put together by Maddison and his World Economy project a variety of geoeconomic arguments have been put forward about the decline and the rise of Asia and the rise and decline of the West. The key statistic that has become the backbone of considerable theorising on both geopolitical and geoeconomic change has been the data on changing shares of world national income and trade of Europe, US, China and India. Maddison showed how at the beginning of the 19th century China and India accounted for almost half world income, while the combined share of Europe and the US was just about a quarter of world income. By the middle of the 20th century, the combined share of Europe and the US was more than half of world income, while China and India together accounted for less than 10 per cent. Thus, the resurgence of China and India (continental and civilisational nations) it may be argued, stands apart from that of most other emerging economies. However, in recognising the primacy of China and India among the 'Rest' one should not ignore the importance of other Asian, African and Latin American economies in altering geoeconomic and geopolitical equations.

4. Angus Maddison's original monograph was titled *Monitoring the World Economy 1820-1992* and was published by the Development Centre of the Organisation for Economic Co-operation and Development, Paris, in January 1995 . This and his subsequent work is available at *www.theworldeconomy.org*

The rise of the 'Rest' is, after all, not just an economic phenomenon. It has geopolitical implications. Already China's rise has impacted international relations and institutions in Asia and globally. In focusing only on this we miss the geopolitical relevance of the rise of the 'Rest'. The global economic shift has also contributed to changing political alliances between the West and others among the 'Rest'. New political equations have emerged and are shaping the global 'rules of the game' with respect to trade, environment and intellectual property protection. "It is essential to recognize" says Nayyar, "that the significance of developing countries in the world would be shaped not only in the sphere of economics but also in the sphere of politics."[5]

Indeed, apart from the other rising economies of Asia, Africa and Latin America that Amsden and Nayyar identify as the new poles of economic activity, other major powers like Russia, Japan and Germany are bound to assert their political role globally. In his classic treatise *Arthashastra*, Kautilya famously suggested "From the strength of the treasury, the army is born."[6]

Thus, if the dispersal in economic activity is accompanied by a complementary shift in defence spending and military capability there would be a shift in the global balance of power in real terms. Such a shift would create multiple centres of power, and, in a balance of power system prevent any one power from asserting its global role. In short, the rise of the 'Rest' has the potential to create a multipolar global balance of power system in which the US, EU, Russia, China, India and Japan may emerge as dominant powers but no one should under estimate the margin for manoeuvre that other powers from among the 'Rest' will seek and retain. As Nayyar observes, "the outcome, fifty years later, is likely to be a multipolar world in which dominance might not be so striking."[7]

However, such a shift in military balances is not yet upon us. As the International Institute of Strategic Studies (IISS) on the Military

5. Nayyar (2013: 184).

6. Kautilya, *Arthashastra* ,

7. Nayyar (2013: 185).

Balance has recorded that the defence spending of the Rest is rising sharply, and faster than that of the West. Moreover Asia as a whole now spends more on defence than member countries of National Atlantic Treaty Organisation (NATO). But, the US has a defence budget that is larger than that of the next ten powers taken together (China, Russia, Saudi Arabia, UK, India, France, Japan, Germany, South Korea and Brazil).[8] China has emerged as the second biggest spender and is rapidly increasing its defence budget and capability. Even though China's defence budget is still just a quarter of the US, the geopolitical impact of its rising defence spending, a consequence of its geoeconomic rise, is already being felt in Asia.[9]

If the West wishes to prevent a return to a 'bipolar' system with China replacing the former Soviet Union as the other pole, it should in fact invest in the growth of parallel centres of prosperity and of power across the globe. It is in the interests of the West that democracies like Brazil, India, Indonesia and South Africa emerge as independent centres of economic activity and political assertion so that no one country like China can in fact challenge it. The pursuit of such supportive multilateralism may benefit countries that the West is not particularly inclined to support, like Iran and Russia, but it is in the interests of all, that a more dispersed multipolar balance of power system emerges at the global level than the one in which the dominance of one set of powers is replaced by another.

While the idea of a G-2 condominium may be seductive to some and the appeal of a China containment strategy may induce others to push the 'Rest' to make an 'us-or-them' choice between the US and China, the wiser strategy would indeed be to promote the development of the 'Rest'. This will imply a change of US-EU strategy in the management of international economic institutions. Rather than continue to keep the 'Rest' outside the boards of management of multilateral institutions, while creating new mega-regional blocs, it would be wiser for the West to share power with the Rest and democratise the management of global institutions. The fear that

8. International Institute of Strategic Studies (2016).

9. See Chapters 1 and 6 in International Institute of Strategic Studies (2016).

power would slip away from the West to the East, or from the US to China, is highly exaggerated. The others, among the 'Rest', would never allow the global system to move from one unipolarity to another, nor would other rising powers wish to return to another bipolar world. If the growth processes of the past half century, analysed by Nayyar, persist into the next, the global balance of power system would indeed be characterised by multipolarity.

For all the reasons, cited above, the global balance of geoeconomic power is likely to move in the direction of multipolarity, rather than bipolarity or a new unipolarity centred around China. The notion that China's geoeconomic rise will mimic that of the United States in the 20th Century and, therefore, China would establish its 'economic dominance' is an idea that is neither informed by history nor the nature of power in the international system. In his analysis of China's economic rise, economist Arvind Subramanian (2011) draws a parallel between Great Britain's 'economic dominance' in the 19th century, US economic dominance in the 20th and the emerging Chinese economic dominance in the 21st based on a set of economic indicators like a country's share in world income, trade and net capital flows. Based on these and other such economic indicators, Subramanian jumps to the conclusion that just as the US and the Dollar replaced Britain and the Pound Sterling after Britain ceded its global economic dominance to the US, so too China and the Yuan replaced the US and the Dollar, asserting China's global economic dominance.

What is missed in this economic determinist argument is an understanding of the nature of global power and dominance. Britain did not become 'great' merely because of its economic dominance. It did so by acquiring colonies and establishing a global empire through the deployment of military power. While the US did not acquire 'colonies', its power in fact grew during the era of decolonisation, it acquired 'allies' and through the alliances it maintained and through the assertion of its military power it acquired access to markets and resources and thereby ensured its global economic dominance.

China has neither colonies, unless one regards Tibet and Xinjiang as colonies, nor has it important military alliances that would enable it to acquire the kind of control over markets and resources that

Great Britain and the US have enjoyed in turn as dominant global powers. There is no doubt that China is a major geoeconomic power. However, it remains to be seen if it can translate its economic power into geopolitical power and dominance.

Structural Shifts and Economic Shocks: Drivers of Strategic Change

The rise of China and indeed of other newly industrialising economies of Asia, as well as the rise of other 'Emerging Economies, denotes a 'structural shift' in the locus of growth in the world economy.[10] This constitutes an enduring geoeconomic shift that has already had and will continue to have geopolitical consequences, with attendant political risks and opportunities. This 'structural shift' must, however, be distinguished from 'economic shocks', like a financial crisis or an energy shock, that can have their own geoeconomic consequences, sometimes accelerating the underlining structural shifts, sometimes slowing them down. This is the central thesis of our argument. Any analysis of the geopolitical consequences of economic change and the economic consequences of geopolitical trends and events must make a distinction between long-term shifts and short-term shocks, even as one recognises and takes account of the impact of one on the other.[11]

Thus, China's economic rise is undoubtedly a long-term shift in the global economy that would be impacted by economic shocks such as a global debt crisis or an energy shock. The impact of economic 'shocks' on structural 'shifts' may be benign for some countries and malign for others. An oil shock would hurt China and India while benefitting Russia and Iran, but while it may slow down the rise of China and India, it is unlikely to alter the fact that the long-term global shift is in fact in favour of China and India compared to Russia and Iran.

The reason for this is that the 'structural' or 'institutional' factors that have contributed to what are now very clearly long-term

10. See Chapter 9 of the present volume and Nayyar, 2013.

11. On the idea and estimation of such long-term shifts see Maddison (2011).

structural 'shifts' in the global economy are more enduring than the factors contributing to random economic shocks. There are at least four such factors that have come to define the geoeconomics of the post-Cold War period. They are: knowledge power and demographic transition; fiscal capacity of the state; global economic competitiveness; control over natural resources; and these may be called the geoeconomic 'drivers' of strategic change.

Knowledge Power and Demographics

After the Second World War and in the context of the end of the 'Empire', Winston Churchill famously told a Harvard University audience that the "empires of the future are the empires of the mind", highlighting not just the strategic importance of values and ideas, but of education and the investment in science and technology. Cutting edge knowledge in modern science offered a strategic advantage to the victors of the war. Knowledge, that is human capability, is the single most important attribute of power in the modern world.

In a policy note to Jawaharlal Nehru, the Chicago economist Milton Friedman wrote in 1955, when he was visiting India as an advisor to India's Planning Commission: "The great untapped resource of technical and scientific knowledge available to India for the taking is the economic equivalent of the untapped continent available to the United States 150 years ago." The US remains a technology leader and has retained the capacity to generate new technologies using immigrant skilled labour and reaching out to developing country allies to widen its Research and Development R&D base. Few other developed or emerging powers have this kind of capability. Hence, while the US will remain a technology leader, it is likely that other countries like China and India will emerge as new technology developers. The shifting geography of technological change is yet another geoeconomic driver of strategic change.

Since a nation's knowledge power is embedded in its people, long-term demographic shifts can alter the dynamics of knowledge power and have both geoeconomic and geopolitical consequences. The decline of Japanese power, *vis-a-vis* China for example, is writ into its demographic structure. So also the rise of India. Long-term demographic shifts, if accompanied by investment in human capabilities, can shift the production possibility frontier of economies in decisive ways.

One way in which nations on the wrong side of the demographic shift can mitigate its consequences would be through being open to in-migration of talent and skilled labour. The US has greatly benefitted from such in-migration of human talent and labour. In Germany, Chancellor Angela Merkel's approach to migration seems informed by its potential benefits for an ageing society. However, less pluralistic and open societies may be at a disadvantage. Japan has lost momentum partly on account of its cultural inhibition to in-migration. Prime Minister Shinzo Abe has been trying to address this problem by seeking in-migration of talent from friendly Asian nations like India.

The rise of China and India is in large part a consequence of the combination of a demographic shift and investment in human capability. Transient economic shocks need not necessarily reverse the long-term shifts underway as a consequence of these demographic trends. One of the findings of centre for strategic and International Studies (CSIS) reveals that the median age in most Western, especially European and North American, countries is rising and will be above 40 by 2030.[12] Some countries, including Asian nations like Japan and South Korea, will see the median age of their population rise above 50 by 2030. Many developing countries, especially China and even more so India, will have a much younger population. A key conclusion of the study is that: "In the developed world, the transformation will have sweeping economic, social, and political consequences that could undermine the ability of the United States and its traditional allies to maintain security." On the other hand, among developing countries this transformation will have "more varied consequences—propelling some countries toward greater prosperity and stability, while giving rise to dangerous new security threats in others."

Taken together, these geoeconomic trends will alter the global distribution of power. Four different outcomes are likely:

12. Centre for Strategic & International Studies (2008).

(i) Developed countries that are open to immigration and can develop technologies that mitigate the impact of working population decline, like the US, will be much less impacted.
(ii) Developed countries that are socially conservative and discourage immigration, while at the same time, are incapable of developing technological solutions to the problem of declining population, will experience a loss of power.
(iii) Developing countries that experience a baby boom without a commensurate increase in economic growth and employment opportunities, like many Asian and African nations, will experience domestic social and political strife.
(iv) Developing countries that are able to generate income and employment will increase their share of world income and trade. China falls into this category and so would India.

The geo-political weight of the 2nd and the 3rd category countries will decline, while that of the 1st and the 4th category will increase. National governments can and will adopt policies to adapt to mitigate the impact of this demographic shift. The logic of demographics can be altered by proactive migration policies, just as they can be altered by new technologies.

Fiscal Capability of the State

Apart from its impact on a country's productivity demographic transition will also impact the fiscal capacity of nation. Ageing societies become less fiscally flexible. Even the most modern and dynamic economy requires an effective government, that has adequate financial and human resources at its command—that will then enable it to project power. That is: the translation of development into power requires the mediation of an effective and efficient state.[13]

The foundation of such a state system is built on its fiscal capacity. As the ancient Indian strategist Kautilya wrote, "From the strength of the treasury the army is born."[14] The fiscal empowerment of the State,

13. Ferguson (2001).

14. Kautilya, *Arthasastra* (circa 400 BC). This is an idea that informs Kennedy's theory of 'imperial overstretch' and Ferguson's hypothesis about the 'square of power' in Ferguson (2001).

a consequence of high growth and improved governance, creates the fiscal resources required; both for welfare and infrastructure spending and for building technological and military capability. This too is a long-term phenomenon.

A combination of demographic change and rising welfare expenditure in many developed countries is constraining state capacity to invest in defence. Weak fiscal management has forced many developed country governments to adopt fiscal stabilisation policies with a consequent impact on defence spending and power projection. Clearly, then, fiscal constraint is emerging as an important geoeconomic driver of strategic change.

Predatory and rent extracting states may be able to easily amass the resources required for war effort and projection of power, but this is not a sustainable strategy. On the other hand, as a country's national income grows bigger and economic capabilities improve on a long-term and sustainable basis, its ability to garner resources required to acquire and project power also grows. Thus, China's sustained economic growth has generated the resources required to fund a larger and larger defence budget. On the other hand, economic incapacity contributed to the implosion of the Soviet Union, whose low productivity economy was weighed down by the burden of high defence spending.

The construction of a nation's fiscal capacity is a structural shift that can be temporarily reversed by economic shocks; but if the economy is big and productive enough it would have the resilience to bounce back and continue to generate higher incomes and high rates of saving and investment.

Global Economic Competitiveness

Nothing illustrates the geoeconomic potential of economic competitiveness better than the rise of Asia in the second of the 20th century, culminating in the rise of the two Asian giants, China and India. It is neither through colonialism nor through the establishment of military alliances that Asian economies have been able to increase their share of world income and trade. They have done this by establishing economically competitive industries and services. It is by adhering to the 'rules of the multilateral game'; observing the disciplines of the General Agreement on Trade and Tariffs (GATT) and the World Trade Organisation (WTO)—that Asia's newly industrialising economies have enhanced their geoeconomic power and potential. Increasing share of world trade is one way of measuring the competitiveness of an economy. However, one could also argue that increasing ability to ensure import substitution, while adhering to the discipline of the 'rules of the game' of multilateral trading system, and localising production of goods and services also contributes to a nation's geoeconomic power and potential.

Developing countries that have not been able to improve their competitiveness and developed economies that have not been able to retain theirs have yielded space to these 'emerging economies', some of whom are also 'rising powers.'

Access to Markets and Natural Resources

The acquisition of markets and resources, whether 'trade follows the flag' or 'the flag follows trade'—has been an important geoeconomic driver of strategic change. In the post-War period, the United States provided leadership for the creation of an open global trading regime through the GATT. Immediately after the end of the Cold War a new multilateral trading regime was put in place, again under US and EU leadership but with the participation of emerging economies in the form of the World Trade Organisation. However, after the successful completion of the Uruguay Round, the WTO has been unable to launch a new round, called the Doha Development Round, because of the growing clout of new trading nations, especially China and India.

The WTO's *World Trade Report 2013* has discussed at length what has been termed as the new "balance of power in the multilateral trading system" resulting from the rise of these new trading powers. Unable to secure an outcome of its liking from the Doha Round, as a consequence of the rise of new trading powers, the US is trying to step out of the existing multilateral system and launch two new plurilateral initiatives—TPP and the TTIP.

Edward Luttwak (2012) views these initiatives as an attempt at what may be termed as the 'geoeconomic containment' of China However, it is more than that. By excluding not just China but the BRICS as a whole, TPP and TTIP may well serve to contain the rise of emerging powers, which is why they have responded with Regional Comprehensive Economic Partnership (RCEP). From the days when trade has followed the Flag, the search for markets has been a geoeconomic driver of strategic change.

The search for markets and resources, including energy, has been an important geoeconomic driver of strategic change. Here too, new technologies can mitigate the importance of traditional resources, (for example, shale gas, solar energy and other energy sources are likely to reduce the strategic importance of oil) but control over resources—minerals, oil, gas, water, food—is the essence of the geography of power. The geoeconomics of resources explains to a great extent the geo-politics of the modern world. In resource rich regions, while the players change, the motives endure. Yesterday it was Europe in Africa, in South America, in the Antarctic; today it is Asia, China, Japan and India that seek resources. In the Gulf, the US may well yield space to China and India as security providers as these two Asian economies become the dominant consumers of Gulf energy.

Here again demographics plays a role. New markets are being created in regions with younger populations, like Asia and Africa. Many of these economies are resource constrained. Hence their eagerness to use national power to acquire resources. The race for resources will emerge as an important source of tension between emerging powers as well as between developed economies and emerging powers.

Each of the four factors we have outlined above is an important determinant of geoeconomic and geopolitical power of a country. These are, however, long-term structural factors and there can be year to year fluctuations in the ability of countries to address these challenges. Long-term projections of national power will have to be based on likely trends in each of these phenomenon. Analysts at the China Academy of Military Sciences have long sought to measure 'Comprehensive National Power' based on such geoeconomic phenomenon as domestic economic capability, scientific and technological capability, social development, government capability and so on.[15]

While being mindful of such long-term shifts, the analysis of economic and political power and risk must at any point in time be based on the near term ability of nations to deal with economic shocks that could have an impact on these long-term trends. A financial or fiscal crisis can have serious implications for long-term growth and comprehensive national power. The Asian and the trans-Atlantic financial crises, as well as the European debt crisis, were 'economic shocks' that have had the effect of either accelerating or decelerating the long-term 'structural shifts' underway. An energy shock today, in the event of a war in the Gulf, would have a similar impact on national capabilities.

In trying to understand the interplay between economic and political risk one must make a distinction between the risk of structural shifts that are predictable and against which nations can seek insurance through planned policy intervention; and the risk of economic shocks that may be less amenable to planned policy intervention.

In its analysis of 'Global Risks 2012' the World Economic Forum (2012) lists five different types of risks—economic, environmental, geopolitical, societal and technological It is easy to see that not all are risks of the same type from a policy and time perspective. In the short run, policy intervention can deal with certain types of risks and not others.

Thus, Europe can formulate a policy response to its debt crisis, but can do very little to offset the likely impact of the demographic transition. A 'water supply crisis', which is ranked as the fifth most important global challenge, after 'severe income disparity', 'chronic fiscal imbalances', 'rising greenhouse gases' and 'cyber attacks' is not as easily addressed in the short-term as the other top four sources of risk. Further, the ability of governments to deal with one risk is

15. See Chapter 3 "Conceptualising Economic Security" in Baru (2006: 76).

contingent upon its ability to deal with another. Thus, 'chronic fiscal imbalances' can be more easily addressed if governments have the political mandate and will to redress 'severe income disparities'.

Nowhere is the interplay between political and economic risk more obvious than in national policy. Governments faced with economic challenges at home constantly weigh the political pros and cons of various policy options. In the end, it is the dynamics of power that shapes choice. In international affairs too there are similar choices to be made. Political choices, like a military attack on Iran, has economic consequences, like an increase in oil prices. Germany's ability and willingness to step in and help Greece is as much a function of the economic costs of such an intervention as of the political costs and the geo-political consequences. Geoeconomics impinges upon geopolitics as much as economics impinges upon politics.

Power is as much a function of prosperity as prosperity is a function of power. There can be episodic disengagement between the two. That is, a country may be able to exercise or project more political or military power than is warranted by its true economic capability. The Soviet Union of the 1970s is a good example. Similarly, a prosperous country may be able to exercise influence in excess of its military and geopolitical power. Japan of the 1980s is a good example. Neither has been able to sustain this imbalance between economic and political power because they lacked the four elements of geoeconomic power.

References

Amsden, Alice (2001). *The Rise of the Rest: Challenges to the West from Late Industrialising Economies.* Oxford, UK: Oxford University Press.

Baru, Sanjaya (2006). "The Asian Economic Crisis and India's External Economic Relations", in *Strategic Consequences of India's Economic Performance*. Delhi: Academic Foundation.

Bergstein, Fred (2008). "A Partnership of Equals: How Washington Should Respond to China's Economic Challenge", *Foreign Affairs*, July-August. Accessed at: *https://www.foreignaffairs.com/articles/asia/2008-06-01/partnership-equals*

Cecchini, Paolo, Michael Catinat and Alex Jacquemin (1988). *The European Challenge, 1992: The Benefits of a Single Market.* Gower.

Centre for Strategic & International Studies (2008). *The Graying of Great Powers*. Washington DC. Accessed at: *http://csis.org/files/media/csis/pubs/080630_gai_majorfindings.pdf*

Ferguson, Niall (2001). *The Cash Nexus: Money and Power in the Modern World, 1700-2000.* Allen Lane The Penguin Press.

International Institute of Strategic Studies (2016). *The Military Balance 2016.* Chapter 2. February London: Routledge.

Luttwak, Edward (2012). *The Rise of China vs the Logic of Strategy.* US: The Belknap Press, Harvard University.

Maddison, Angus (2011). *The World Economy: A Millennial Perspective.* Paris: OECD.

Nayyar, Deepak (2013). *Catch Up: Developing Countries in the World Economy.* UK: Oxford University Press

Stiglitz, Joseph (2015). "The Chinese Century", *Vanity Fair*, January. Accessed at: *http://www.vanityfair.com/news/2015/01/china-worlds-largest-economy*

Subaramanian, Arvind (2011). *Eclipse: Living in the Shadow of China's Economic Dominance.* Washington DC: Peterson Institute for International Economics, PIIE Press. p.44.

World Economic Forum (2012). *Global Risks 2012*. Geneva.

An earlier version of this chapter was published in *Survival*, Aug-Sept 2015. Accessed at: *https://www.iiss.org/en/publications/survival/sections/2015-1e95/survival--global-politics-and-strategy-august-september-2015-c6ba/57-4-11-baru-re-b3de*

3

India and the Geoeconomics of the Trans-Atlantic Financial Crisis

The fiscal, trade, industrial, financial and banking sector reform that India undertook in the early 1990s helped her weather the consequences of the 'Asian financial crisis' in the late 1990s. India undertook further reforms and economic policy initiatives to overcome the impact of economic sanctions imposed on it by some developed countries in response to the nuclear tests conducted in the summer of 1998, following which India declared itself a 'nuclear weapons power'. Consequently, India's economic growth rate did not decline as sharply as that of the East and the South-east Asian economies in the late 1990s (See Figure 3.1).

Figure 3.1

Impact of Asian Financial Crisis on India's Real GDP Growth

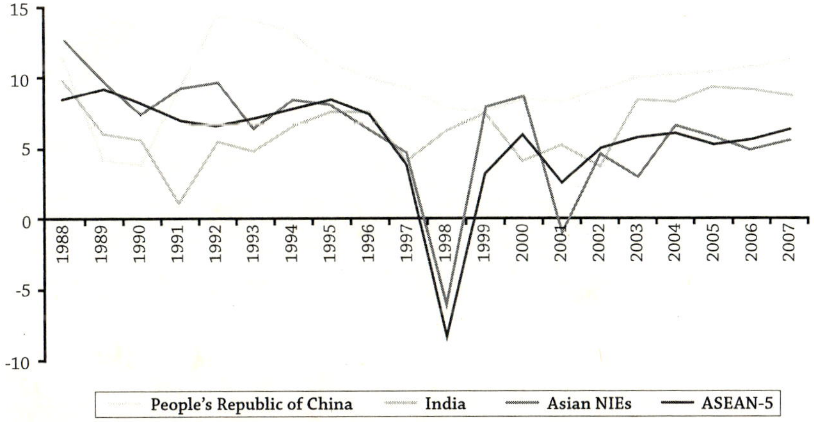

Source: Asian Development Bank (2008: 36), Figure 2.4.

While India survived the initial impact of the trans-Atlantic financial crisis in 2008-09 despite being a more open and globally integrated economy, it did finally feel the impact of the global slowdown.

The Indian economy is on a long-term path of accelerating economic growth. Maddison's (2011) study funded by the Organisation for Economic Cooperation and Development (OECD), of historical trends in the national income of major world economies shows that at the beginning of the 18th century Europe, China and India had more or less equal shares of world GDP and the two Asian economies have been recovering their lost space, albeit at a different pace, over the past half century (Figure 3.2).

Figure 3.2

Historical Trends in Distribution of World Income

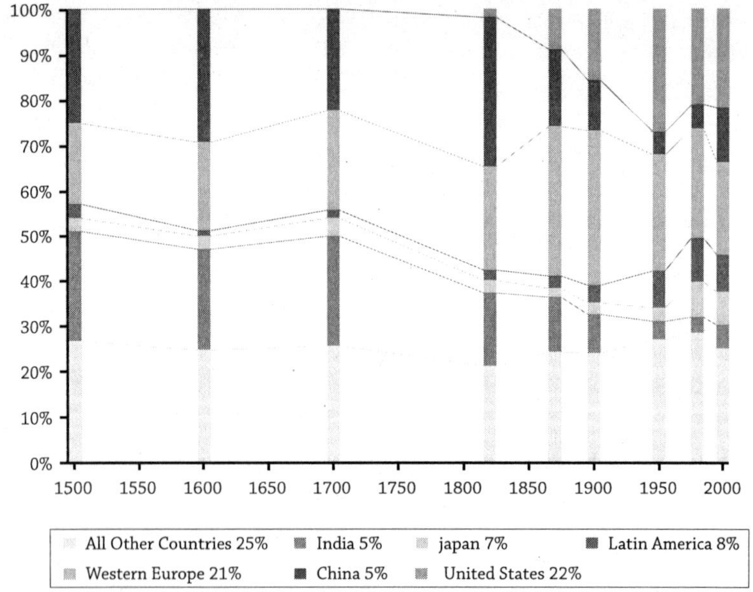

Source: Maddison 2001.

The Indian economy has grown at an annual average of 3.5 per cent in 1950-1980, close to 6.0 per cent in 1980-2004 and at close to 9.0 per cent since 2004 (Figure 3.3).

Figure 3.3

Trends in GDP Growth: 1952-2009

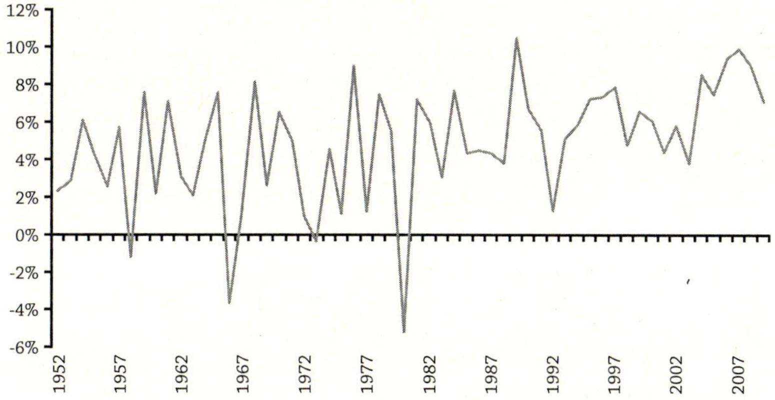

Source: Economic Advisory Council to Prime Minister, Government of India, March 2009.

India's more recent growth acceleration, since the early 1990s, has followed a shift in the macroeconomic policy framework, with greater external and internal economic liberalisation. India's economic rise, as a 'free market democracy', and her reintegration into the global economy, creating new relationships of interdependence both globally and regionally, has shaped her strategic and foreign policies.[1]

Policy Impact of the Triple Crises of the 1990s

India's management of the 'triple crises'-fiscal, balance of payments and financial crises—experienced sequentially between the late 1980s and the mid 1990s, set the stage for India's response to the Asian and, more recently, the 'trans-Atlantic' financial crises.

First came the fiscal crises of the 1990s. Responding to an unsustainable rise in budgetary and fiscal deficits, India adopted a fiscal stabilisation programme, subsequently enacting a Fiscal Responsibility and Budget Management Act, ensuring a reduction in revenue and fiscal deficits. However, the recent fiscal stimulus packages put in place in response to the current slowdown have forced the Government to breach the provisions of the Fiscal Responsibility and Budget Management Act (FRBM).

1. Baru 2006.

Second came an external payments crisis in 1991. India has since undertaken transformative changes in her trade, tariffs and foreign investment policies. These have helped improve India's external economic profile, including a reduction in external debt to GDP ratios, an increase in trade/GDP and foreign investment/GDP ratios, and, most importantly, enabled India to accumulate foreign currency reserves. India's increased openness to global trade and capital flows has, however, increased her vulnerability to global crises and recession.

Third came the financial sector crisis of the early 1990s, which included a stock market crash and problems in the banking sector. India has since undertaken comprehensive financial sector reforms; put in place a world class regulatory and supervisory system for the equities market and the financial and banking sectors and recapitalised banks and improved their asset position.

While undertaking these internal reforms, India opted for gradualism in external sector liberalisation, adopting full currency convertibility only on the current account and eschewing it on the capital account. The cumulative impact of the reforms undertaken since 1991 has been to make the Indian economy more resilient to external shocks, and at the same time more open to external flows, enabling India to sustain an acceleration of her economic growth within a more open economy framework.

India's low inflation tolerance (the average rate of inflation for fifty years, 1950-2000, has been around 8.0%) has meant that fiscal and monetary policies have been largely conservative, with brief episodes of high inflation and fiscal laxity. It was the easing up of this fiscal conservatism that contributed to the 1990 crisis. Though India returned to a more conservative approach in fiscal policy, the current crisis has forced the government to adopt a liberal fiscal stance.[2]

In his authoritative review of India's new economic policies Panagariya (2008) concludes, "India has had a history of maintaining a relatively stable macroeconomic environment, ...", and says of India's external sector management in recent years, "The judicious

2. See Joshi and Little 1994.

handling of the monetary and exchange rate policies must be largely credited with price stability in the domestic market and a broadly competitive exchange rate that facilitated a healthy growth of international trade."[3]

In short, India's experience with handling the triple economic crises it confronted in the early 1990s has helped put in place a regime of policies that have contributed to an acceleration of economic growth and a strengthening of the Indian economy. This has helped India deal with the current slowdown with a greater degree of confidence.

Closing the Two Gaps

In the past, India's growth process has been constrained by what economists referred to as the 'two gaps'—a domestic savings gap and an external financing gap. Rising domestic savings and increased inflow of foreign capital have helped bridge both gaps, contributing to higher growth. For a long time India's savings rate was below 20 per cent, even as East and South-east Asian economies saw their savings rates exceed 30%. In the 1990s India caught up. India's more recent growth acceleration has been facilitated by a sharp rise in the savings and investment rates (See Table 3.1).

Traditionally India had bridged the 'external gap' through foreign aid and concessional debt. However, after 1991 India reduced its dependence on aid and debt flows, and has allowed private capital flows to bridge the gap. The share of foreign investment in India's GDP has gone up and foreign capital inflows have increased on account of higher remittances from overseas Indians (See Table 3.2 and Table 3.3).

Following the Asian financial crisis and, more importantly, after facing economic sanctions, in the wake of the 1998 nuclear tests, imposed (among others) by the United States and Japan, India chose to accumulate foreign exchange reserves as a hedge against risk of currency shortage. This explains the sustained rise in foreign currency assets since 2000 (Table 3.3).

3. Panagariya 2008: 207.

Table 3.1

Growth Rate of GDP, and Investment and Savings Rates

Financial Year	GDP Growth	Investment/GDP	Savings/GDP
	%	%	%
2000-01	4.4	24.3	23.7
2001-02	5.8	22.8	23.5
2002-03	3.8	25.2	26.3
2003-04	8.5	28.2	29.8
2004-05	7.5	32.2	31.7
2005-06	9.5	35.5	34.3
2006-07	9.7	35.9	35.6
2007-08 QE	9.0	37.4	37.8
2008-09 AE	7.1	35.5	35.9

Note: QE = quick estimate; AE = advance estimate.

Source: Prime Minister's Economic Advisory Council, Govt. of India 2009.

Table 3.2

External Economy Indicators

Financial Year	Foreign Investment/ GDP (%)	Foreign Investment/ Exports (%)	Import Cover of Foreign Exchange Reserves (Months)
1990-91	0.0	0.6	2.5
1995-96	1.4	14.9	6.0
2000-01	1.5	14.9	8.8
2005-06	2.6	20.3	11.6
2007-08	5.2	38.8	15.0

Source: Reserve Bank of India Database.

The share of external trade in India's national income has doubled since 1991 (Table 3.4). India's trade/GDP ratio, at over 33 per cent, is higher than that of the US (around 25%). While increased trade dependence has made India more vulnerable to external shocks, her relatively low export dependence compared to other newly industrializing economies in Asia (China's trade/GDP ratio is close to 80%) has helped to limit the negative impact of a global slowdown.

Table 3.3

Foreign Investment and Income Flows into India

Financial Year	*Foreign Direct Investment (US$Mn)*	*Portfolio Investment (US$Mn)*	*Total Foreign Investment (US$Mn)*	*Net Private Income Transfers (US$Bn)*	*Foreign Currency Assets (US$Bn)*
1990-91	97	6	103	2.07	2.24
1995-96	2144	2748	4892	8.51	20.81
2000-01	4029	2760	6789	12.85	39.55
2005-06	8961	12492	21453	24.46	145.11
2007-08P	32435	29395	61830	40.78	299.23

Note: P = Provisional.

Source: Reserve Bank of India Database.

Table 3.4

Trends in Trade/GDP Ratio

Financial Year	*Exports/GDP*	*Imports/GDP*	*X+M/GDP*
1980-81	6.2	9.8	16.0
1985-86	5.6	8.5	14.1
1990-91	7.3	9.9	17.2
1995-96	11.2	14.5	25.7
2000-01	13.0	14.7	27.7
2007-08	13.5	21.2	34.7

Source: *Economic Survey* (Various Issues), Ministry of Finance, Govt. of India.

Table 3.5

Trends in External Debt Indicators

Financial Year	*Debt Stock-GDP Ratio*	*Debt-Service Ratio*	*Short-term Debt to Total Debt Ratio*
1990-91	28.7	35.3	10.3
1995-96	27.1	24.3	5.2
1999-00	22.0	16.0	4.1
2005-06	17.2	9.9	14.1
2007-08	18.8	5.4	20.0

Source: Reserve Bank of India Database at *www.rbi.org.in*

The policy of ensuring reduced dependence on external debt flows has, therefore, been accompanied by a policy of increased openness to investment and income inflows (Table 3.5). In response to the current global slowdown India has further liberalised her foreign investment rules to attract increased capital flows. Inward remittances of income earned by Indian workers abroad, especially in the Persian Gulf region, have increased in importance as a source of foreign currency earnings for India. Nearly 3.5 million Indians work in the member-countries of the GCCt. They send home monthly remittances which constitute a bulk of the US$40 billion that India received in 2007-08, and the US$55 billion it is estimated to receive in 2008-09 (Table 3.6). The slowdown of economic activity in the Middle East could result in a decline in such repatriated incomes. This is an important concern for India's balance of payments management.

India is also concerned about a decline in the number of H1B visa holders in the US, since many of them would also be repatriating some part of their income to families based in India. The downside of the high profile skilled manpower and services exports from India is an increased exposure to the risk of a global slowdown in demand.

Increased openness and external integration have made the Indian economy more efficient, increasing India's share in world trade from 0.5 per cent in 1991 to over 1.0 per cent by 2008. India has also been able to draw on foreign savings. However, for these very reasons, the current global slowdown could be expected to have a higher negative impact on India's economic growth compared to the Asian crisis of 1997-98 or earlier episodes of global recession.

Already India's trade deficit and current account deficit have gone up, and India has had to draw down its foreign exchange reserves defending the rupee, which has depreciated against the dollar by close to 30 per cent in the past year, with a sharp fall in February 2009.

From a national security perspective it is relevant to note that India's policy of external economic liberalisation after 1991 has focused on increasing non-debt inflows, including foreign equity and inward private remittances. India has never pursued a mercantilist trade policy. Rather, it has always run a trade deficit that has been financed by inflows on the capital account. These inflows have contributed to an accumulation of foreign currency reserves.

Table 3.6

India's Balance of Payments

	2004-05 R	*2005-06 PR*	*2006-07 (P)*	*2007-08 (P)*	*2008-09*		
					H1	*H2*	*year*
Merchandise Exports	85.2	105.2	127.1	158.5	96.7	86.1	182.9
Merchandise Imports	118.9	157.0	192.0	248.5	165.9	137.7	303.6
Merchandise Trade Balance	-33.7	-51.8	-64.9	-90.1	-69.2	-51.6	-120.7
	-4.8%	-6.4%	-7.1%	-7.7%	-11.5%	-8.6%	-10.1
Net Invisibles	31.2	42.7	55.3	72.7	46.9	51.1	97.9
o/w Software & BPO	14.7	24.6	31.2	37.0	22.2	25.0	47
Private Remittances	20.5	24.1	27.9	40.8	25.8	29.5	55.3
Investment Income	-4.1	-4.9	-6.0	-5.2	-1.6	-4.5	-6.1
Current Account Balance	-2.5	-9.2	-9.6	-17.40	-22.3	-0.5	-22.9
	-0.4%	*-1.1%*	*-1.0%*	*-1.5%*	*-3.7%*	*-0.1%*	*-1.9%*
Foreign Investment	13.0	17.2	15.5	44.8	9.0	2.7	11.8
o/w FDI (net)	3.7	4.7	8.5	15.5	14.6	3.0	17.6
Portfolio capital	9.3	12.5	7.1	29.3	-5.5	-0.3	-5.8
Loans	10.9	6.1	24.5	42.0	7.3	-14.3	-6.9
Banking capital	3.9	1.4	1.9	11.8	4.8	-0.4	4.4
Capital Account Balance	28	23.4	45.8	108.0	19.9	-9.9	10.0
	4.0%	*2.9%*	*5.0%*	*9.2%*	*-3.3%*	*-1.7%*	*0.7%*
Errors & Omissions	0.6	0.8	0.6	1.5	-0.1	0.0	-0.1
Accretion to Reserves	26.2	15.1	36.6	92.2	-2.5	-10.5	-13.0
	3.7%	*1.9%*	*4.0%*	*7.9%*	*-0.4%*	*-1.7%*	*-1.1%*

Note: BPO = business process outsourcing; P = Provisional. Figures in italics denote percentage of GDP.

Source: Economic Advisory Council to Prime Minister (2009).

Figure 3.4

Nominal Exchange Rate of Indian Rupee

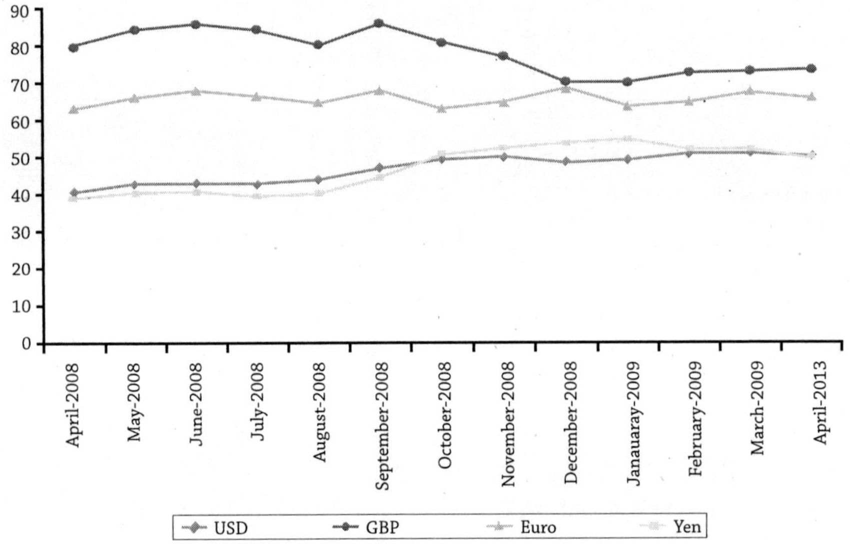

Popular resistance to approaching the IMF (as in much of the developing world), has encouraged India to shift its source of external financing away from debt and aid flows, including multilateral and bilateral aid and official development assistance, to increased trade and private equity flows.

Banking and Finance

The 'third' dimension of India's reform and stabilization programme has been financial and banking sector reform. A stock market 'scam' in the early 1990s, that brought issues of banking supervision and use of bank funds in the equities market into focus, kick-started the first phase of banking and equities market reform. The Asian financial crisis and the Government's decision to prepare a road map for capital account convertibility defined the second phase of banking and financial sector reform in the late 1990s. A third wave of financial sector reform was initiated by the bursting of dotcom bubble and its impact on the Indian stock market.

India's decision to attract foreign currency inflows through the capital market by opening up the stock market to foreign institutional investors also forced the authorities to undertake institutional reform. Consequently, India put in place a more efficient and transparent regulatory system for the equities market and the banking and financial sectors.[4] The relatively high standards of governance and institutional credibility of the Reserve Bank of India (RBI) and the Securities and Exchange Board of India (SEBI) have helped.

It has been widely commented that India's banking sector has not been impacted by the banking and financial sector crises of 2008, that preceded the global slowdown.[5] The Governor of the RBI, D. Subba Rao (2009) has claimed that, "The Indian banking system has had no direct exposure to the subprime mortgage assets or to the failed institutions. It has very limited off-balance sheet activities or securitized assets." The RBI has been credited with taking pre-emptive action that has minimized the vulnerability of Indian banks to the ripple effects of the US subprime crisis and the crisis in the equities market. In fact, in an early public statement on this, former RBI Governor, Y.V. Reddy (2008) claimed:

> Financial stability in India has been achieved through perseverance of prudential policies which prevent institutions from excessive risk taking, and financial markets from becoming extremely volatile and turbulent. As a result, while there are orderly conditions in financial markets, the financial institutions, especially banks, reflect strength and resilience. While supervision is exercised by a quasi-independent Board carved out of the RBI Board, the interface between regulation and supervision is close in respect of banks and financial institutions, and on market regulation, a close coordination with other regulators exists.

The RBI also took counter cyclical and precautionary measures to limit the exposure of banks to high risk lending, especially in real estate and housing. According to Reddy (2008):

> In the year 2000 the Reserve Bank of India (RBI) conducted a stress test of the banks' investment portfolio in an increasing interest rate

4. See Reddy 2004.
5. Mohan 2008.

scenario, when the general trend then was decreasing interest rates. At that time, banks in India were maintaining a surrogate capital charge for market risk, which was at a variance from the Basel norms.

On the basis of the findings, in order to equip the banking system to be better positioned to meet the adverse impact of interest rate risk, banks were advised in January 2002 to build up an Investment Fluctuation Reserve (IFR) within a period of five years. The prudential target for the IFR was 5 per cent of their investments in 'Held for Trading' (HFT) and 'Available for Sale' (AFS) categories. Banks were encouraged to build up a higher percentage of IFR up to 10 per cent of their AFS and HFT investments. This counter-cyclical prudential requirement enabled banks to absorb some of the adverse impact when interest rates began moving in the opposite direction in late 2004. Banks have been maintaining capital charge for market risk as envisaged under the Basel norms since end-March 2006.

Fiscal Policy

Higher economic growth had enabled India to reduce its budgetary and fiscal deficits over the past decade. This had also created the fiscal space for increased public investment in infrastructure development, defence modernisation and the development of strategic capabilities, including maritime. The current slowdown will undoubtedly exert a fiscal pressure on such strategic investments. The Government has pursued a counter-cyclical fiscal policy and provided a fiscal stimulus, variously estimated to be between 3 per cent and 4 per cent of GDP during 2008-09. However, a large part of such spending would naturally go into counter-cyclical safety nets and employment generation programmes. This would reduce the funds available for defence and strategic modernisation.

The Indian government can view some of the defence spending as part of the fiscal stimulus. However, given the high import intensity of defence spending in India, and the capital intensive nature of defence modernisation, there are limits to how much defence spending can be a counter cyclical activity.

To sum up, while India's reintegration into the world economy in the 1990s has made her more vulnerable to global crises, her pursuit of gradual reform and prudent regulation seem to have helped her minimize the negative impact of the trans-Atlantic financial crisis and the global economic slowdown. From a strategic policy perspective, therefore, India can claim that her model of 'gradual' and 'graduated' economic liberalisation, and of risk averse prudential regulation in the banking and financial sector have helped limit her exposure to the Asian and trans-Atlantic financial crises and the subsequent global economic slowdown.

While India still lags behind China, in terms of her share of world trade and capital flows as well as her share of global currency reserves, her strategy of gradual reintegration into the world economy has yielded strategic dividends. India has been able to increase its share of world income, trade and capital flows, emerging as a participant at the G-7 plus forums, along with China, Brazil and South Africa, and a member of the G-20 Summit. India has also increased its economic linkages with East and South-east Asia, and is a founder member of the East Asian Summit. Finally, the improved economic performance has enabled India to find resources for defence modernisation and to upgrade her maritime and strategic capabilities. Slower growth will exert a fiscal pressure that would adversely affect investments in these areas.

India and the Global Slowdown: New Vulnerabilities

In underscoring the new post-reform resilience of the economy, we do take account of new vulnerabilities that could hurt the growth process. First, the higher trade/GDP ratio and the consequent increased dependence on the global market in both goods and services. Second, the increased importance of foreign capital inflows —portfolio, direct investment, ECB (external commercial borrowing) of Indian private corporate sector and private remittances by overseas Indians. While India's recent growth acceleration benefitted from this external connectivity, the global crisis would hurt economic growth in the near term on account of the importance of these linkages[6] (See Figure 3.5).

6. Kumar et al. 2009.

In a candid rejection of the so-called 'decoupling thesis', namely that higher growth based on domestic savings and investment, and the greater reliance on domestic demand has 'decoupled' the Indian economy from the global economy. RBI Governor D. Subba Rao (2009a) told the Confederation of Indian Industry:

> The reason India has been hit by the crisis, despite mitigating factors, is clearly India's rapid and growing integration into the global economy. The contagion of the crisis has spread to India through all the channels—the financial channel, the real channel, and importantly, as happens in all financial crises, the confidence channel.

Figure 3.5

India's Increasing Global Linkages

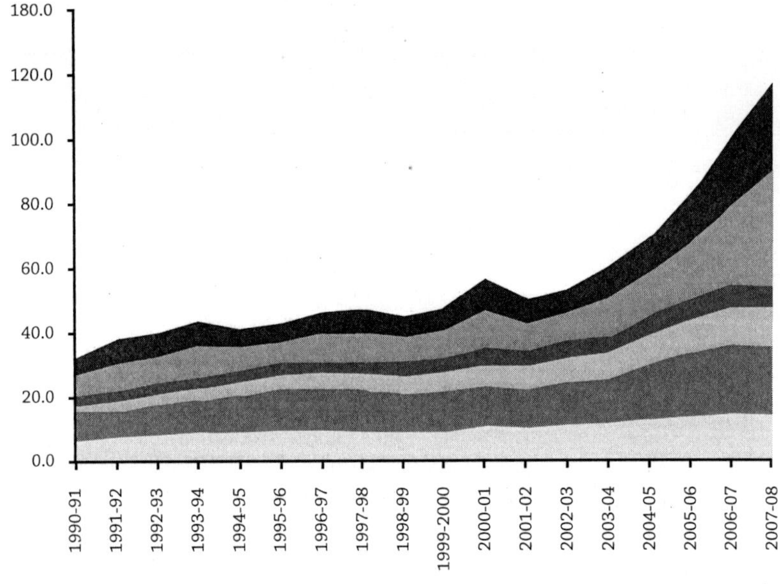

Source: Kumar et al. (2009)

Both public and private sector companies in India have become more dependent on the capital market for securing equity and debt finance, and India's equity market is fully integrated with global markets; though the debt market is not. Indian companies are estimated to have raised US$41 billion (net of repayment) as overseas debt through external commercial borrowing and fully convertible commercial debentures.[7] Even in the period October to December 2008 Indian companies were able to raise a total of US$4.5 billion from global debt markets. But these flows are expected to weaken given increased risk aversion in global markets. The decline in global merchandise trade has also slowed down growth of India's exports, and for the first time in seven years export growth has been negative in the first quarter of 2009.

Apart from these macro linkages and the overall increase in the trade/GDP ratio, the changes in the geographical pattern of trade also points to increased vulnerability to a slowdown. The depreciation of the Rupee is a reflection of these external vulnerabilities. India has had to draw down its foreign exchange reserves through the last quarter of 2008 and the first quarter of 2009 largely in defence of the Rupee. While India's reserves are denominated in a basket of currencies, the US dollar is the principle foreign currency in which India's external transactions are denominated. The US and EU still account for over a third of India's exports, but Asia's share has increased in recent years. The share of Japan and Russia has gone down, but that of China, South Korea and ASEAN economies has increased (Table 3.7). Each of these economies has experienced a slowdown in growth and a consequent decline in trade.

Tables 3.5 and 3.7 refer to merchandise exports. The growth of inward remittances from expatriate Indian workers, especially in the Persian Gulf region, and earnings from information technology and software services exports has increased the importance of services exports to India's balance of payments management. While low-skilled manpower exports are mainly belonging to the Organisation of the Petroleum Exporting Countries (OPEC) member countries of the Persian Gulf and Middle East, high skilled services exports are mainly to the United States and to the other Countries belonging to the OECD. In 2008-09, inward remittances amounted to US$55

7. *Money & Finance*, ICRA Bulletin, March 2009. New Delhi.

billion, while export earnings from IT and BPO business was estimated to be US$47 billion.

Table 3.7

Geographical Direction of India's Exports

Region	*1960-61*	*1970-71*	*1980-81*	*1990-91*	*2000-01*	*2006-07*
EU	36.2	18.4	21.6	27.5	22.7	21.3
US	16.0	13.5	11.1	14.7	20.9	14.0
Africa	6.3	8.4	5.2	2.1	3.2	6.7
L America	1.6	0.7	0.5	0.4	2.1	3.4
USSR	4.5	13.7	18.3	16.1	2.0	1.0
Russia						0.7
Asia (non-Oil)	6.9	10.8	13.4	14.3	21.4	31.6
Asia (incl Oil)						49.8
OPEC	4.1	6.4	11.1	5.6	10.9	-
Japan	5.5	13.3	8.9	9.3	4.9	2.2
ASEAN				3.0	7.5	10.0
China					1.0	6.6
S. Asia						5.1

Source: *Economic Survey* (various issues), Ministry of Finance, Govt. of India.

The information technology, IT services and business process outsourcing industry is now estimated to account for almost 6.0 per cent of India's GDP. Two-thirds of the US$72 billion business is accounted for by exports, mainly to trans-Atlantic economies. Spokespersons of the National Association of Software Services Companies (NASSCOM) in India, have expressed optimism that their exports would not be hurt if developed economies do not resort to protectionist measures. Since firms in OECD economies would increase their demand for lower cost Indian software services in a downturn, NASSCOM (2009) has forecast a reduction in export earnings in 2009-10. Growth in IT enabled services exports is expected to be around 15 per cent in 2009-10, compared to annual growth rates of around 25 per cent in recent years.

Speaking at the London Summit of the G-20, Prime Minister Manmohan Singh summed up the official thinking in India on the impact of the trans-Atlantic financial crisis and the global economic slowdown in these words:

> We in India have been fortunate in having weathered the global downturn better than many others. Our growth rate, which was close to 9% in the previous 5 years, will fall below 7% in 2008-09. Like other countries, we have made aggressive use of both monetary and fiscal policy, with a total fiscal stimulus or expansion of the fiscal deficit above the planned level of almost 4 percentage points of GDP in 2008-09. We hope to be able to achieve a similar growth rate in 2009-10, with continuing reliance on monetary and fiscal policy. We recognize the importance of fiscal sustainability and it is our firm intention to return to a fiscally sustainable path after 2010. The additional fiscal stimulus we have undertaken will raise our debt to GDP ratio by a few percentage points above what it would otherwise have been, but this is relatively modest compared to what would have happened had our banks suffered a financial crisis. Effective regulation of the banking system has gained us much more than any additional strain imposed by temporary fiscal expansion. Besides, since most of the fiscal stimulus will be directed to increased investment in infrastructure, it will in the medium term contribute to growth and thus help reduce the debt ratio automatically.
>
> Expansionary policy at home in an environment where exports are weak and private capital flows have dried up would normally lead to pressure on the balance of payments. In our case this has been partly offset by the fall in oil prices, but even so, India's current account deficit in 2009-10, is likely to be about 1.4. per cent of GDP. We expect to be able to finance this without difficulty and in any case our strong foreign exchange reserves position enables us to cope with any shortfall in capital flows we may experience.[8]

This sense of optimism is based on India's growth experience in the past decade. In the period 2002-2008 the global economic environment was benign for India. By 2003 the Governor of India's central bank, Bimal Jalan, was declaring that "there is no longer

8. Singh (2009).

any external constraint on growth."[9] This marked a turning point in Indian thinking about globalisation and external dependence.

Jalan's view was shared by Singh who often spoke of how India had overcome external constraints on growth and that the remaining constraints are essentially domestic.[10] Singh saw this as symbolising the success of India's economic openness and globalisation. Even as recently as in March 2007 he told The Economist Roundtable:

> An important strength of the Indian economy today is that we no longer face any insurmountable external constraint on growth. The global environment, both political and economic, is largely benign from our point of view. There are, of course, issues and trends that cause concern but these are generally applicable to most countries. For example, we are all concerned with high energy prices and uncertainty in the oil-producing regions of the world. We are all equally concerned about terrorism and threats to global peace and stability. Finally, we are all equally concerned about global warming and climate change. We are also concerned about the growth of protectionism in major developed countries. But these are global challenges and merit a global response.[11]

While this optimism about future growth prospects has been dented by recent events, there is as yet no anti-globalisation or protectionist sentiment in India. However, such protectionism in the OECD economies, and the pursuit of 'beggar-my-neighbour' policies by her economic partners may make India less sanguine about globalisation, given the new external vulnerabilities.[12]

---

9. Interview with RBI Governor Bimal Jalan, *The Financial Express*, Mumbai, 18 August 2003. Available at: *http://www.financialexpress.com/news/there-is-no-longer-an-external-constraint-to-growth/90535/0*

10. "I have often said that there are no external constraints to our growth. The world wants India to do well. The global community will be happy to see us participate more actively in the global exchange of goods, services, ideas and people. If at all there is a constraint, it is at home. The constraint of illiteracy, ill-health, low incomes, poverty, poor infrastructure—in short, the constraint of inadequate investment in people and in their capabilities." Prime Minister Manmohan Singh, India International Trade Fair, New Delhi, 14 November 2005. Available at: *http://pmindia.nic.in/speech/content.asp?id=220*

11. Available at: *http://pmindia.nic.in/speech/content.asp?id=510*

12. It is significant that the election manifestos of all the major mainstream political parties in the 2009 elections to the Indian Parliament do not adopt a protectionist stance. In fact the global crisis and slowdown has not encouraged a protectionist sentiment at home, even though there is increased awareness of and concern with China's rising global profile.

Globalisation, Geopolitics and India's Grand Strategy

India's economic rise and the success of its gradual outward-orientation have brought economics to the centre of its strategic thinking, influencing India's grand strategy. In the early years after its Independence India did see its economic rise as key to its re-emergence as a great power.[13] However, the Cold War interregnum, and India's relatively unimpressive economic performance during that period, saw high politics displace economics in the conceptualization of India's grand strategy. Bringing the economy to the centre of India's strategic weltanschauung, Prime Minister Manmohan Singh told a "Commanders Conference" in 2005:

> Our strategy has to be based on three broad pillars. First, to strengthen ourselves economically and technologically; Second, to acquire adequate defence capability to counter and rebut threats to our security, and third, to seek partnerships both on the strategic front and on the economic and technological front to widen our policy and developmental options...
>
> In the *Arthashastra*, Kautilya wrote that a healthy economy is a sound foundation for well-funded armed forces. 'From the strength of the treasury', he said 'the army is born'. But it is not only for fiscal reasons that the health of our economy is important for our national security. A healthy, growing and stable economy in itself enhances security. New notions of 'Comprehensive National Power' give high weightage to economic, social, scientific, technological, educational and cultural aspects of power. Military strength alone no longer guarantees a nation's security. Knowledge power and economic capabilities are equally important.[14]

This view of India's grand strategy firmly embeds it on the foundations of her economic performance. It is only as a 'growing and globalizing economy' that India can be a 'rising power'. Hence,

13. In his first major foreign policy speech to the Indian Constituent Assembly, in December 1947, India's first Prime Minister Jawaharlal Nehru said: "Talking about foreign policies, the House must remember that these are not just empty struggles on a chess board. Behind them lie all manner of things. Ultimately, foreign policy is the outcome of economic policy." See Baru (2006: 58), Chapter 2.

14. Manmohan Singh, Address to Combined Commanders Conference, New Delhi, 20 October 2005. Available at: *http://www.pmindia.nic.in/speeches.htm*

safeguarding the environment for economic growth, albeit as a 'free market democracy', is critical to India's re-emergence as a 'great power'.[15]

China's rise as a 'socialist market economy', globally and regionally integrated with major industrial and newly industrialising economies, has only added urgency to India's efforts to boost domestic economic growth and build economic bridges with the rest of the world.

Improved economic performance has also enabled India to become more globally and regionally integrated with her Asian neighbours. In the 1990s India had launched a 'Look East Policy' aimed at closer economic integration with East and South-east Asia. A decade later India felt confident enough to seek a free trade agreement with ASEAN. This was preceded by an India-Sri Lanka Free Trade Agreement (FTA) and the launch of negotiations for a South Asian Free Trade Agreement (SAFTA). India launched a series of FTA negotiations with her other Asian neighbours (Table 3.8).

The geopolitical dimension to these trade agreements is obvious. Nevertheless, in defending the India–ASEAN FTA against domestic criticism, that it may hurt Indian farmers, Prime Minister Manmohan Singh pointedly drew attention to its geopolitical dimension. Writing to Congress President Sonia Gandhi on the merits of the India-ASEAN FTA, Manmohan Singh said:

> Our approach to regional trade agreements, in general, and FTAs, in particular, has been evolved after careful consideration of our geopolitical as well as economic interests. Although India has a large domestic market, our experience with earlier relatively insular policies, as also the global experience in this regard, clearly bring out the growth potential of trade and economic cooperation with the global economy.[16]

15. In an official banquet speech on his visit to Tokyo, Prime Minister Manmohan Singh told his Japanese hosts: "India and Japan share a proud civilisational heritage and a common Asian identity. Our two nations have converging long-term political, economic and strategic interests. We have a common commitment to democracy, human rights, the rule of law and a free market economy. India and Japan are thus natural partners with a mutual stake in each other's progress and prosperity." 15 December 2006. Available at: *http://pmindia.nic.in/visits/content.asp?id=149*

16. See Baru (2008).

Table 3.8

Preferential, Free and Regional Trade Agreements and Comprehensive Economic Cooperation/ Partnership Agreements Being Pursued by India

Mauritius–CEPA	SAARC–FTA/CECA
South Africa Customs Union–PTA	Gulf Coop Council–FTA
Africa–PTA/CECA	New Zealand–FTA
Australia–FTA	Japan–CEPA
Chile–PTA	Israel–FTA
South Korea–CEC/PA	BIMSTEC–FTA
India, Brazil S Africa–CECA	Mercosur–PTA
South Korea–CEPA	ASEAN–FTA/CECA
Singapore–FTA/CECA	Sri Lanka–FTA/ CECA
China–FTA	Russia–CECA
Malaysia–CECA	EU–FTA
Egypt–PTA	Thailand–FTA

Note: FTA= Free Trade Agreement; PTA= Preferential Trade Agreement; CECA= Comprehensive Economic Cooperation Agreement; CEPA= Comprehensive Economic Partnership Agreement. * indicates concluded.

Source: Ministry of Commerce, Govt. of India. 2008.

Even the India-Sri lanka FTA was sealed at the highest political level in the face of opposition from farm and business lobbies. Such opposition was muted in the past since the Indian economy has been performing well. Any economic slow down can intensify such opposition to external liberalisation, with consequent geopolitical implications in an increasingly integrated economic region.[17]

The strategic significance of being actively engaged in the processes of Asian economic integration cannot be over emphasised. India's improved economic performance since 1990, and especially since 2003, helped ensure that the imperatives of globalisation worked in tandem with the logic of geopolitics. As a 'rising power' India felt more confident dealing with a 'rising China' and was able to mentally 'de-hyphenate' itself from slow-growing Pakistan. It

17. This has already delayed finalisation of the India-ASEAN FTA, though the official reason given is that the summit meeting has been postponed due to the situation in Thailand and that India is now into election season. It is possible that the global slowdown may have encouraged both sides to go slow on the FTA.

also felt encouraged to participate more actively in the processes of East and South-east Asian regionalism. India's membership of the ASEAN Regional Forum (ARF) was a stepping stone to closer strategic engagement with the region. Closer economic relations with countries of the region has enabled India to participate in the East Asia Summit and the regional community building efforts.

China's rise and globalisation has encouraged India's own policy transition. China has emerged as a key economic partner for most Asian economies, including Japan and South Korea. It has overtaken India as an economic partner of South and Central Asian economies as well, and is well on its way to emerging as a major economic partner for Africa.

While India's share of global trade, merchandise and services, has doubled in the past decade it still lags way behind China's. In 2007 India's share of world merchandise trade was around 1.2 per cent and of commercial services trade it was estimated to be around 2.5 per cent, while respective shares for China were 8.0 per cent and 3.5 per cent respectively. But India's lower level of global integration has in fact made it less vulnerable to the global downturn than China.

Hence, there are two ways of viewing the implications of globalisation for national power. On the one hand, it creates new relationships of global inter-dependence that add to a country's global influence and power; on the other hand, this also creates new vulnerabilities that less globally integrated economies do not face. For India, sustaining her recent growth acceleration and increasing the competitiveness of the Indian economy remain vital strategic objectives, but the gradualism of India's globalisation has yielded dividends in dealing with a global economic downturn. Given that, India's growth acceleration has also helped alter her global and regional profile; sustaining this process is vital to its grand strategy.

The Re-hyphenation with Pakistan

In the past decade an important perceptional gain for India in strategic terms was its 'de-hyphenation' from Pakistan and a new 're-hyphenation' with China in the popular and intellectual imagination, especially in the West. Rather than view India only as a 'South Asian' economy, western investors and analysts began viewing her in the context of Asia's rise. In recent years the idea of 'Chindia'—a joint assessment of the rise of China and India—had gained currency.[18] This new 'hyphenation' with China, and 'de-hyphenation' with Pakistan was firmly embedded in the relative economic performance of each of the three countries. The period since 1991 has been a turning point for India in terms of global appreciation of her economic prospects relative to China, Pakistan, South-east and other South Asian economies.

Till the 1980s, Pakistan had a relatively superior record in economic performance compared to India. This shaped her self-image as well. But the 1990s saw India not only overtaking, but also breaking ranks. Changing economic performance has had its impact on changing strategic perceptions about the two neighbours, both within the region and outside (See Table 3.9).

Table 3.9

Average Real GDP Growth

Period	*Pakistan*	*India*
1954-1958	2.01	
1953-1960	3.80	3.7
1959-1971	3.90	
1961-1970	3.35	3.3
1971-1980	4.81	3.5
1981-1990	6.19	5.4
1991-2000	3.96	6.2
2000-2005	4.98	7.0

Sources: 1. Razmi (2007) and 2. *Economic Survey* (various issues), Ministry . of Finance, Govt. of India.

The overall deceleration in Pakistan's growth comes through even more sharply when we compare per capita income growth. Pakistan's higher population growth rate and the deceleration of India's population growth has widened per capita income disparity between the two South Asian neighbours.

18. The word 'Chindia' got 177,000 hits on google. A selection of 'Chindia' books includes: Ramesh (2005), Sheth (2007), Meredith (2008), Winters and Yusuf (2007), Engardio (2006), Smith (2007), Emmott (2008).

Table 3.10

Growth Rate of Per Capita National Income (Percentage/Year)

Country/ Period	*1975-90*	*1990-2003*
India	2.8	3.8
Pakistan	3.4	1.4

Source: Ahmed (2006).

In more recent years Pakistan has been able to improve its economic performance due to a huge infusion of aid from the United States and multilateral financial institutions. However, the overall deterioration in Pakistan's security environment has meant that this marginal improvement in her economic performance has not yet altered the changed perceptions of the economic weight and performance of India and Pakistan. This could well be one reason why jehadi terrorists with links to Pakistan have specifically targeted important economic centres in India like Mumbai, Delhi, Hyderabad and Bangalore.[19]

India's superior economic performance in the 1990s had the effect of subduing Pakistani bravado, on the one hand, and encouraged India to adopt a more accommodative stance towards Pakistan, and its other South Asian neighbours. This is reflected in India's policy of 'asymmetric liberalization' within the South Asian Association for Regional Cooperation (SAARC) region. At the Dhaka, Delhi and Colombo Summits of the SAARC, India proposed a series of initiatives to boost regional economic cooperation.[20]

An economically stronger and stable India has felt encouraged to pursue a policy of 'asymmetric' or non reciprocal liberalisation in South Asia, offering duty free access to less developed countries. This policy would also be reassessed as a consequence of the economic slowdown. On the other hand, if Pakistan feels emboldened by the

19. Speaking in Parliament on the 26 November 2008 terrorist attacks in Mumbai, Prime Minister Manmohan Singh drew pointed attention to the targeting of India's economy: "As far as Mumbai is concerned, it was a very calculated and sinister attack, intended to cause widespread terror and damage to the image of India. The forces behind these attacks wanted to destabilise our secular polity, create communal discord and undermine our country's economic and social progress", Lok Sabha, 11 December 2008. Available at: *http://www.pmindia.nic.in/speeches.htm*

20. See Baru (2008).

renewed injection of economic and military assistance and aid from the West it may spur new adventurism within the military leadership. Any slowing down of the Indian economy would only encourage such adventurist elements in Pakistan.

Pakistan is the source of India's biggest security problem—jehadi terrorism. However, India faces a strategic dilemma. It is in India's interests that Pakistan should stabilise as a nation, a society and an economy. It is in India's interest that Pakistan economy should do well, a moderate and peace-loving middle class and business class gains ascendance and that democratic institutions take root. However, if improved economic performance, aided by US assistance, emboldens Pakistan to return to adventurist tactics vis-à-vis India, the security environment in the region would only deteriorate.

The impact of the slowdown on the US economy and politics, and the challenge of US budget management, could also shape US response to the challenge of terrorism in South Asia. If domestic economic and political pressures encourage the US Administration to pursue a so-called 'AfPak' strategy that is not in line with Indian security perceptions, India would be constrained to develop its own response to the threat of regional instability. How US policy response to the global economic crisis influences its policy on jehadi terrorism in South Asia would, therefore, have a direct bearing on India's strategic environment.

India's growth acceleration since 2003 has also enabled it to adopt a more liberal stance towards other Least Developed Countries (LDCs) in Asia and Africa. The policy of non reciprocal trade liberalization involving duty free access was extended to all African LDCs at the India-Africa Summit in New Delhi in April 2008, and to the countries in South-east Asia Cambodia, Myanmar, Laos and Vietnam (CMLV). There are clearly two distinct strands of Indian strategic policy defining these initiatives. On the one hand, India's traditional policy of building bridges with other developing countries and promoting South-South cooperation; on the other hand, the need to keep pace with China in providing aid and assistance to other developing countries, especially LDCs.

Liberal unilateral trade concessions, even if to LDCs, would come under attack from producers' lobbies and politicians in a slow growing India. For example, India's trade concessions to Viet-nam, a friendly country, in commodities such as coffee have already come in for sharp attack from even the Communist Party led State Government of Kerala, where coffee growers have political clout. Apart from unilateral trade concessions, India has also stepped up aid and technical assistance to other developing countries. Indian external aid budget has increased substantially in recent years, with a significant share of it going to Afghanistan and Bhutan[21] (Table 3.11).

Table 3.11

Budget Allocations for External Aid Financing (in ₹)

	2008-09	*1998-2009*
Foreign grants	1,92,643	5,604
Foreign loans	1,386	2,730
Total grants and loans	20,64,950	8,334
Of which MEA budget for, ITEC	650	
Africa	800	110
Afghanistan	4,450	
Bhutan	8,184	4,500
Nepal	1,400	700
Myanmar	560	510
Contributions to IOs[7]	3,531	1,621
Allocations to IFIs	171	-
Of which, AfDB	144	
Exim Bank interest equalisation subsidy	2,320	
Total estimated foreign aid	2,66,712	9,955
Exim Bank loans and guarantees	3,50,039	21,013

Source: Chanana (2009)

While strategic interests in South Asia and traditional commitment to South-South cooperation drive India's aid budget, competition for influence with China, both within South Asia and in

21. See Chanana (2009).

the developing world as a whole, is also a major driver. India's growth acceleration in the past decade has enabled her to find the resources for such aid. Any deceleration in growth and consequent fiscal pressures would impose constraints. This would most certainly be an adverse strategic consequence of the extant economic slowdown.

The G-2 Challenge

The bigger challenge for India, however, is to ensure that the current global economic slowdown does not constrain it from catching up with China. Without doubt the rise of China is India's main long term strategic challenge. Already China's influence in Asia is rising. China had long overtaken India as the main business partner of many South Asian economies, not to mention East and South-east Asia.[22] China has also emerged as a major source of external financial support through its contribution to the Chiang Mai Initiative and direct financial assistance to various countries.[23]

The two Asian giants are already engaged in a race for resources and markets in Asia and Africa, with China far ahead of India. A deceleration in China's growth could blunt the edge of this competition. But it will not go away. Rather, it is likely to accentuate as India catches up in the growth race. As a consequence of the current global slowdown, we can conjecture three alternative scenarios of regional growth.

First, India is able to recover more easily than China, due to its lower dependence on global markets and lower exposure to the US economy. Second, India is unable to regain its growth momentum, while China does. Third, no relative change in the status of India and China in the world economy.

How the global slowdown impacts this bilateral relationship will shape the overall strategy of both the Asian powers. It will also impact on their relations with other Asian economies as well as Western powers. It will shape the process of institution building in Asia, and the structure of regional economic and security architecture. The

22. See Baru (2006), Chapter 38.

23. See Henning (2009).

resolution of the problem of the savings consumption imbalance between China and the US will have a profound impact on the emerging global strategic balance. A US-China 'condominium' could alter India's strategic environment and options.

The idea of such a condominium was first proposed by Fred Bergsten (2008), who called for a US-China G-2 working together to deal with the challenge of global imbalances and other issues like climate change and the completion of Doha Round negotiations. The idea of 'Chimerica' captured popular imagination in the western media on the eve of the London Summit of the G-20, but Chinese commentators have so far reacted cautiously.[24]

A US-China condominium could go beyond the management of global imbalances and crises. If it encapsulates multilateral trade negotiations and discussions on global warming and climate change, it would have an even greater impact on India's strategic environment. India seeks a benign global environment for trade and investment that will enable it to sustain higher rates of economic growth.

The US offered such a 'benign' economic environment for the reconstruction of post-War western Europe and East Asia. Its' policies also facilitated the rise of China. How open the US remains towards India, keeping her markets open, being liberal with H1-B visas, being supportive in multilateral economic institutions, will have a bearing on India's growth process.

India's strategic perspective on trade and climate change negotiations has been defined in the framework of economic development, employment generation and poverty eradication. So far India and China have been able to work together on these issues. If China breaks ranks and arrives at an understanding with the US that does not meet India's needs, India would have no option but to join ranks with other developing countries and other powers to secure its own interests. Here too the US could adopt a supportive stance

24. The phrase 'Chimerica' was first popularized by Ferguson and Schularick (2007). However, Ferguson has himself since expressed scepticism about the idea. "The End of Chimerica", *StandPoint*, Available at: *http://www.standpointmag.co.uk/node/399/full*. Also see Economy and Segal (2009).

towards India or adopt postures that would revive old North-South divisions on global economic issues.

The global economic slowdown has increased the salience of trade and climate change negotiations since the outcomes of these negotiations will shape the overall environment for India's economic development. India has often been portrayed as a 'spoiler' both in the Doha Round and in the climate change negotiations. This is not true. India has a 'strategic stake' in multilateralism on both counts. However, its priority lies in defending the environment for economic growth and poverty eradication. Without a 'development' dimension to the trade and climate change negotiations India would be hard put to join a multilateral agreement.

A US-China condominium, with its attendant implications for relations with Pakistan, would force India to rethink its own strategy of global engagement. It would certainly strengthen anti-US and anti-China sentiment in India. It would encourage India to return to its leadership role in the developing world, imparting new momentum to the IBSA forum and to its relations with other powers like Russia, EU and Japan. Indeed, if the G-20 gets reduced to a G-2, then IBSA could become the core of a new G-77, the developing countries forum. It remains to be seen if China would risk yielding the leadership space in the developing world to India.

The management of the global economic crisis has forced the pace of events with respect to the reform of institutions of global economic governance. The G-7 have realised the need to bring China, India and other major developing economies into the institutions of global governance like the IMF and the Financial Stability Board (FSB). For India the challenge would be to ensure that China does not once again steal a march over it, as it did in the creation of the UN Security Council, in the anticipated reform of global institutions and the creation of new regional institutions.

Finally, India would want to see how the changing relationship between the US and China would shape global negotiations on trade, finance and climate change, and impact on dealing with the challenges of food and energy security. The US and India have a shared stake in reducing their dependence on imported petroleum and natural gas, and in the development of nuclear and non-conventional energy. Given India's low per capita domestic availability of energy and other natural resources, ensuring access to these resources is vital to India's development process and national security.

Crisis Management, Regional Stability and Implications for India-US Relations

It is an appreciation of the strategic importance of sustained growth of a free market democracy in the developing world, and the assurance of energy security for it, that helped define an improvement in India-US relations in recent years, especially during the Bush Administration. The US came to appreciate that India's economic success within the framework of a secular and plural democracy is of strategic importance to all open societies and open economies.

Condoleezza Rice (2008) best articulated this view when she wrote:

> India stands on the front lines of globalisation. This democratic nation promises to become a global power and an ally in shaping an international order rooted in freedom and the rule of law. .... the United States has a vital stake in India's rise to global power and prosperity, and relations between the two countries have never been stronger or broader. It will take continued work, but this is a dramatic breakthrough for both our strategic interests and our values.

Responding to this supportive stance of the US and seeking long term US commitment to both democracy and development in India, Prime Minister Manmohan Singh told the United States Congress in July 2005:

> Democracy is one part of our national endeavour. Development is the other. Openness will not gain popular support if an open society is not a prosperous society. This is especially so in developing countries, where a large number of people leave legitimate material expectations which must be met. That is why we must transform India's economy, to raise the standard of living of all our people and in the process eliminate poverty.

> India's aspirations in this respect are not different from those of other developing countries. But we are unique in one respect. There is no other country of a billion people, with our tremendous cultural, linguistic and religious diversity, that has tried to modernise its society and transform its economy within the framework of a functioning democracy. To attempt this at our modest levels of per capita income is a major challenge. We are determined to succeed in this effort.[25]

President Obama's first important statement on US-India relations, conveyed through a letter written when he was still a candidate in the presidential elections, to Prime Minister Singh, adopted a forward looking and supportive position on US-India relations, underscoring the importance of India's democratic development. Obama said:

> I strongly support civil nuclear cooperation, because I believe it will enhance our partnership and deepen our cooperation on a whole range of matters. Importantly, it will help India to meet its growing electricity demands while aiding in the important effort to combat global warming. But I see this agreement only as a beginning of a much closer relationship between our two great countries. I would like to see US-India relations grow across the board to reflect our shared interests, shared values, shared sense of threats and ever-burgeoning ties between our two economies and societies.
>
> As a starting point, our common strategic interests call for redoubling US-Indian military, intelligence and law enforcement cooperation. The recent bombings remind us that we are both victims of terrorist attacks on our soil, and we share a common goal of defeating these forces of extremism. India and America should similarly work together to promote our democratic values and strengthen legal institutions in South Asia and beyond. We also should be working hand-in-hand to tap into the creativity and dynamism of our entrepreneurs, engineers and scientists to promote development of alternative sources of clean energy. Imagine our two democracies in action: Indian laboratories and industry collaborating with American laboratories and industry to discover innovative solutions to today's

25. Prime Minister Manmohan Singh's Address to the Joint Session of the US Congress, Washington DC, July 19 2005. Available at: *http://www.pmindia.nic.in/speeches.htm*

energy problems. That is the kind of new partnership I would like to build with India as President.[26]

However, the Obama Administration has so far not shown strong and visible commitment to this vision of US-India relations. It is instructive to remember that the September letter was written when the financial crisis was just unfolding and few had foreseen the depths of the impending global economic downturn. In the months following this statement, not only has the economic crisis become worse but the situation in Afghanistan and Pakistan has sharply deteriorated.

In dealing with the economic crisis the US has moved closer to China, in dealing with terrorism it has become more dependent on Pakistan. It is, therefore, possible that these remarks do not any longer fully reflect the world view of President Obama. The Obama Administration's outreach to China, on the one hand, and its so-called 'AfPak' strategy in South Asia, on the other, have not been viewed favourably in India.[27]

Any dilution of the focus on shared democratic values could make US policy excessively transactional and less value-based in Asia. US-India relations have been defined both by "ideals and interests", to use a phrase used by Rice, and "principles and pragmatism", to use a phrase used by Singh.[28]

Faced with an economic deceleration, India's priority would be to regain the growth momentum of the past decade. US strategy in Asia will shape the strategic environment within which India is trying to improve her economic prospects. Stabilising the economy is also vital for India to deal with the instability of her neighbourhood. Apart from Pakistan, Sri Lanka too is in turmoil and both Nepal and Bangladesh remain potentially unstable polities. In each of these

26. Letter of President Barack Obama to Prime Minister Manmohan Singh, 23 September 2008. Available at: *http://en.wikisource.org/wiki/Barack_Obama's_Letter_to_Prime_Minister_Manmohan_Singh*

27. The Obama administration's 'AfPak' strategy has come in for critical comments in India and experts are already expressing doubts about the durability of the 'strategic partnership' that President Bush and Prime Minister Singh sought. See for example Sibal (2009).

28. See Rice (2008) and Manmohan Singh *op. cit.* no. 25.

countries we see China's growing influence and interest. China has also arrived in the Indian Ocean with its naval fleet and is once again flexing its muscles on the status of Arunachal Pradesh. Its influence is growing in Pakistan, Nepal, Sri Lanka, Myanmar and Bangladesh. Chinese leaders have visited the Indian Ocean islands of Seychelles and Mauritius, and China is probing the newly democratic Bhutan.

Against the background of a rising China that is increasingly influential in her troubled neighbourhood India cannot afford to see a weakening of its own growth process that underpins her strategic capabilities.

The global economic crisis has reopened a debate that many thought was buried by the debris of the collapse of the Soviet Union and the end of the Cold War; the debate about 'State vs Market' and the pros and cons of a free market democracy.[29] The debate is significant for the future of policy in the developing countries democracies around the world, as China's success increases the appeal of its model of single party based Statist rule. India's world view, of the importance of a developing country becoming economically better off within the framework of a democracy, is losing salience as that of China's 'socialist market economy' gains ground.

The issue at stake is not the extent of government intervention in markets and State support for private enterprise. Most economies are 'mixed economies' anyway. The issue is the political basis of governance. Has democracy been devalued by the economic crisis? India, like the US, has a strategic stake in ensuring that democratic institutions are not so delegitimized.

How nations and peoples respond to the current global economic crisis will determine the ideological and political foundations of the world order in the 21st Century. Many in East Asia are already suggesting that China's model of the 'development state', based on benign authoritarianism, is more relevant to developing countries than western models of multi-party democracy that are handicapped by internal political dissent. Claims are being made that a 'Beijing Consensus' on economic policy is replacing the disgraced 'Washington

29. Bremmer (2009).

Consensus' (a phrase used to describe policies that defined IMF conditionality in the past two decades).[30]

There was much that was wrong with the policies of the so-called 'Washington Consensus'. But the answer for a democracy like India cannot be the economics of a 'Beijing Consensus'. India has a strategic stake in the success of its model of a liberal democracy and a mixed economy—a 'New Delhi Consensus', if you like. The Great Depression of the 1930s gave rise to non-democratic political movements in the wake of popular resentment against the failure of democratic governments to deal with the challenge of an economic downturn. The US and India have the opportunity to work together in ensuring that the current recession does not encourage non-democratic political movements and systems. Rather, the global economic downturn offers an opportunity for the world's largest democracies and market economies to work together to strengthen the foundations of open societies and open economies, by creating a global order that is supportive of India's developmental aspirations and the aspirations of all developing country democracies, like Brazil, Indonesia and South Africa.

References

Ahmed, Sadiq (2006). *Explaining South Asia's Development Success*, The World Bank.

Asian Development Bank (2008). *Emerging Asian Regionalism: A Partnership for Shared Prosperity*. Available at: *http://www.adb.org/Documents/Books/Emerging-Asian-Regionalism/chapter02.pdf*

Baru, Sanjaya (2006). "Introduction", in *Strategic Consequences of India's Economic Performance*. Delhi: Academic Foundation.

———. (2008). "India and the World: Economics and Politics of the Manmohan Singh Doctrine in Foreign Policy", *Working Paper* No. 53, Institute of South Asian Studies, Singapore. November. Available at: *http://www.isasnus.org/events/workingpapers/52.pdf*

Bergsten, Fred C . (2008). "A Partnership of Equals: How Washington Should Respond to China's Economic Challenge, *Foreign Affairs*, July-August. Available at: *http://www.foreignaffairs.com/articles/64448/c-fred-bergsten/a-partnership-of-equals*

Bremmer, Ian (2009). "State Capitalism Comes of Age: The End of the Free Market?", *Foreign Affairs*, May-June. Available at: *http://www.foreignaffairs.com/articles/64948/ian-bremmer/state-capitalism-comes-of-age*

---

30. "It is very possible that the Beijing Consensus can replace the Washington Consensus," said Cui Zhiyuan, a professor of public policy at Tsinghua University who edited a recent book on the subject. "Since the crisis, the world doesn't have as much confidence in the U.S. economic model as before." See Chag (2009).

Cha, Ariana Eunjung (2009). "China Uses Global Crisis to Assert Its Influence: Along With Aid to Other Nations, Beijing Offers Up Criticism of the West", *The Washington Post*, 23 April. Available at: *http://www.washingtonpost.com/wp- dyn/content/article/2009/04/22/AR2009042203823.html?wpisrc=newsletter*

Chanana, Dweep (2009). "India as an Emerging Donor", *Economic and Political Weekly.* 21 March. Available at: *http://www.epw.in/uploads/articles/13314.pdf*

Economic Advisory Council to Prime Minister (2009). *Review of the Economy, 2008-09.* New Delhi: Government of India. March.

Economy, Elizabeth C. and Adam Segal (2009). "The G-2 Mirage", *Foreign Affairs*, May-June 2009, Available at: *http://www.foreignaffairs.com/issues/2009/88/3*

Emmott, Bill (2008). *Rivals: How the Power Struggle Between China, India and Japan Will Shape Our Next Decade.* London: Harcourt.

Engardio, Pete (ed.) (2006). *Chindia: How China and India Are Revolutionizing Global Business.* New York: McGraw Hill.

Ferguson, Niall and Moritz Schularick (2007). "Chimerica and Global Asset Markets", *International Finance* 10(3): 215-29 (Winter).

Henning, C. Randall (2009). "The Future of the Chiang Mai Initiative: An Asian Monetary Fund?" Available at: *http://www.iie.com/publications/pb/pb09-5.pdf*

Jairam, Ramesh (2005). *Making Sense of Chindia: Reflections on China and India.* New Delhi: India Research Press.

Joshi, Vijay and IMD Little (1994). *India: Macroeconomics and Political Economy, 1964-1991.* New Delhi: Oxford University Press.

Kumar, Rajiv Mathew Joseph, Dony Alex, Pankaj Vashisht, Debosree Banerjee (2009). "Indian Economic Outlook, 2008-09 and 2009-10", *ICRIER Working Paper* No. 234. March. Available at: *www.icrier.res.in*

Maddison, Angus (2001). *The World Economy: A Millennial Perspective.* Paris: OECD. Available at: *http://www.visualizingeconomics.com/category/angusmaddison/*

Meredith, Robyn (2008). *The Elephant and the Dragon: The Rise of India and China and What it Means for All of Us.* New York: W.W. Norton & Company.

Ministry of Commerce (2008). *Annual Report.* New Delhi: Government of India.

Mohan, Rakesh (2008). "Global Financial Crisis and Key Risks: Impact on India and Asia", Remarks prepared for IMF-FSF High-Level Meeting on the *Recent Financial Turmoil and Policy Responses* at Washington D.C. 9 October. Available at *www.rbi.org.in*

National Association of Software Services Companies. (2009). *Report on IT Software and Services: Performance and Prospects.* Available at: *www.nasscom.in* & *http://www.nasscom.in/upload/60387/Key_Highlights.pdf*

Razmi, Arslan (2007). "Analyzing Pakistan's Economic Prospects in an Increasingly Integrated World: External Constraints on Sustainable Growth", *ISAS Working Paper*, March. Available at: *http://www.isasnus.org/2007MaySymposium/Panel%20Three%20-%20Presentation%20Paper%20-%20Dr%20Arslan%20Razmi.pdf*

Rao, D. Subba (2009). "Impact of the Global Financial Crisis on India : Collateral Damage and Response', Speech delivered at the Symposium on *The Global Economic Crisis and Challenges for the Asian Economy in a Changing World.* Institute for International Monetary Affairs, Tokyo.18 February 18. Available at: *www.rbi.org.in*

———. (2009a). *India: Managing the Impact of the Global Financial Crisis.* 29 March. Available at: *http://www.rbi.org.in/scripts/BS_SpeechesView.aspx?Id=413*

Reddy, Y.V. (2004). "Monetary and Financial Sector Reforms in India: A Practitioner's Perspective", in Kaushik Basu (ed.), *India's Emerging Economy*. Oxford University Press.

———. (2008). *Global Financial Turbulence and Financial Sector in India: A Practitioner's Perspective.* Reserve Bank of India. July. Available at: *http://rbidocs.rbi.org.in/rdocs/Speeches/PDFs/85529.pdf*

Rice, Condoleezza (2008) "Rethinking the National Interest: American Realism for a New World", *Foreign Affairs*, July- August. Available at: *http://www.foreignaffairs.com/articles/64445/condoleezza-rice/rethinking-the-national-interest?page=show*

Sheth, Jagdish N. (2007). *Chindia Rising*. New Delhi: McGraw Hill India.

Sibal, Kanwal (2009). "Promise of Indo-US Ties Diluted by Obama", *Mail Today (New Delhi)*. 21 April.

Singh, Manmohan (2009). *Statement at G-20 Summit, London.* 2 April. Available at: *http://www.pmindia.nic.in/lspeech.asp?id=784*

Smith, David (2007). *The Dragon and the Elephant: China, India and the New World Order*. London: Profile Books.

Winters, Alan and Shahid Yusuf (eds.) (2007). *Dancing with Giants: China, India, and the Global Economy*. World Bank.

4

The Economic Imperative to Indian Foreign Policy

From its inception Indian foreign policy has been shaped by two, not necessarily competing though potentially contradictory, imperatives. On the one hand, the political leadership's requirement to address free India's developmental needs and aspirations and, on the other hand, democratic India's urge to continue to inspire anti-colonial and liberation struggles, and play a leadership role within the developing world.

As a predominantly agrarian society with starving millions, desperate to re-industrialise and widen employment opportunities India was required to build bridges with economies that had the capital surplus and the modern technology it needed, both in manufacturing and agriculture. As a nation that had inspired anti-colonial movements and liberation struggles in Asia and Africa, with the leadership of Mahatma Gandhi, India could not have but extended its solidarity to new nations in the making.

Clearly, the challenge for the architects of Indian foreign policy was to combine the 'idealism' of a new post-colonial democratic republic with the 'realism' needed to address a backward economy's developmental needs. Jawaharlal Nehru, India's first Prime Minister, a thinker, a writer and a nation builder, immediately grasped the nature of this dilemma. Addressing the Constituent Assembly months after India's independence, on 4th December 1947, Nehru said:[1]

1. Jawaharlal Nehru, *Address to the Constituent Assembly*, 4 December 1947. Reprinted as Appendix in Baru (2007).

> Talking about foreign policies, the House must remember that these are not empty struggles on a chess board. Behind them lie all manner of things. Ultimately, foreign policy is the outcome of economic policy ... It is well for us to say that we stand for peace and freedom; and yet that does not convey much to anybody, except a pious hope. We do stand for peace and freedom. ... There is some meaning when we say that we stand for the freedom of Asian countries and for the elimination of imperialistic control over them. ... But a vague statement that we stand for peace and freedom by itself has no meaning ... What then do we stand for? Well, you have to develop this argument in the economic field.[2]
>
> [......] Whatever policy you may lay down, the art of conducting the foreign affairs of a country lies in finding out what is most advantageous to the country. ...in the ultimate analysis, a government functions for the good of the country it governs....[3]
>
> [......] Therefore whether a country is imperialistic or socialist or communist, its Foreign Minister thinks primarily of the interests of that country.[4]

While India did often walk the high road of universal principles in defending its foreign policy, every now and then it has had to come to terms with the compulsions of the low road of interests in defining it.[5] Even as India stayed away from Cold War military alliances it did not shy away from reaching out to the United States (US) and to the Soviet Union, from time to time, for economic and military assistance. I have argued elsewhere that economic performance and capability are a necessary, though by no means sufficient, foundation of political and diplomatic influence and military power.[6] India's priority at the time was to build such economic capability.

The 'implosion' of the Soviet Union under the burden of its economic weightlessness, and the rise of China as a major power on the back of rapid economic growth stand testimony to the vital

2. Baru, 2007: 455
3. Ibid.: 459
4. Ibid.: 460
5. Baru, Sanjaya (2007a).
6. Baru, 2007: 31, Chapter 1.

importance of economic capacity and capability of a State. It is not economic growth in itself, to be sure, but the nature of that growth process that holds the key to a country's global profile and power, its strategic role and relevance. By 'nature' we mean the distributional aspects of growth, the impact of growth on human capabilities and skills, on global competitiveness and the sectoral composition of that growth, that is the extent of industrialisation, and its fiscal sustainability.

The fiscal sustainability of growth has become increasingly important as nation's find their resources stretched. Governments need finances both for diplomacy and defence. To the extent that the effectiveness of a country's foreign policy is shaped by its defence capability and the link between fiscal capacity, defence capability and international relations is manifest. No country can project power nor extend influence externally if it is internally fiscally stressed.

Planning and Foreign Relations

Aware of these links between India's domestic capability and its external profile, between its economic capacity and national aspirations, Nehru emphasised the strategic importance of economic development. This at a time when both the national movement and domestic business interests shaped a world view in which India sought to minimise its external dependence in re-building its economy. This attitude influenced Indian thinking about foreign direct investment and foreign trade. India's First Five Year Plan put it pithily:

> That a plan of development today must, in the main, rely on domestic resources can hardly be over-emphasised. In the first place, the conditions governing international investment are no longer what they were when some of the highly industrialised countries of today like the US, Australia and Canada began their career of development. Secondly, external assistance is acceptable only if it carries with it no conditions explicit or implicit, which might affect even remotely the country's ability to take an independent line in international affairs.[7]

7. Planning Commission (1952).

The link between an independent foreign policy and national economic development was directly drawn. This also reflected the thinking and the interests of Indian business leaders. As the authors of a plan for post-Independence economic development, popularly named the 'Bombay Plan', India's top industrialists including J.R.D. Tata, G.D. Birla, Lala Shriram and Purshothamdas Thakurdas, invited the government to step in and fill the investment gap rather than allow FDI (foreign direct investment) to do so.[8]

The Bombay Plan preferred drawing on foreign savings through external loans and aid rather than FDI. The First Five Year Plan's preference for aid over investment reflected this bias. It was a bias that was reversed in 1991, as we shall show later, when India opted for FDI and trade to bring in foreign exchange resources over loans and aid. The First Plan did recognise that even aid can come with conditions that may not serve national interest, but opted for it as the best of a bad bargain. In the words of the Plan document:

> There are also obvious risks in excessive reliance on foreign aid which depends on the domestic political situation in lending countries and which might be interrupted by any untoward international developments. And yet, external resources at strategic points and stages can be of so much assistance in a period of rapid development that it is desirable, consistently with other objectives, to create conditions favourable to their inflow.[9]

Even in Nehru's time, there was a dichotomy between how Indian diplomats and the architects of Indian foreign policy viewed the world and how its economic planners and the managers of the fisc did. The thinking within the foreign and strategic policy establishment was greatly influenced by the 'idealist' strand in Nehru's thinking, seeking a larger international role for India commensurate with her standing as a leading post-colonial democracy inspired by the idea of the solidarity of developing countries, especially the post-colonial nations of Asia and Africa. On the other hand, the thinking on external economic policy was shaped by another set of Nehru's disciples

8. Thakurdas et al. (1945).
9. Planning Commission (1952a).

who were 'realists' in their appreciation of India's capabilities and needs. Their view was further bolstered by the pragmatism of 'non-Nehruvian' economic policy makers like John Mathai, Morarji Desai and T.T. Krishnamachari.[10]

Thus, even as India offered encouragement to anti-imperialist struggles in Asia and Africa, Nehru's government was pragmatic enough to recognise the importance of attracting foreign investment and maintaining good relations with the rising developed economies of the time, especially the US. In October 1949, Nehru undertook a major tour of the US partly with a view to attracting American private sector investment into India. Before embarking on the trip his government issued a policy statement, in April 1949, that assured equal treatment to domestic and foreign business.[11] It is a different matter that the US was more focused at the time on post-War reconstruction in western Europe and East Asia and had little interest in India's development. Even so, and despite limited US interest in India at the time, Indian communists chastised Nehru for keeping India under the "American shadow."[12]

The foreign exchange crisis of 1957-58, dubbed the 'sterling crisis' due to the sharp and speedy decline in India's sterling reserves in the post-Korean War period, forced the Government of India to adopt more inward-oriented economic policies aimed at conserving foreign exchange. These policies, quite naturally, also had protectionist consequences. Domestic business, which had in fact explicitly come out in favour of loans and aid and against FDI, supported this shift in policy. India's neglect of foreign trade reflected both the 'export-pessimism' of its policy makers and the 'inward-orientation' of its industrialists. Even though the Indian sub-continent was at the crossroads of pan-Asian trade for centuries before the arrival of European traders in the Indian Ocean, India's national movement was greatly influenced by its more recent historical experience where

10. For an elaboration of this theme see Baru (2013).

11. Kidron (1965).

12. Natarajan (1952).

in trade was viewed as 'exploitative' and 'enforced' rather than as beneficial to development and growth.[13]

Thus, even as India's share of world trade declined from 2.0 per cent in 1950 to 0.5 per cent by 1980, her share of both bilateral and multilateral aid increased significantly, with India emerging as a major beneficiary of such assistance. In the period 1960s and 1970s India's share of total ODA (official development assistance) was 10 per cent, with South Asia as a whole receiving as much as the whole of Africa in ODA. In the period 1960-2003, India was the third largest recipient of the US aid, next only to Israel and Egypt.[14]

The critical importance of foreign aid and its influence on foreign policy was brought home to Indian political leadership in the mid to late 1960s when India faced an acute food shortage, following failed monsoons in 1965-66 and an acute shortage of foreign exchange after the war with Pakistan. India led what was popularly called a 'ship-to-mouth' existence, dependent on food imports from the US. In exchange for offering this assistance the US expected India to open up its economy and devalue the Indian rupee. At the same time, ironically, the US stepped forward to assist India's Green Revolution programme that aimed to reduce India's dependence on imported food. Each of these economic choices had important foreign policy consequences, shaping India's bilateral and multilateral relations.

This phase of economic development, characterised by 'state capitalism'—that is public investment creating the foundations for private sector development—mirrored in a way Indian foreign policy that sought to maintain a balance in India's relations between the capitalist West and the socialist East.[15]

Non-Alignment and Mixed Economy

The realist view of the policy of non-alignment would suggest that it was aimed at making use of Cold War divisions, steering clear

---

13. For a classic left wing statement of this view see Chandra (1966). For a liberal academic presentation of both sides of the debate see: Kumar et al. (1982).
14. Gupta et al. (2006).
15. Bettelheim (1971).

of military alliances but securing aid from both the US and the USSR. While the US aid was focused on agriculture, Soviet aid went into the creation of public sector industry and defence manufacturing. World Bank aid, which was also 'US' aid, in a manner of speaking, went into irrigation and power. Indeed, through the Cold War period India sought the US and European assistance for her developmental effort as it indeed did from the Soviet Union. The Polish macroeconomist Michal Kalecki (1972) captured this aspect of Indian policy of non-alignment well in the metaphor of the "clever calf that sucks two cows".

Kalecki's reflections on non-alignment were in the context of what he dubbed "intermediate regimes"—mixed economies in which the middle class had acquired power through the institutions of democratic governance. To quote Kalecki (1972),

> On the international scene, the internal position of the ruling lower-middle class finds its counterpart in the policy of neutrality between the two blocs; an alliance with any of the blocs would strengthen the corresponding antagonist at home (capitalists in the case of the US, working class in the case of the USSR—sb) ... The intermediate regimes are the proverbial clever calves that suck two cows; each bloc gives them financial aid competing with the other. This has made possible the 'miracle' of getting out of the USA some credits with no strings attached as to internal economic policy.

In other words, non-alignment was no strategy, much less a 'grand strategy' or 'high principle'. It was clever self-serving tactics responding to India's developmental needs and political compulsions. As a non-aligned country India utilised the strategic autonomy available to her to promote national industrial development, facilitating the rise of national business. The public sector became the foundation for the growth of an indigenous private sector.

While India's private sector remained open to greater engagement with the US, the government built public sector capacities with the help of the Soviets. Thus, a tactical policy of non-alignment facilitated the emergence of a mixed economy and the rise of the state sector strengthened the economic relationship between India and the Soviet Union. While India often took positions at variance with Western developed nations in the United Nations and within the Non-aligned Movement, on the boards of international financial institutions, dominated by the US and western Europe, Indian officials remained pragmatic, always aware of the fact that as a potential borrower India needed the support of the IFIs (international financial institution) and their key shareholders.

As a 'founding member' of the International Monetary Fund (IMF) and the World Bank India felt entitled to draw funds from both. The 1967 devaluation episode, when India felt the US was not supportive enough, strained the equation between the Indian government and the 'Bretton Woods sisters'. In 1969 India entered into a formal alliance with the Soviet Union, became a critic of the world economic order, cemented a new relationship with the Non-Aligned Movement, created the G-77 and other developing country forums and became an advocate of the New International Economic Order, a platform that was critical of the Bretton Woods institutions and the so-called 'Washington Consensus'—conservative macroeconomic policies that were aimed at encouraging debtor nations to reduce fiscal and budget deficits, privatise public enterprises, liberalise external trade and open up capital markets to external flows.[16]

It was only after the 1967-69 experience, and in the wake of India's strategic alliance with the Soviet Union, in the 1969-77 period, that India became wary of approaching the US-dominated IMF. India returned to the Fund for assistance only in 1981 after Indira Gandhi's return to power. Indira Gandhi's nuanced position on the Soviet invasion of Afghanistan in 1979, which India did not endorse, and her meeting with the US President Ronald Reagan at Cancun, Mexico, in October 1981 were indicative of a softening of her view of the US and of 'US-led institutions'. However, in response to a renewed political attack against her by the Left Front, which targeted her decision to seek IMF assistance, she opted to give up the last installment of the loan and pre-pay the loan, making it a symbol of her independence of action.[17]

16. See Williamson (1994).

17. Patel (2002).

The 1981 episode is instructive. India's application for IMF lending met with initial resistance from the US. India's case was presented starkly by her executive director on the IMF board, M. Narasimham, who told his US counterpart that if the US blocked IMF support, India would have no option but to turn to the Soviet Union for financial assistance. The US chose to abstain on the vote in the IMF board thereby enabling India to get access to IMF support, while at the same time expressing her disapproval of Indian policies at the time by not actually voting in favour of the loan application. This was probably the last time that India could, to deploy Kalecki's metaphor, try 'suck two cows', bargaining with the Cold War rivals to get what she wanted.

As the Indian economy became more private sector oriented, more open to foreign investment, more dependent on foreign trade and as India's key 'socialist' ally, the Soviet Union, imploded, Indian foreign policy too began to re-orient itself. Both Indira Gandhi and Rajiv Gandhi reached out to the US. Rajiv sought to mend fences with China, which too was now pursuing a more pragmatic economic and foreign policy. The gradual shifts in India's economic orientation in the 1980s, began to reflect themselves in similarly gradual shifts in foreign policy, culminating in the Indian decision to permit the over flight of US air force planes over Indian territory during the first Gulf War in 1990.

The Post-Cold War–Post-Liberalisation Era

It was not a mere coincidence that India faced its worst external economic crisis just around the time its strategic ally was on the verge of disappearing. The implosion of the Soviet Union, the popular uprising in eastern Europe and the end of the Cold War ran parallel to a sharp deterioration in India's economic performance. The BoP (balance of payments) crisis of 1990-91 was triggered in part by shifts in the global balance of power and the refusal of the Organisation for Economic Co-operation and Development (OECD) economies to help India tide over a payments crisis till it undertook major structural economic reforms, and perhaps a rethinking of its foreign policy.

Thus, the new turn in India's economic policies was in part a consequence of shift in India's foreign policy priorities. First, India reached out to the US, by nuancing its views on the situation in Afghanistan and the Gulf aimed at not annoying the US. Second, India stopped viewing the Association of South-east Asian Nations (ASEAN) as a pro-US cabal and treated her South-east Asian neighbours as important economic partners. Prime Minister Narasimha Rao launched a new 'Look East Policy' aimed at reviving India's long standing economic and people-to-people links with the region. Third, India extended diplomatic recognition to Israel and has, over time, become Israel's defence and strategic partner. Fourth, in opening up the economy to foreign trade and investment India reached out to both developed economies, especially the US, Japan and the European Union, and to developing economies, especially her immediate neighbours.[18] For the first time, India placed its economic growth and development at the centre of its neighbourhood policy by suggesting that the rise of India as an economic power would benefit its South Asian neighbours. While the seed of this idea is to be found in Narasimha Rao's approach to Pakistan, Bangladesh and other neighbours, Prime Minister I.K. Gujral enthusiastically promoted the idea as the 'Gujral Doctrine'.[19]

The link between the new turn in economic policies and foreign policy was directly established by Prime Minister Narasimha Rao when he told a news magazine in 1992,

> Now the Cold War is over. There is an element of cooperation instead of confrontation. It is a new situation. And we have to respond to that also. So certain policy reorientations will take place to ensure that our national interest does not suffer.[20]

Several factors contributed to this shift in Indian thinking on relations with the world and the role of economic and business interests in international relations.[21]

---

18. For a detailed discussion of the influence of economic policy changes on post-Cold War Indian foreign policy see Kim (2006).
19. Baru (2007b).
20. P.V. Narasimha Rao quoted in Sunday magazine 29 September 1991.
21. Baru (2008).

First, the collapse of the Soviet Union and the consequent disruption of an important external trade relationship. In 1989, the Soviet Union accounted for 16 per cent of India's foreign trade. By 1992, this share was down to 2.0 per cent. Soon thereafter, Russia began to demand an end to the Rupee-Rouble bilateral trading arrangement and wanted trade payments settled in US Dollars. This at a time when India was still feeling the pressure of low foreign exchange reserves.

Second, the BoP crisis of 1990-91 forced India to reach out to the US, Japan and the European Union and adopt a stabilisation and adjustment programme to secure financial support from the IMF and the World Bank. All three demanded major changes in Indian economic policy, with a focus on greater openness to foreign trade and investment, in exchange for extending support.

Third, as a consequence of the BoP crisis, as a result of new thinking within the policy making establishment, and thanks to new trends in remittance inflows and foreign trade, India chose to move away from external aid and debt as major sources of BoP support and opt for foreign trade, especially services trade, and investment, especially portfolio flows, as sources of foreign exchange.

Fourth, the 1990s saw a major change in India's approach to foreign trade in general and to a multilateral trade regime in particular. India changed its stance in 1992, departing from its earlier opposition to the launch of the Uruguay Round of trade negotiations under the General Agreement in Trade and Tariffs (GATT) to became a founding member of the World Trade Organization (WTO). India agreed to bring the services sector under WTO purview, but has insisted that the 'movement of natural persons' be governed by multilateral trading rules. India's 'Look East' policy and its interest in increasing its economic interaction with the Indian Ocean Rim countries also shaped India's relations with its wider 'Southern Asian' neighbourhood. India sought regional and bilateral trade agreements on a parallel track and supported the idea of a South Asian Free Trade Agreement (SAFTA), negotiated an FTA (free trade agreement) with ASEAN and a range of countries including South Korea, Israel and the countries of the Gulf Cooperation Council (GCC).

Fifth, China's rise as an open economy and a trading nation had a profound impact on political and academic thinking within India and shaped public policy both with respect to domestic and external economic policy and with respect to India's foreign and strategic policy.

Sixth, as the 1990s progressed, and more in the first few years of the new century, India discovered its global prowess in the field of information technology. The business generated by the so-called "Y2K" problem followed by the growth of Indian IT (information technology) and IT-enabled services business, the 'software and outsourcing' boom, and the growth in trade in services greatly changed attitudes towards globalisation and global integration, in particular towards relations with the United States.[22]

Seventh, the outward-orientation of Indian business has increased with an easing of regulations on capital inflows and outflows. The emergence of a new class of 'Forbes Billionaires' in sectors with global markets, like IT, telecom and pharmaceuticals, shaped the attitudes of a new generation of Indian enterprise, altering the attitude of Indian business to globalisation. The acquisition of firms in OECD economies and increased South-South trade and investment flows has increased the stake of Indian business in improving India's relations with these countries.

Finally, the increased outward-orientation of Indian business has made business organisations such as the Federation of Indian Chambers of Commerce and Industry (FICCI) and the Confederation of Indian Industry (CII) active players in Indian diplomacy. Both FICCI and CII have been actively engaged in trade and economic diplomacy, working closely with Indian and foreign governments. Indian diplomats, traditionally averse to dealing with private business, now increasingly find their time taken up by trade, corporate and related issues. Nowhere was the influence of business on foreign policy more evident than in the bringing to fruition of the India-US civil nuclear energy cooperation agreement.[23]

22. On the role of the IT sector in promoting India-US relations see Baru (2007c).

23. Baru (2009).

A change of government, with the ostensibly more 'ideologically' driven Bharatiya Janata Party (BJP), coming to power in 1998, did not alter the realist principles guiding post-Cold War foreign policy. In an assertion of realism Prime Minister Atal Behari Vajpayee chose to conduct nuclear weapons tests, declare India a nuclear weapons power and then, unilaterally, imposed a moratorium on further testing while adopting a 'no first use' doctrine. While the US, Japan and some other countries imposed sanctions on India after the tests were conducted, Vajpayee's pragmatic follow up decisions, including the moratorium, the doctrine and the diplomacy blunted the edge of sanctions. His government then pushed for greater economic opening up to build new bridges of inter-dependence both with major powers and India's neighbours. It was Vajpayee who gave concrete shape to the so-called Gujral Doctrine by signing the India-Sri Lanka FTA in 1998.[24]

By the turn of the century the idea that economic inter-dependence can improve relations between countries had come to influence thinking on Indian foreign policy. The successful opening up of the Indian economy in the 1990s, with the economy's growth rate rising as the share of trade in national income rose, imparted a strategic edge to India's trade policies.

Prime Minister Manmohan Singh captured this best in his reply to Sonia Gandhi when she cautioned him against the India-ASEAN FTA in 2006. "Our approach to regional trade agreements, in general, and FTAs, in particular," he told her, "has been evolved after careful consideration of our geo-political as well as economic interests. Although India has a large domestic market, our experience with earlier relatively insular policies, as also the global experience in this regard, clearly bring out the growth potential of trade and economic cooperation with the global economy."[25] Pragmatism is writ large on India's post-Cold War foreign policy. Almost all bilateral relationships, regional associations and multilateral priorities are now defined by

24. Baru, 2007, Chapters 1-7

25. Prime Minister's Letter to UPA Chairperson, 20 April, 2006. See "Manmohan allays Sonia's FTA Concerns", *Indian Express*, 8 May 2006.

India's primary concern of ensuring sustained and rapid economic development and ensuring her national security.

Economic Inter-dependence and International Relations

From 1950 to 1980, the Indian economy grew at around 3.5 per cent per year. This was the era of inward-oriented development, when India's share of world trade remained at around 0.5 per cent, compared to a 2.0 per cent share it had at the time of Independence. Foreign investment inflows were minimal and India depended almost entirely on aid and debt flows to meet its foreign exchange requirements. From 1980 to 2000, the Indian economy grew at the rate of around 5.5 per cent. This acceleration of growth was associated both with a rise in domestic savings and investment rates and an increase in the share of trade in India's national income. After 2000, and till the trans-Atlantic financial crisis and the global economic slowdown impacted India, the economy grew at an average rate of 7.5 per cent per year, maintaining an all-time high rate of close to 9.0 per cent per year in 2003-2008. This acceleration of growth and the rise in India's share of world trade, to around 1.5 per cent by the end of the first decade of this century, shaped Indian external economic and foreign policy. India concluded a series of FTAs and further opened up its economy to FDI.

Five elements have come to define Indian foreign policy during this phase of greater outward-orientation of the economy.[26]

First, the single most important objective of Indian foreign policy has come to be defined as the 'creation a global environment conducive to her economic development and the well-being of the people of India'.

Second, the idea that India would benefit from greater integration with the world economy and that India should be more closely integrated with other Asian economies as an active member of a future Asian Economic Community. India began to recognise the benefits of economic inter-dependence when it saw a country like South Korea refuse to impose sanctions on it in the wake of the

26. Baru (2014).

Pokhran tests and, on the other hand, signalled unhappiness with Scandinavian countries that did impose sanctions by cutting off their aid programmes.

Third, India's relations with major powers, especially the US, have increasingly been shaped by economic factors, including a concern for energy security and access to high technology.

Fourth, greater regional cooperation and integration, through better connectivity, in South Asia is viewed as a win-win proposition for all countries, restoring to the sub-continent the status of being the 'crossroads' of Asia.

Fifth, India's experiment of pursuing economic development within the framework of a plural, secular and liberal democracy is seen to have a global relevance, redefining relations with many countries. As the Prime Minister put it:

> Economists quantify our engagement with the world in terms of our share of world trade and capital flows; strategic analysts look at military and political alliances. I submit to you for your consideration the idea that the most enduring engagement of a people with the world is in the realm of ideas and the idea we must engage the world through is the 'idea of India'—the idea of *Vasudhaiva Kutumbakam*. The idea that even as nations may clash, cultures and civilisations can co-exist.[27]

Launching the *Indian Foreign Affairs Journal*, a journal of the Association of Indian Diplomats, in February 2006, Manmohan Singh captured the essence of this approach to foreign policy when he said:

> As we strive to realize our due place in the comity of Nations, any policy must stand the test of one simple question: how will it affect our quest for development and our need to provide a secure environment for government to deliver to our people. For this, it goes without saying that the realization of our goal lies in widening,

27. Manmohan Singh, Hindustan Times Summit, 5 November 2004. Accessed at: *http://pmindia.nic.in/speech-details.php?nodeid=37*
C. Raja Mohan clubbed these ideas together and dubbed them the 'Manmohan Singh Doctrine' in his: Mohan (2005).

> deepening and expanding our interaction with all our economic partners, with all our neighbours, with all Major Powers.[28]

Conclusion

Even though Nehru recognised early the economic underpinnings of foreign policy, as long as the Indian economy was inward-oriented and grew slowly, placing limited demands on the global economy and on its own neighbourhood, the economy imposed fewer constraints on foreign policy options. Moreover, India's global appeal as a post-colonial democracy with a secular Constitution was larger than the economic opportunity it was willing to and capable of offering the world. Thus, India could rally the developing world against neo-colonialism and seek a 'new international economic order' in the place of the one designed and dominated by the West.

As the economy grew bigger and more open, the benefits and the imperatives of global inter-dependence came to shape India's relations with the world. Economic, in particular business, interests became more pronounced in defining her relations with the world. Rather than campaign against the global order, India began to demand a role in the rule-making processes. On the occasion of the 50th anniversary of the Bandung Conference, where newly independent Asian and African nations gathered to unite against the existing world order, Prime Minister Manmohan Singh told the Africa Asia Conference in Indonesia, in 2005:

> At the global level, we must devise instrumentalities to deal with imbalances built into the functioning of the international political and economic order. We should aim to expand the constituency that supports the processes of globalization.

India's decision to shift away from aid and debt dependence to trade and investment changed the nature of her interaction with the world and the choice of partners. Like many other Asian economies, India too embraced globalisation and a more inter-dependent world worrying, however, that a crisis-ridden West may now be becoming more protectionist and insular.

---

28. Manmohan Singh, Address to Association of Indian Diplomats, 15 February 2006. *www.pmindia.nic.in*

While external dependence on energy has defined the foreign and strategic policy of many countries, including India, an additional element that India became increasingly conscious of in articulating its foreign policy was the economic clout of, for want of a better word, the Indian diaspora—both PIOs (people of Indian origins) and NRIs (non-resident Indians).

Nowhere has this role of P2P (people-to-people) interaction, involving the economic interests of PIOs and NRIs been more evident than in India's relations with the US and the countries of the Gulf. Thus, P2P and B2B (business-to-business) interests have come to define India's foreign policy priorities. This is now widely recognised and acknowledged by India's policy makers.[29]

However, if the Indian economy reverts to a more inward-oriented policy, reducing the inter-dependencies that have been enabled by the opening up of the economy and the acceleration of growth, her foreign policy would still be primarily influenced by her developmental priorities. That was Nehru's message to the Constituent Assembly in 1947, and remains relevant event today.

References

Baru, Sanjaya (2007). *Strategic Consequences of India's Economic Performance.* London: Routledge. pp.453-64.

———. (2007a). "The Economic Dimension of India's Foreign Policy", in Sanjaya Baru, *Strategic Consequences of India's Economic Performance.* London: Routledge. pp.57-74.

———. (2007b). "National Security in an Open Economy", in Sanjaya Baru, *Strategic Consequences of India's Economic Performance.* London: Routledge. p.125.

———. (2007c), "IT and the e-Economy: The Ballast for India-US relations", in Sanjaya Baru, *Strategic Consequences of India's Economic Performance.* London: Routledge.pp 294-329.

———. (2008). "India and the World: Economics and Politics of the Manmohan Singh Doctrine in Foreign Policy", *ISAS Working Paper* No. 53. Singapore, Institute for South Asian Studies. Accessed at: *iiss-me-fsprn01/home/barus/Downloads/ISAS_working%20 paper_52_21102009183722.pdf*

———. (2009). "The Influence of Business and Media on Indian Foreign Policy", *India Review* 8(3).

29. "In today's economically integrated world, economic relationships are the bedrock on which social, cultural and political relationships are built. A strategic relationship that is not underpinned by a strong economic relationship is unlikely to prosper. On the other hand, a web of economic relationships intensifies both business-to-business and people to people contacts, promoting a deeper and better understanding between countries," Manmohan Singh address to US-India Business Council, Washington DC, 23 November 2009. Accessed at: *http://pmindia.nic.in/speech-details.php?nodeid=818*

———. (2013). "The Economic Imperative to India's Multilateralism" in W.P.S. Sidhu, P.B. Mehta and B. Jones (eds.), *Shaping the Emerging World: India and the Multilateral Order.* Washington DC, Brookings Institution Press.

———. (2014). "The Manmohan Singh Doctrine", in Sanjaya Baru, *The Accidental Prime Minister: The Making and Unmaking of Manmohan Singh*. Chapter 9. New Delhi: Penguin/Viking.

Bettelheim, Charles (1971). *India Independent*. New York: Monthly Review Press.

Chandra, Bipan (1966). *The Rise and Growth of Economic Nationalism in India: Economic Policies of Indian National Leadership.* New Delhi: People's Publishing House.

Gupta, Sanjeev, Pattillo, Catherine and Wagh, Smita (2006). "Are Donor Countries Giving More or Less Aid?", *Working Paper* WP/06/1, Washington DC: International Monetary Fund. Accessed at: *www.imf.org/external/pubs/ft/wp/2006/wp0601.pdf*

Kalecki, Michal (1972). "Observations on Social and Economic Aspects of Intermediate Regimes", in Michal Kalecki, *Selected Essays on the Economic Growth of the Socialist and the Mixed Economy.* Cambridge: Cambridge University Press.

Kidron, Michael (1965). *Foreign Investments in India*. London: Oxford University Press.

Kim, Chan Wahn (2006). *Economic Liberalisation and India's Foreign Policy.* Delhi: Kalpaz Publications.

Kumar, Dharma, Tapan Raychaudhuri, Irfan Habib and Meghnad Desai (eds.) (1982). *The Cambridge Economic History of India.* Vols. 1 & 2. Cambridge: Cambridge University Press.

Mohan, C. Raja (2005). "Rethinking India's Grand Strategy", in N.S. Sisodia and C. Uday Bhaskar (eds.), *Emerging India: Security and Foreign Policy Perspectives*. New Delhi. IDSA and Bibliophile South Asia.

Natarajan, L. (1952). *American Shadow Over India*. Delhi: People's Publishing House.

Patel, I.G. (2002). *Glimpses of Indian Economic Policy*. Delhi, Oxford University Press. Chapter 7.

Planning Commission (1952). *First Five Year Plan, 1952*. Government of India. Accessed at *http://planningcommission.nic.in/plans/planrel/fiveyr/index1.html*

Planning Commission (1952a). "Introduction", in *First Five Year Plan, 1952*. Government of India.

Thakurdas, P. Tata, J.R.D., Birla, G.D. et al. (1945). *A Brief Memorandum Outlining a Plan of Economic Development for India*. Bombay, Penguin.

Williamson, John (ed.) (1994). *The Political Economy of Policy Reform*. Washington DC. Institute for International Economics.

5

The Political Economy of Post Cold War Indian Foreign Policy

Much of the political and public discourse on Indian foreign policy in recent years has come to focus too narrowly on the diplomacy around the civil nuclear energy cooperation agreement that India has engaged in with the United States of America (US) and the 45-member Nuclear Suppliers Group (NSG). While this is undoubtedly a major initiative of Prime Minister Manmohan Singh, his other foreign policy pre-occupations have been the diplomacy associated with India's participation in the East Asia Summit and the building of an East Asian Community; the revitalisation of the South Asian Association for Regional Cooperation (SAARC), with a focus on normalising relations with Pakistan; and, increased South-South cooperation, with a focus on development cooperation in Africa. Economic issues have been at the core of each of these initiatives. Singh's primary objective has been to improve the global and regional environment for sustaining India's growth process and overall development.

In an early comment on the foreign policy initiatives of Prime Minister Singh, C. Raja Mohan (2005) outlined four elements of what he dubbed as the Manmohan Singh Doctrine. These four elements are:

i) the changing weight of India in the global economy as a factor shaping its weight in global affairs;
ii) recognition of the new opportunities available to India, as a consequence of its economic growth and openness, to improve relations with all major powers;

iii) positive impact of a new approach to the developing world, based on India's economic globalisation, on regional integration in South Asia and bilateral relations with neighbours; and
iv) the recognition that as an open society and an open economy India can build bridges with the world on the foundations of its democratic, liberal, plural and secular credentials.

A closer look at his views on India and the world over a longer period of time and an examination of his major initiatives as Prime Minister allows us to elaborate further on Raja Mohan's formulation. Singh's diplomatic initiatives as Prime Minister cannot be the only basis for the articulation of a doctrine. This paper is based on Singh's articulation of a foreign policy vision dating back to his days as Union Finance Minister. Singh's remarks, in his very first budget speech in July 1991, mark the point of departure for a new phase in Indian foreign policy thinking. His views on India's relations with the world in the post-Cold War era and in the era of globalisation, and the initiatives taken by the P.V. Narasimha Rao Government, have shaped the policy of successive governments in India. Hence, it is fair and relevant to talk of a 'Manmohan Singh Doctrine', albeit one that is painted on a wider canvas than his tenure as Prime Minister.

In elaborating Raja Mohan's four propositions, we draw attention to Singh's persistent focus on economic development as the central objective of India's relations with other countries,and his enunciation of the idea of "inclusive globalisation"; his articulation of the notion of "creating a web of inter-dependencies"; and, his pursuit of "asymmetric liberalisation" with less developed economies. We suggest that the Manmohan Singh Doctrine is premised upon:

i) India's ability to sustain the recent growth momentum, of an annual average growth rate of national income of close to nine per cent;
ii) assurance of energy security, food security and livelihood security;
iii) the growth process being socially and regionally more inclusive and balanced;

iv) fiscal and price stability and the fiscal empowerment of the State;
v) the pursuit of employment creating industrialisation and rural development;
vi) remaining a globally open economy, while pursuing closer integration with the economies of South, West, Southeast and East Asia; and
vii) remaining an open and plural society, socially and politically inclusive, liberal and secular.

In his very first budget speech in Parliament, in July 1991, Singh linked India's global standing with its economic performance. After spelling out his strategy to deal with an immediate crisis—a BoP (balance of payments) and fiscal crisis—Singh firmly anchored his economic initiatives in a wider strategic setting. He ended his historic speech with the now famous quote from Victor Hugo ("No power on earth can stop an idea whose time has come") and added:

> I suggest to this August House that the emergence of India as a major economic power in the world happens to be one such idea. Let the whole world hear it loudcand clear. India is now wide awake. We shall prevail. We shall overcome.

Six years later, recalling this speech in an interview published in the inaugural edition of a new international affairs journal, *World Affairs*, Singh underlined the foreign policy implications of the 'new economic policies' unveiled by the Narasimha Rao government.[1] There was no doubt in Singh's mind that the liberalisation of the Indian economy and the 'new turn' in its economic policies were part of a new strategic policy orientation taken in the context of the collapse of the Soviet Union, the rise of China and East Asian economies, and India's own economic rise in the 1980s.

Indeed, Rao himself so explained his foreign policy initiatives. In one of his first media interviews, explaining his foreign and economic policies, Rao said, "now the Cold War is over. There is an element of cooperation instead of confrontation. It is a new situation. And we

1. Interview with Manmohan Singh, "Liberalisation and Globalisation: Where is India Heading?", *World Affairs* (Delhi) I(1), January-March 1997.

have to respond to that. So certain policy orientations will take place to ensure that our national interest does not suffer."[2] In 1991 this 'national interest' was defined essentially in economic terms, given the crisis at hand and the need to pull India back from the brink of bankruptcy.

However, it was not merely the compulsions of crisis management that forced a rethink on foreign policy priorities. The crisis had been anticipated by many economists and there was a long period of rethinking on economic policy priorities preceding the 1990-91 crisis. This rethinking was triggered by the development experience of East and Southeast Asian economies and that of China, which had launched its own "Four Modernisations" policy a decade earlier, as part of a general reorientation of its strategic policy and its relations with the outside world.

In an interview given to this writer in February 1991, three months before he assumed charge as India's finance minister, Singh told *The Economic Times* (Delhi) that India has to learn from the East Asian experience and reorient its economic policies.[3] He reminded Indians that, in 1960, South Korea and India were on par in economic terms, including their level of industrial development but by the late 1980s, Korea had become a "newly industrializing economy", an "Asian Tiger", while India still lagged behind. He returned to this theme in his last Budget Speech in February 1995, "It is this vision, of a resurgent India taking her rightful place as an economic power house in Asia, which has inspired our economic policies".

In relating India's economic capabilities to its global profile and influence Singh was in fact drawing on early "Nehruvian realism" that had been forgotten during the intervening years when Indian foreign policy was shaped more by the "low politics" of the Cold War era and the "high politics" of post-colonialism. It was an interregnum

2. P.V. Narasimha Rao quoted in *Sunday*, 29 September 1991. For a detailed discussion see Kim (2006). These issues have also been discussed in Dixit (1996) Dutt (1999).

3. Manmohan Singh's interview to Sanjaya Baru, 30th Anniversary Special Edition, *The Economic Times*, 15 March 1991.

in which "non-alignment" became an "ideology" rather than the "strategy" that it initially was.[4]

In his very first speech on foreign policy as Prime Minister of free India, Jawaharlal Nehru had observed,

> Talking about foreign policies, the House must remember that these are not just empty struggles on a chessboard. Behind them lie all manner of things. Ultimately, foreign policy is the outcome of economic policy, and until India has properly evolved her economic policy, her foreign policy will be rather vague,rather inchoate, and will be groping. ...a vague statement that we stand for peace and freedom by itself has no particular meaning, because every country is prepared to say the same thing, whether it means it or not. What then do we stand for? Well, you have to develop this argument in the economic field. As it happens today, in spite of the fact that we have been for some time in authority as a Government, I regret that we have not produced any constructive economic scheme or economic policy so far ...When we do so, that will govern our foreign policy more than all the speeches in this House.[5]

In a further elaboration of this "realist" and "instrumentalist" perspective on foreign policy, Nehru added, "Whatever policy we may lay down, the art of conducting the foreign affairs of a country lies in finding out what is most advantageous to the country." It is this original Nehruvian 'realist' perspective that Singh brought back to Indian thinking on foreign policy. Several factors contributed to this shift in Indian thinking on relations with the world and the role of economics and business in international relations.

First, the collapse of the Soviet Union and the consequent disruption of an important external trade relationship. It was not just the economic and strategic fallout of this that was debilitating for India, but also the political and diplomatic fall-out. The Soviet Union was an importance "balancer" from India's point of view in its negotiations with Organisation for Economic Co-operation and Development (OECD) countries, and with multilateral financial

4. On the idea that "Nehruvian non-alignment" was a "strategy" rather than an "ideology", which is what it became subsequently and especially in the 1970s and 1980s, see Baru (2006).

5. For reference see Baru (2006), Chapter 2.

institutions. As recently as in 1980 Indira Gandhi used the "Soviet Card", as it were, in her negotiations with the International Monetary Fund (IMF) to secure improved terms for an extended financing facility loan[6].

Second, the BoP (balance of payments) crisis of 1990-91 and the need to adopt a stabilisation and adjustment programme to secure financial support from the IMF and the World Bank. India also reached out to Japan for bilateral assistance and found Japan unwilling to extend such support without India adopting a clear programme of reform and adjustment. Finance Minister Yashwant Sinha had to return from Tokyo empty-handed, after having been kept waiting for an appointment with his counterpart.

Third, as a consequence of the BoP crisis, as a result of new thinking within the policy making establishment, and thanks to new trends in remittance inflows and foreign trade, India chose to move away from external aid and debt as major sources of BoP support and opt for foreign trade, especially services trade, and investment, especially portfolio flows, as sources of foreign exchange.

Fourth, the 1990s saw a major change in India's approach to foreign trade in general and to a multilateral trade regime in particular. India became a founding member of the World Trade Organization (WTO) and committed itself to multilateral rules of engagement in trade. India also began to seek regional and bilateral trade agreements on a parallel track and supported the idea of a South Asian Free Trade Agreement (FTA), to begin with, and soon expressed interest in an India-ASEAN FTA. India's 'Look East' policy and its interest in increasing its economic interaction with the Indian Ocean Rim countries also shaped India's relations with its wider "Southern Asian" neighbourhood.

Fifth, China's rise as an open economy and a trading nation had a profound impact on political and academic thinking within India

6. India's executive director on the IMF Board, M. Narasimham, told this writer in an interview years later that the US was dragging its feet on voting in favour of the Indian loan application on the IMF Board. It was a threat from Mrs Gandhi to turn to the Soviets for help, after having criticised them an year before for their invasion of Afghanistan, that encouraged the US administration to direct its Governor on the IMF board to "abstain" on the India loan application vote and allow it to go through.

and shaped public policy both with respect to domestic and external economic policy and with respect to India's foreign and strategic policy.

Sixth, as the 1990s progressed, and more in the first few years of the new century, India discovered its global prowess in the field of information technology. The business generated by the so-called "Y2K" problem followed by the growth of Indian IT (information technology) and IT-enabled services business, the "software and outsourcing" boom, and the growth in trade in services greatly changed attitudes towards globalisation and global integration.

Seventh, in more recent years the outward-orientation of Indian business has also increased. First inspired by the experience of IT firms such as Tata Consultancy Services, Infosys and WIPRO and, subsequently, by that of pharmaceutical majors like Ranbaxy and Dr. Reddy's, Indian business groups began to move away from their earlier inward-looking "Bombay Club" mentality to a more global orientation. The recent listing of Indians among "Forbes Billionaires" is only one visible symbol of Indian business making its mark outside. Such success, howsoever limited as yet, and new attitudes of a new generation of Indian enterprise, has encouraged Indian business to push for more aggressive globalisation. This 'outward orientation' of Indian business has shaped India's relations with many OECD economies, including the United States. It has also made Indian business organisations such as the Federation of Indian Chambers of Commerce and Industry (FICCI) and the Confederation of Indian Industry (CII) active players in Indian diplomacy. The 'business diplomacy' of FICCI and CII has shaped public and political opinion at home and won new friends for India outside.[7]

Impact of Successful External Liberalisation

The impact of the economic reform and liberalisation programme launched in 1991 was felt soon enough on the performance of the economy. Compared to an average annual rate of growth of 3.5 per cent in the period 1950-1980 and about 5.5 per cent in 1980-1990,

7. For a detailed discussion of the rising influence of business in foreign policy see: Baru (2008).

the Indian economy grew by close to 7.5 per cent in 1992-1997. There was a slowdown after that till the revival of 7.0 per cent plus growth after 2003. The net impact of this accelerated growth was to take India away from its historical comparison with South Asia and Pakistan into a new league where its performance was increasingly compared with that of China and ASEAN. This had its own geo-political and strategic consequence.[8]

India's improved macroeconomic performance in the decade of 1991-2001 had more than a positive impact on its external economic and diplomatic profile. India's trade/GDP (gross domestic product) ratio went up, and so did her foreign exchange reserves. There was a sharp decline in external debt and debt service ratio. After 2000, services exports went up from around US$10 billion in 1999 to over US$60 billion by 2006. A third of this was accounted for by software services exports. India's share of world services exports rose to over 2.5 per cent of world's services exports and its share of world merchandise exports doubled from 0.5 per cent in 1990 to 1.0 per cent by 2005 and to 1.5 per cent by 2007-08.

India's external economic liberalisation strategy can be described as a 'stable and successful' strategy. It was characterised by policy stability and a step-by-step approach that helped it escape the Asian financial crisis in 1997-98, weather trade sanctions after the nuclear tests in 1998, accumulate foreign exchange reserves, ensure exchange rate stability, reduce external debt burden and increase its share of global capital flows.

All this reflected itself in a more robust engagement of the outside world. India went into the Doha Development Round of WTO negotiations with a forward-looking strategy focused on securing better market access to industrial products, agricultural goods and to skilled services. Singh took a pro-active stance on multilateral and regional trade negotiations. Early in his term as Prime Minister, he created a new institutional mechanism for coordinated policymaking on the external front in the form of the Trade and Economic Relations Committee (TERC). TERC was chaired by the Prime

8. See Baru (2006a).

Minister and included the Ministers of External Affairs, Finance, Industry and Commerce, and Agriculture, and the Deputy Chairman of the Planning Commission and the National Security Advisor. TERC remained an active body in the period 2004-2008, pushing forward the India-ASEAN FTA and defining India's stance on a range of other bilateral, regional and multilateral trade negotiations.

Singh was a strong proponent of the view that India had a "strategic stake" in the multilateral system managed by the WTO. "We have as a nation, a great stake in a rule based international system, a system that is rule based and not deal based," Singh would often say, and repeatedly reaffirm India's commitment to "the successful functioning of the multilateral trading system and to broadening the agenda of the WTO with an increasingly liberal flow of goods, services and labour." Contrary to western media perception, India is not responsible for the current impasse in the Doha Round negotiations, since India has a strategic stake in multilateralism.[9] India would like the Doha Round to adhere to its original mandate of being a "development round".

Without diluting its commitment to multilateralism, India also pursued regional and bilateral FTAs. Successive Indian Finance Ministers, beginning with P. Chidambaram in 1997, set the policy objective of "lowering our tariffs at least to ASEAN levels."[10] Singh would reiterate as Prime Minister that this was a "policy priority for us".

Making India a member of the East Asian Community became a policy imperative for Prime Minister Singh. "I have stated my commitment to the idea of creating an Asian Economic Community, an arc of prosperity across Asia, in which there are no barriers to trade and investment flows and to the movement of people" he told the CII Partnership Summit in Kolkata in January 2005.

---

9. The propaganda in western media that Indian trade minister Kamal Nath was responsible for stalling Doha Round negotiations is not valid. However, it is true that Indian trade ministers are quite happy to be portrayed in the West as obstructionists in trade negotiations since this plays well in domestic politics. I recall former trade ministers Murasoli Maran and Arun Jaitley defending their stance at the Doha and Cancun WTO Ministerial Meetings on these grounds. Prime Minister Singh remains firmly committed to a successful conclusion of the Doha Round, as long as it protects the interests of India's small and marginal farmers.

10. Budget Speech, 28 February 1997.

While greater openness to external trade has increased the importance of external relations, the changing geographical pattern of that trade has quite understandably changed the relative importance of different countries. During the Cold War period, the Soviet Union was an important economic partner for India. Apart from defence purchases, India depended on the Soviet market to sell a range of commodities through what came to be described as "rupee trade". With the collapse of the Soviet Union, the Soviet market disappeared. In its place, and apart from the United States and European Union, ASEAN and the East Asian markets emerged as an important destination for Indian exports. Even in defence-related trade, Russia is no longer a dominant player, with India diversifying its defence imports.

India's integration into the world economy has more recently manifested itself in increased outward investment by Indian 'multinational' companies.[11] Outward FDI (foreign direct investment) by India shot up from less than US$2 billion in 2003-2005 to US$14.4 billion in 2006-07, and continues to rise as large Indian companies take over multinationals in a range of industries such as pharmaceuticals, steel, telecom and automobiles. Business leaders like Lakshmi Mittal, the Ambani Brothers and Ratan Tata have acquired a profile in India's relations with a wide range of countries. Their influence and that of business organisations such as CII and FICCI in foreign policy choices has grown over the years.

Apart from increased trade and capital flows, India has also benefited from out-migration of skilled labour and brain power. Inward remittances of migrant labour constitute an important source of foreign capital inflows. The presence of several million Indian workers in the Middle East and in OECD economies has become a strategic asset for the Indian economy, creating a strategic stake for India in the smooth functioning of the global economy and in the stability of the regions where overseas Indians live and work.

11. Ramamurti ansd Singh (2009) discusses in some detail this phenomenon of Indian multinational enterprise.

Singh also viewed the growing economic importance of overseas Indians as a by-product of the policies of economic liberalisation he introduced in 1991. At the annual gathering of over seas Indians and people of Indian origin, the Pravasi Bharatiya Diwas, in January 2005, Singh said:

> There is, of course, something more tangible than emotion that brings us closer today. This is the opportunity we are creating at home for overseas Indians to once again relate in a meaningful way to their ancient motherland. The process began with the measures we took in 1991 to liberalise and modernise the Indian economy. The many subsequent steps taken by successive Governments have enabled Indians abroad to invest at home and to travel freely to and from India.
>
> More recently it has also become possible for many to simultaneously pursue professional careers and businesses both in their host countries and in their home country... I feel particularly happy that the economic policies we initiated at home in the past decade have enabled us to connect with you more vigorously and to engage you in meaningful ways in the reconstruction of our Motherland.
>
> These policies have significantly contributed to the emergence of India as a major global player in the economic world. Together with the tremendous strides our country has been making in the knowledge based sector, there is no doubt that the 21st century is going to be an Indian century.

Apart from expanding trade and seeking foreign investment, India's global economic diplomacy was focused on two other important objectives—first, energy security; and second, regional integration. We return to these issues in the next section.

II

It should be clear from our discussion thus far that sustaining India's economic growth and outward orientation, and ensuring the sustainability of that process, became an important driving element shaping Indian foreign policy in recent years. The key objectives were market access, energy security and access to high technology. These objectives gained greater salience in the context of the rise of

Asian economies, and the consequent competition for markets and resources. The energy security objective became even more important in the context of global fears pertaining to global warming and climate change.

Against this background, we should expect Singh to take a pro-active stance in dealing with the consequences of the global financial crisis and economic slowdown. He has already stated that this remains his top priority.[12]

Taken together, these developmental objectives shaped Indian policy towards the major powers, especially the United States, and towards its wider neighbourhood, especially ASEAN and East Asia, the developing world and major global issues of the day, including climate change.

In a major policy speech at the India Today Conclave, in February 2005, Singh said:

> Our relations with major powers, especially the United States, and more recently China, have increasingly been shaped by economic factors... In the case of the United States, an acceleration of people-to-people contact and the consequent business-to-business interaction has forged closer state-to-state relations. Shared values and growing economic links have enabled a closer strategic engagement.[13]

Singh went on to underscore the role of business and commerce in shaping India's relations with European Union, Russia, China, Japan, Korea, ASEAN and the rest of the world. This statement elaborated Singh's view that "government-to-government' bilateral relations were increasingly shaped by "people-to-people" and "business-to-business" contacts.

---

12. It is pertinent to note that during the week when India was hit by renewed terrorist attacks, Prime Minister Singh told the media that his "first priority" was to ensure that the Indian economy was insulated from the fallout of the global financial crisis and his second prioritywas to fight terrorism. He viewed the financial and economic threat as more deserving of his immediate attention rather than terrorism. *www.rediff.com/*September 30, 2008. Singh's statement in Parliament on 20 October, 2008—*www.pmindia.nic.in/speeches.htm*—and his remarks in Tokyo on 22 October 2008, suggest that India will remain pro-active in dealing with the impact and consequences of the financial crisis and the global economic slowdown so as to ensure that is not hurt by them and it is able to sustain its growthprocess. If India can succeed in doing this, and if Pakistan slips into an economic crisis and China slowsdown, India's strategicenvironment would improve.
13. Full text in Government of India (2005).

Summarising his approach to strategic and foreign policy at his first interaction with the senior leadership of the armed forces, Singh said:

> Greater economic integration will be a basis for greater security, enhanced cooperative efforts and stable relations. Consequently, we may have to revisit some of the traditionally accepted notions of 'self-sufficiency' and 'self reliance'.[14]

Singh was more expansive at the subsequent Combined Commanders in October 2005 where he summarised his approach to strategic policy:

> Our strategy has to be based on three broad pillars, first, to strengthen our selves economically and technologically; second, to acquire adequate defence capability to counter and rebut threats to our security; and third, to seek partnerships both on the strategic front and on the economic and technological front to widen our policy and developmental options.

In the same vein, he said at the 40th anniversary celebrations of the Institute of Defence Studies and Analysis a few days later:

> Our engagement with the major powers and indeed with the world must be set in this wider perspective. We must balance the pursuit of national interests with a clear appreciation of what other nations perceive as their core interests. To advance our own security interests, we must engage in cooperative, constructive and mutually beneficial relations with all major powers of the world. Most of all,we must engage in pro actively strengthening multilateral mechanisms for financial, economic and political security.[15]

The United States and Major Powers

While Singh's first visit abroad was to Bangkok for the Bay of Bengal Initiative for Multisectoral Technical and Economic Cooperation (BIMSTEC) Summit, his first important meeting was

---

14. Prime Minister Manmohan Singh, Address to Combined Commanders Conference, Defence Headquarters, New Delhi, 26 October 2004. Abridged version only in Selected Speeches, Vol.1 *www.pmindia.nic.in/speeches.htm*

15. Institute of Defence Studies & Analysis, 11 November 2005. *www.pmindia.nic.in/speeches.htm*, Selected Speeches, Vol.2.

with President George Bush of the US on the sidelines of the United Nations General Assembly in September 2004. Rising crude oil price was on both their mind so the conversation naturally focused on the subject. Singh told Bush that India's dependence on imported oil had gone up and if India had to sustain high growth over the long term it had no option but to explore alternative energy options. India's desire to expand civil nuclear energy was constrained by a discriminatory global regime. Bush quickly understood the problem. If China and India continue to rise at high rates of growth their per capita consumption of energy will go up, agreed Bush. If the world community had to ensure that this did not result in a sharp rise in oil prices, which would of course hurt American consumers, then India must have the ability to explore the nuclear energy option. Bush readily conceded the argument and hoped that the United States and India would be able to work together to help India exercise the nuclear energy option.

That is how the civil nuclear energy issue first came up. This conversation on energy security and helping India sustain its growth process was taken forward at their next meeting in Moscow in early May 2005. It is important to note that in the Joint Statement issued by the two leaders after the summit meeting at the White House on 18 July 2005, the civil nuclear energy issue was one among many other equally important initiatives aimed at promoting India's economic and technological development.

What began as a bilateral initiative between India and the United States, reflecting their shared concern with rising oil prices and their shared interest in developing nuclear and alternative energy sources, evolved into a major global diplomatic initiative for India. The agreement with the United States was contingent upon India signing a Safeguards Agreement with the 145-member International Atomic Energy Agency (IAEA) and the 45-member NSG.

The agreements that have now been signed—with IAEA and NSG and the United States and France, and Russia is to follow—pave the way for an expansion of India's civil nuclear energy potential. These agreements, based on a "separation plan" that fire walls India's military nuclear programme from the civil energy programme, also imply a de factor ecognition of India as a nuclear weapons power.

Singh pursued this initiative mainly with the aim of widening India's development options by enhancing its energy security and ending restraints imposed on trade in high technology. While the civil nuclear cooperation agreement with the United States may have other strategic and political dimensions, it was primarily motivated by Singh's concern for India's long-term energy security.[16] The sharp rise in crude oil prices in the past few years only served to add a sense of urgency to this agreement. The purely "ideological" critics of the agreement, on the Indian political 'Left' and 'Right', refused to accord the same weight as Singh did to the economic significance of the agreement. The Left rejected the agreement on the grounds that it would entail closer strategic relations with the United States, and the Right on the grounds that it would impinge on India's strategic autonomy. Singh viewed the agreement as necessary to an expansion of India's nuclear energy capacity, overall energy security, and to open up new avenues for cooperation in high technology areas, contributing to India's growth potential.

Singh also viewed the agriculture and knowledge initiatives as equally important. He has often emphasised the supportive role of United States assistance in India's 'first' Green Revolution and underscored the potential for such cooperation in launching a "second Green Revolution". It was in this context that he sought United States investment in agricultural research and development. Similarly, he sought United States support in the further development of India's knowledge economy. The entire focus of the joint statement was,therefore, on a broad range of growth-oriented priorities.

The Prime Minister's statement in Parliament on 17 August 2006 on the civil nuclear cooperation agreement was the most

16. In September 2004 at the first meeting between Prime Minister Manmohan Singh and President George Bush rising energy prices were on top of both their minds, since both were grappling with the problem at home. The conversation about developing India's nuclear energy option came up in the context of rising oil prices. It should be noted that this was not the only subject on the agenda of the two leaders. As the July 18th Joint Statement clearly shows, both placed great emphasis on economic cooperation, including in the fields of agriculture, and on human resources development.

comprehensive statement he had made on the subject. While the second part of the statement was prepared by officials, the first few paras were spoken extempore. Singh defended the nuclear agreement only on the grounds of energy security and even went to the extent of boldly stating that India's nuclear programme in fact began as a civil energy programme and not as a military weapons programme. No Indian Prime Minister after Jawaharlal Nehru has had the courage to say that in Parliament. Singh said:

> Sir, it is my solid conviction that mass poverty can be removed only if we have a fast expanding economy... If India has to grow at the rate of 8 percent to 10 per cent and, maybe, more, India needs rising amounts of energy... In this context, we must never forget the primary motivation for India's nuclear programme was the production of energy, defence came much later... all development is about widening human choices. And, when it comes to energy security, widening our choices means that we should be able to make effective use of nuclear power. If the need arises, if the economic calculus demands that this is the most cost-effective means.[17]

India's engagement of all major powers is sharply focused on trade, investment and movement of skilled people. While political issues like terrorism and India's membership of the United Nations Security Council get discussed at summit-level meetings, and find reflection in joint statements, the key to all major bilateral relationships has become the extent, range and depth of economic engagement. Even the difficult India-China relationship has been sustained by a sharp increase in bilateral trade, with discussions on the border stuck in a groove.

Singh's approach to the developed world, especially the G-8, was summed up in his comment to the media after the Helligendamm Summit that the G-5 developing countries were happy to participate in the meeting with G-8 as long as they had an opportunity to shape thinking within the G-8 on global issues of the day and not just as mute observers. Singh refused to attend the G8 Summit in Japan when it was first indicated that the hosts had arranged only

17. *See www.pmindia.nic.in/speeches.htm,*

for an hour's interaction between G-8 and G-5 leaders, and that too over breakfast. Singh secured G-5 support for his stand that the so-called "outreach meeting" made no sense unless G-5 concerns were incorporated into the G-8 statement. This required interaction between the G-8 and G-5 'before' the G-8 joint statement had been drafted and adopted, rather than after.

India and Immediate Neighbours

Next in importance to the civil nuclear cooperation agreement that Singh has successfully negotiated with members of the NSG and the United States, was Singh's initiatives with respect to the relationship with Pakistan and his attempts to "resolve" the issue of Jammu and Kashmir. Singh invited President Pervez Musharraf of Pakistan to visit New Delhi in April 2005 to witness a cricket match between teams of the two countries. The visit evolved into a summit meeting that put out a wide-ranging joint statement, taking forward the dialogue process from where Musharraf and Atal Behari Vajpayee had left it in January 2004.

While announcing his decision to invite President Musharraf in Parliament, Singh enunciated a new idea of more informal interaction among South Asian leaders. Singh was aware of the fact that excessive protocol and ceremony had come to stultify contact among South Asian leaders. Each meeting, especially between Indian and Pakistani leaders, became the focus of media hype and often excessive expectation resulting in disappointment. The infamous Agra Summit fiasco only under-scored this sad reality. Hence, Singh put forward a new theory of greater informal contact, though he has not been able to practice it as often as he may have liked. Putting forward this idea in Parliament, Singh said,

> Relations between nations are after all nothing more than relations between their people. I am sure that time will work to heal our wounds and create an environment of shared prosperity and peace in the sub-continent... Sir, I am happy to inform Hon. Members of the House that I have decided to invite President Musharraf to come to India to watch the cricket match between our two teams. It is my earnest desire that the people in our neighbouring country and their

> leaders should feel free to visit us whenever they wish to do so. Be it to watch a cricket match; be it to do some shopping; or be it to meet friends and families—India is proud to be an open society and an open economy.[18]

The bilateral engagement that began at this summit has kept its focus on increased 'people-to people' interaction and greater economic interaction between the two neighbours as a means of resolving the long standing dispute over Jammu and Kashmir. On the eve of his becoming Prime Minister in May 2004, Singh told journalist Jonathan Power (*Statesman*, 20 May 2004, it was an off-the-record conversation that Power published without Singh's permission), "Short of secession, short of re-drawing boundaries, the Indian establishment can live with anything. Meanwhile, we need soft borders—then borders are not so important."

This is precisely the idea that Singh has pursued in office. At the official banquet on the eve of their summit meeting in New Delhi in April 2005, Singh told Musharraf:

> Our people and our common destiny urge us to make an earnest attempt to find a lasting solution to all issues. In a globalising and increasingly integrated world, borders have lost meaning for much of the world. The journey of peace must be based on a step-by-step approach.

This theme of the "irrelevance of borders in a globalised world" Singh has repeated on many occasions in the context of Jammu and Kashmir. The persistence of terrorist attacks and, more importantly, the political developments inside Pakistan slowed down the engagement that Singh and Musharraf began. However, initiatives based on the Singh Doctrine, of increasing "people-to-people" and "business-to-business" interaction, as a means of resolving"government-to-government" differences, have moved ahead. There is today greater connectivity between the two sides of the Line of Control. Singh spoke of his "dream" and his "vision" that one day he could have "breakfast in Amritsar, lunch in Lahore and dinner in Kabul" moving with ease from one country to another. Step by step initiatives are being taken in that direction.

18. Manmohan Singh in Lok Sabha, 10 March 2005. *www.pmindia.nic.in/speeches.htm*

While the outline of an eventual solution to the problem of Jammu and Kashmir is not yet clear, President Musharraf shared his thinking on the subject with A.G. Noorani (*Frontline*, August 2006):

> Kashmir will have the same borders but people will be allowed to move freely back and forth in the region, ii) the region will have self-governance or autonomy, but not independence; iii) troops will be withdrawn from the region ina staggered manner; and iv) a joint supervision mechanism ('institutional arrangement') will be set up, with India, Pakistan and Kashmir represented on it.

Recent initiatives to strengthen cross-border trade and further improve connectivity between India and Pakistan must be viewed in this perspective. The recent visit of Nepal's new President Prachanda to India also reinforced the importance of strengthening trade and connectivity between the neighbours.

Asymmetric Trade Liberalisation

An important element of the Manmohan Singh Doctrine, flowing directly from the ideas of the South Commission, of which he was the Secretary-General, is what I would call the idea of 'Asymmetric Liberalisation'. In the South Asian context, this idea has been referred to as "non-reciprocal" liberalisation. India's smaller neighbours expected India to do more in terms of providing market access than they would be asked to do for India. In recent foreign policy literature the acceptance of this principle has been attributed to former Prime Minister I.K. Gujral, and has been dubbed the so-called 'Gujral Doctrine'. The idea precedes Gujral's term as Prime Minister and was first advocated by Singh during his tenure as finance minister in the Narasimha Rao government.[19]

While many analysts and earlier governments had only spoken of 'non-reciprocal liberalisation' only in the South Asian context, Singh

19. The phrase 'Gujral Doctrine' was in fact promoted by I.K. Gujral himself. I recall being asked to interview him on Doordarshan when he was Prime Minister, as part of a panel that comprised Kuldip Nayyar and Jasjit Singh. Before the recording Gujral expressed the hope that the interview would seek his elaboration on "what people have been referring to as the Gujral Doctrine". Nayyar, who wasGujral personal friend, appointed High Commissioner to UK by Gujral in 1989 (when Gujral was foreign minister in the V.P. Singh government) and subsequently nominated to the Rajya Sabha by Gujral in 1997 (when he was Prime Minister), readily obliged and asked him to define the 'Gujral Doctrine'!

extended this idea to all LDCs (least developed countries). First, in Southeast Asia, when he extended non-reciprocal trade preferences to ASEAN's CMLV countries (Cambodia, Myanmar, Laos and Vietnam). At the Delhi Summit of SAARC in 2006, this policy was extended to all South Asian LDCs. At the India-Africa Summit in 2008, it was extended to all LDCs.

Singh has taken the idea of "asymmetric liberalisation", whereby India does more for its neighbours without any expectation of immediate reciprocity, forward in India's relations with all its neighbours. The offers made by India at bilateral meetings and at the SAARC Summits at Dhaka, Delhi and Colombo reflect the Manmohan Singh Doctrine.[20] Singh personally took interest in creating an agenda for SAARC when he offered asymmetric trade concessions, offered opportunities for coordinated research and policy making on issues like climate change, disaster management, improved road, rail and air connectivity and the creation of the South Asian University.

A similar approach of building long-term relationship through investment in its neighbour's progress has marked Singh's approach to other South Asian neighbours as well. In the neighbourhood, however, the 'fourth dimension' of the Manmohan Singh Doctrine of contributing to the strengthening of democracy has come to play in a significant way. We will return to this in the last section.

India and Wider Asian Neighbourhood: East Asian Community

Singh has, in fact, attached even greater importance to economic integration with East and Southeast Asia. India's participation in the East Asian Summit and the creation of an East Asian Community with India in it have been important foreign policy priorities for him. His first visit abroad as Prime Minister was to Bangkok for the first Summit of the BIMSTEC in July 2004. India's full participation in an East Asian Community became the main focus of India's 'Look East' policy during Singh's four years in office so far. Towards this end, he has vigorously pursued an India-ASEAN FTA, in the face of

20. The notion of "non-reciprocal liberalisation", popular in the diplomatese of the 1990s, is what we call "asymmetric liberalisation".

considerable opposition at home, from business interests that feared competition, and political resistance within ASEAN, initially from Malaysia and, subsequently, from Indonesia.

He told the Third India-ASEAN Business Summit in New Delhi in October 2004:

> A decade ago we unveiled our 'Look East' policy. This is more than a mere political slogan, or a foreign policy orientation. It has a strong economic rationale and commercial content. We wish to 'Look East' because of the centuries of interactions between us... We envision an Asian Economic Community, which encompasses ASEAN, China, Japan, Korea and India. Such a community would release enormous creative energies of our people. One cannot but be captivated by the vision of an integrated market, spanning the distance from the Himalayas to the Pacific Ocean, linked by efficient road, rail, air and shipping services. This community of nations would constitute an "arc of advantage", across which there would be large-scale movement of people, capital, ideas, and creativity.

Once again, the focus was on how people-to-people and business-to-business links would eventually shape government-to-government links in the region. But he saw the FTA with ASEAN as a step towards a larger engagement with the region. When some elements in the Congress Party sought to raise alarm over the impact of the ASEAN FTA on the plantation sector in Kerala and encouraged the Congress Party President Sonia Gandhi to write to the Prime Minister urging caution on the India-ASEAN FTA, Singh wrote back to Gandhi stating:

> Our approach to regional trade agreements, in general, and FTAs, in particular,has been evolved after careful consideration of our geo-political as well as economic interests. Although India has a large domestic market, our experience with earlier relatively insular policies, as also the global experience in this regard,clearly bring out the growth potential of trade and economic cooperation with the global economy.[21]

Such a strategic perspective and a steadfast commitment to the ASEAN FTA has finally ensured the completion of negotiations. Singh

21. Prime Minister's Letter to UPA Chairperson, 20 April 2006. See "Manmohan allays Sonia's FTA concerns", *Indian Express*, 08 May 2006.

will sign the India-ASEAN FTA at the East Asian Summit in Bangkok later this year. At each of the East Asian Summits he participated in, Singh kept emphasising the growing and deepening economic engagement between India and East and Southeast Asia. Eventually, he realised, it is hard economics that will shape regional politics and diplomacy and drive the process of India's integration with East Asia.

Singh also launched a new 'Look West' policy in the neighbourhood by strengthening relations with the Gulf States. The historic visit to India of the King of Saudi Arabia and the initiative to seek closer economic relations with member countries of the Gulf Cooperation Council (GCC) shifted the emphasis away from politics to economics in India's relations with the Arab nations.

Singh has also repeatedly emphasised the vital economic role of the Indian community in the Persian Gulf region for India's economic security. In his words:

> India owes a lot to thepeople of Indian origin in the Persian Gulf region whose regular financial remittances homehave played an important role in building our foreign exchange reserves that now amount to over US$130 billion.

Singh always emphasised the 'economic significance' of the region for India and that of the Indian community living in the region. He told a session of the All India Congress Committee (AICC) in November 2007:

> We have had a historic and long-standing relationship with the countries of the Middle-East and the Persian Gulf. Over fifty lakh citizens are working there fortheir livelihood. We have always sought peace in this region—be it Iraq, be it Iran or be it any other country. The bulk of our petroleum and energy requirements come from this region and our energy security is critically dependent on the conditions there. It has been—and will be—our effort to reduce tensions there and promote peace and harmony.

South-South Cooperation

Economics also defined India's engagement of Africa during Singh's tenure. All his major initiatives with respect to Africa focused on economics and human development. While India's own energy needs drove the relationship with a couple of countries like Nigeria and Sudan, the overall strategic relationship with major African countries focused heavily on Indian participation in Africa's educational, technological and economic development.

At the First India-Africa Summit held in New Delhi, Singh took personal initiative to propose a duty free Tariff Preference Scheme for LDCs, 34 out of 50 LDCs being African countries. Under the scheme, India agreed to provide preferential market access for exports from all 50 LDCs, covering 94 per cent of India's total tariff lines and 92.5 per cent of global exports of all LDCs. Products of immediate interest to Africa covered by this scheme include cotton, cocoa, aluminum ores, copper ores, cashew nuts, sugar cane, ready-made garments, fish fillets and non-industrial diamonds.

This major initiative with regard to South-South Cooperation was an important idea of Singh that must be viewed against the backdrop of his association with the South Commission, of which he was the Secretary-General. India has opted to focus on development cooperation in Africa, while encouraging Indian companies to invest in the region and help promote local development. Unlike China, where the government has played an important role as an aidgiver, India has preferred to focus on human development, education and skill development and promote industrial development through private enterprise participation.

New Thinking on Globalisation

A key idea that Singh has brought to the fore in defining India's relations with the world is the notion that "The world wants India to do well. Our challenges are at home."[22] In stating this repeatedly at various forums, including his Party forums, Singh has tried hard to rid India of its "victim" mentality and encourage the idea that

22. "The world wants us to do well. There is today no binding external constraint on our economy, save the pressure exerted by risingenergy prices and the occasional attempts to bring back protectionism through the backdoor of non-tariff barriers by many industrial economies. For us the real challenge is at home and I do hope and believe we can create a national alliance cutting across party political lines in support of a new push to development."

in world affairs today India is expected to be, and can indeed be, a "participant", not merely a "petitioner" or "protestor".

Singh took this view to such important developing country forums as the Asia-Africa Conference in Jakarta, in 2005, and the Summit of the Non-Aligned Movement in Havana in 2006. He told the Non-Aligned Movement (NAM) that it was a "bridge" between "extremes", rather than the 'battleground' that President Mahmoud Ahmadinejad of Iran and President Hugo Chavez of Venezuela tried to make it. At the same time, he told the G-8 Summit in Helligendamm that India was not interested in being a mere 'bystander' at such gatherings and saw no point in attending the so-called 'Outreach' summits if it had no role toplay in shaping the thinking of the G-8 on global issues.

On the two major global issues of the years 2006-2008, namely multilateral trade negotiations, discussions on climate change and management of the global energy, food and financial crises, Singh repeatedly spoke of the need for India's voice to be heard, but committed India to the role of a 'participant' in the management of global issues. India could no longer remain a 'complainant', and certainly not a 'supplicant'. Singh recognised the fact that this called for a "change of mind sets" both at home, about the world, and abroad, about India. Singh's project is to shift India from its traditional anti-colonial "Third Worldism" to a post-colonialnotion of "Inclusive Globalisation".[23]

An important step in this evolution from 'victim' to 'participant' would be a new view of India's relations with 'major powers'. India, like China, must learn to engage the great powers with greater confidence, rather than adopt a victim mentality towards them. It was to trigger this change in thinking that he decided to encourage a more 'balanced' and 'nuanced' view of India's colonial experience. India must learn from history but not become a prisoner of history. It must, for example, be able to deal with a country like Britain, no longer a 'global power' or an 'imperial power', as an equal. This was,

23. The idea of 'inclusive globalisation' is an extension of the idea of 'inclusive growth' that Singh promoted at home as Prime Minister. It was elaborated in his Special Convocation Address to University of Cambridge, UK, in October 2006. See Government of India (2007).

Singh believed, the way Gandhiji and Nehru wanted 'Free" India to relate to post-colonial Britain. It was this idea that Singh elaborated in his famous Oxford University speech on 8 July 2005.[24] The Oxford speech has been pilloried by Singh's critics as genuflection before the Empire. On the contrary, it was a bold statement of self-confidence, urging Indians to look the former ruler in the eye.

The roots of Singh's world view go all the way back to his doctoral dissertation which recognised the importance of foreign trade in India's economic development. However, it was only in the 1980s and more so in the early 1990s that India changed its perspective on integration with the world economy and on the role of trade in national development. As a Finance Minister and, subsequently, as Prime Minister, Singh fully appreciated the strategic dimension of trade. Trade is not just about comparative advantage and market access. It creates "webs of inter-dependencies".

Many years earlier, the trade economist R.N. Cooper had written an essay entitled "Trade Policy is Foreign Policy" (*Foreign Policy*, 1972). However, with the growth of regionalism in trade arrangements, it had become even more obvious that trade creates relationships of inter-dependence that shape political relations between nations. This was the experience of post-War western Europe, and this is what Asia was benefitting from too. India must also enter into mutually beneficial trading arrangements with major powers and neighbours.[25]

The most dramatic shift in India's approach to trade came about during the course of the Uruguay Round of multilateral trade negotiations. India went into the round in the late 1980s adopting

---

24. Manmohan Singh, Oxford University, Special Convocation Address, July 8, 2005. Selected Speeches, Vol. 2 and at *www.pmindia.nic.in/speeches.htm* For example, this telling statement says it all: "It used to be said that the sun never sets on the British Empire. I am afraid we were partly responsible for sending that adage out of fashion! But, if there is one phenomenon on which the sun cannot set, it is the world ofthe English speaking people, in which the people of Indian origin are the single largest component."

25. For a discussion of the idea that trade creates "webs if inter-dependence" and hence can shape India's relations with its neighbours andmajor powers see Baru (2006b), Chapter 4. This chapter, with its presentation of external trade as a means of creating "inter-dependence" between countries, is based on the chapter "Economic Security" written by this writer for the First *Strategic Defence Review* (SDR) presented to the Government of India by the National Security Advisory Board in 1999. At the time when it was written, the author discussed these ideas with Manmohan Singh, who was then Leader of the Opposition in Rajya Sabha.

its traditional posture on trade and resisting calls for a new round of trade liberalisation. The 1991 economic crisis forced the government to change its stance and accept the recommendations of several expert bodies to eliminate quantitative restrictions on imports and reduce tariffs. As a consequence, India changed its negotiating stance in the Uruguay Round and finally became signatory to the creation of the WTO.

Inclusive Globalisation

Deriving from his thinking at the South Commission, Singh came forward with an important concept of development cooperation that he dubbed 'Inclusive Globalisation'. He first unveiled this concept during his intervention at the historic Jakarta Summit of the heads of Asian and African countries marking the 60th anniversary of the Bandung Summit in April 2005, and developed it in his Special Convocation Address at University of Cambridge, United Kingdom, in October 2006. At the Jakarta Summit, Singh eschewed the "old rhetoric" of post-colonialism and put forward a more inclusive notion of globalisation:

> Ours is a world of unprecedented connectivity. Thanks to the communication and information technology revolutions, distance has lost its old meaning. Fifty years after Bandung 1955, we meet in a smaller and more integrated world. Migration and more open economies are creating multi-cultural societies. Globalisation enables instant availability of information and freer competition for opportunities... It is not coincidental that increasing openness, democracy and social awareness follow the process of globalisation. Recent advances in science and technology provides us unparalleled instrumentalities to combat age-old problems of poverty, ignorance and disease. Properly managed, globalisation caneffect a significant improvement in the human condition in the span of a single generation.

Even at the NAM Summit in Havana in September 2006, Singh spoke about 'inclusive globalisation' and said he viewed NAM as a "bridge" between global divides and as a"rejection of extremes." He deliberately differentiated his own "inclusive" perspective from the extremist "exclusive" perspectives of Chavez and Ahmadinijad. Singh told NAM:

> We live in an increasingly interdependent world. The challenge ahead is to promote a balanced and equitable management of this interdependence of nations. As globalisation progresses, national and regional boundaries are becoming less and less relevant. The challenges we face as nations are increasingly less amenable to purely national and autonomous solutions.
>
> Environmental degradation and climate change recognise no national borders. Pandemics like HIV/AIDS, Malaria, TB or Avian Flu can only be contained or overcome through international cooperation. Terrorism anywhere threatens peace everywhere. Our problems are global, so must our solutions be.
>
> The Non-Aligned Movement, encompassing as it does, every religion professed by mankind, every ethnic group and ideological persuasion, is uniquely placed today, once again, to play the role of a bridge of understanding. Our cooperative world view is in itself a rejection of the notion of a 'clash of civilisations'. Rather, our message to the world should be that it is possible to work for a "confluence of civilisations.

At the University of Cambridge, United Kingdom, Singh laid out his perspective on the Doha Development Round of multilateral trade negotiations, on climate change and global warming and on United Nations reform, within this framework of 'inclusive globalisation'. He said:

> Let me say without hesitation that we are committed to the successful functioning of a rule based multilateral trading system. India remains committed to the successful conclusion of the Doha Round of Trade Negotiations at an early date. We do hope that the round keeps in mind the promised development dimension and that it also will addresses the concerns of millions of our subsistence farmers. Trade liberalisation, we recognise, has contributed immensely to our economic growth and to the growth of the world economy as a whole. Lowering trade barriers both at home and abroad has helped us. Our enterprises have become more globally competitive. We shall persist on that path. More importantly, new business activities have grown in response to global opportunities. The successes of our

information technology, automobile and pharmaceutical sectors are a living testimony to the benefits that liberalisation and globalisation have brought us. Sometimes, we do worry that at a time when we are becoming more open, protectionist voices are being heard in developed countries. The lesson we must all draw from the experience of the past century is that no country can reverse the dynamics of social, economic and technological change. Rather we must learn to cope and adapt with change. This is precisely why India chose to join the WTO. India is a founder member of GATT. You will recognise the fact that we have adhered to all our Uruguay Round commitments. In fact, our firms have benefited from these commitments. While we remain committed to these obligations, we must also explore ways in which developing countries can catch up in the race to modernisation. We have affirmed our commitment to the protection of intellectual property rights. But, the global economy, the global community cannot afford the complete privatisation of research, of knowledge generation, especially in fields like medicine. We need to evolve mechanisms that protect intellectual property and at the same time, address the needs of the poor. With the increasing privatisation of research & development in science and technology, modern societies require new approaches to the sharing of knowledge where such knowledge is of benefit to all humankind.[26]

Challenges to the Manmohan Singh Doctrine

It should be clear that the Manmohan Singh Doctrine is a product of the times. It is a manifestation of India's economic resurgence in an era of greater economic openness. India must maintain the recent momentum of high growth, ensuring that it is socially more inclusive and regionally more balanced, to create a domestic economic and political environment conducive to the continuing political appeal and relevance of the Manmohan Singh Doctrine.

The success of India's external liberalisation and the reintegration of the Indian economy into the growth processes of East and Southeast Asian economies have played a vital role in the popular acceptance of the validity of the many postulates of this doctrine. For

26. Fortune Global Forum, New Delhi, 29 October 2007. Selected Speeches, Vol 4.

this reason, the continued relevance of the doctrine will be contingent upon India's continued pursuit of high economic growth within the framework of an open and increasingly globalised economy. It is also contingent upon that process of globalisation being more inclusive. If the global economy slips into a new era of protectionism and if the current financial crisis and the global economic slowdown, with high energy and food prices, generates a backlash against globalisation, it could strengthen the domestic critics of the Manmohan Singh Doctrine in India.

Equally, the doctrine's appeal to the outside world is premised on India remaining a high growth, open economy and an open society, marked by popular commitment to the values ofa liberal, plural and secular democracy. An inward-looking, internally divided, bigoted and illiberal India would have little external standing, and no external appeal. A renewed surge of terrorist and extremist activity in India could also erode the domestic consensus in favour of a liberal, plural and secular political order. This India must always guard against. Equally, China's increased assertiveness on a range of issues, combined with its policy of 'encirclement' around India, could also generate jingoistic responses within India and anti-India sentiments in the neighbourhood that would weaken the appeal of the more benign orientation to the region and the world suggested by the Manmohan Singh Doctrine.

It should, however, be noted that while the doctrine is benign in its orientation to the world, it is by no means supine. The cornerstone of the doctrine is a stronger India, more self confident and more capable and willing to engage the world on more equal terms. That new self-confidence should not become exaggerated, generating either complacency or hubris. India has a long way to go in making its tryst with destiny. But it can only make this tryst, and relate to the world, as an open economy, an open society, a liberal, plural, and secular democracy. It is these aspects of India's personality that encourage the international community to welcome its' rise.

References

Baru, Sanjaya (2006). "The Economics of India's Foreign Policy", in Sanjaya Baru, *Strategic Consequences of India's Economic Performance*. London: Routledge and New Delhi: Academic Foundation.

———. (2006a) "The Economic Consequences of the Kargil Conflict for India and Pakistan", in Sanjaya Baru Sanjaya Baru, *Strategic Consequences of India's Economic Performance*. London: Routledge and New Delhi: Academic Foundation.

———. (2006b). "National Security in an Open Economy", Chapter 4 in Sanjaya Baru Sanjaya Baru, *Strategic Consequences of India's Economic Performance*. London: Routledge and New Delhi: Academic Foundation.

———. (2008). "Domestic Sources of Influence:Business Groups and Media", Paper presented at the *Conference on the Future of India's Foreign Policy*. Centre for the Advanced Study of India, University of Pennsylvania, 18-19 April (To be published).

Dixit, J.N. (1996). *My South Block Years: Memoirs of a Foreign Secretary*. Delhi: UBSPD.

Dutt, V.P. (1999). *India's Foreign Policy in a Changing World*. New Delhi: Vikas Publishing House.

Government of India (2005). *Selected Speeches of Prime Minister Manmohan Singh*. Vol 1. New Delhi: Publications Division.

———. (2007). *Selected Speeches of Prime Minister Manmohan Singh*. Volume 3. Delhi: Publications Division. Also at: *www.pmindia.nic.in/speeches.htm*

Kim, Chan Wahn (2006). *Economic Liberalisation and India's Foreign Policy*. Delhi: Kalpaz Publications.

Raja Mohan, C. (2005). "Rethinking India's Grand Strategy", in N S Sisodia and C. Uday Bhaskar (eds.), *Emerging India: Security and Foreign Policy Perspectives*. New Delhi and Chicago: IDSA and Bibliophile South Asia.

Ramamurti, Ravi and Jitendra V. Singh (eds.) (2009). *Emerging Multinationals from Emerging Economies*. Cambridge University Press, forthcoming 2009.

6

Realism in India's Economic Multilateralism

India has been a strong advocate of multilateralism even when it has preferred a bilateral approach to the political challenges it confronts in South Asia. India is not alone among major powers in adopting such a paradoxical stance. However, the Indian view of multilateral institutions and of multilateralism has evolved over time and has differed in the approach she has adopted in the political and security field as opposed to the economic field. While India has always sought a 'rule based' multilateral order, it has sought with equal vehemence rules that recognise her place in the world as the world's largest democracy, the biggest developing country democracy, a plural, secular and constitutional democracy. India's view of her place in the multilateral political and security order, be her claim for membership of the United Nations Security Council (UNSC) or the Nuclear Non-Proliferation Treaty (NPT) have been defined by this outlook[1].

This chapter discusses India's approach to multilateralism in the realm of economic organisations and regimes. It examines, in particular, India's approach to multilateral economic institutions, namely, the International Monetary Fund (IMF), the World Bank (WB) and the General Agreement on Trade and Tariffs (GATT)/ World Trade Organization (WTO).

It is useful to remember that while a country may have national institutions that help evolve a common approach to international issues and institutions, and this may be even more so under powerful national leaders (like Jawaharlal Nehru and Indira Gandhi), there is

1. For an elaboration of this view see Baru (2000).

always the possibility that the approach to national policy can differ between different segments of government, especially in a plural democracy like India. Analysts in other democracies, such as the United States are all too familiar with different, even conflicting, approaches to international issues adopted by different wings of the Administration, State and Pentagon, and between the White House and the Congress.

In the early years after independence, India's approach to international institutions like the United Nations, and its various organs, had the clear imprint of its first prime minister, Jawaharlal Nehru, and his key foreign and strategic policy advisors. This was equally the case with economic policy—both domestic and external economic policy. However, the thinking within the foreign and strategic policy establishment was greatly influenced by those, including Nehru, who opted for an admittedly 'idealist' posture, seeking a larger international role for India commensurate with her standing as a leading post-colonial democracy inspired by the idea of the solidarity of developing countries, especially the post-colonial nations of Asia and Africa.

On the other hand, the thinking on external economic policy was shaped by another set of Nehru's disciples who were more 'realists' than 'idealists' in their appreciation of India's capabilities and needs. They understood the need for external assistance, even if India were to pursue a more inward-looking strategy of industrial development with less emphasis on foreign trade. India's approach to external economic assistance, in general, and to multilateral and bilateral economic assistance, in particular, was pithily stated in the very first chapter of the First Five Year Plan (1950), written under the direct supervision of Nehru. It summed up the dilemma on seeking external economic assistance in these words, having noted that such assistance could only be a residual and that economic planning must be based on harnessing domestic resources:

> That a plan of development today must, in the main, rely on domestic resources can hardly be over-emphasised. In the first place, the conditions governing international investment are no longer what they were when some of the highly industrialised countries of today

> like the United States, Australia and Canada began their career of development. Secondly, external assistance is acceptable only if it carries with it no conditions explicit or implicit, which might affect even remotely the country's ability to take an independent line in international affairs. There are also obvious risks in excessive reliance on foreign aid which depends on the domestic political situation in lending countries and which might be interrupted by any untoward international developments. And yet, external resources at strategic points and stages can be of so much assistance in a period of rapid development that it is desirable, consistently with other objectives, to create conditions favourable to their inflow.
>
> The Plan document went on to state that while priority would be given to investment through multilateral financial institutions, one must recognise that far more investible funds would be available from foreign governments and from private corporations. It then added the understandable caveat that all such foreign investment would have to be in accordance with "the country's development programme.[2]

It should, however, be noted that even while India's economic planners moved increasingly to an 'inward-oriented' import-substituting strategy of industrial development, they were not averse to either foreign investment or seeking multilateral economic assistance. Aid was preferred over trade partly because of an inherent 'export-pessimism' among policy makers and partly on account of the historically inherited, but flawed, view that much of Indian export trade was 'forced' on India by the East India Company and its inheritors, European multinationals.[3] Even though the Indian sub-continent was at the crossroads of pan-Asian trade for centuries before the arrival of European traders in the Indian Ocean, India's national movement was greatly influenced by its more recent

2. Planning Commission (1950).
3. On India's export pessimism see Singh (1964); Bhagwati and Desai (1970). On the view that exports were a product of "forced commercialisation" there is a vast post-colonial literature. In India this view found its earliest academic exposition in Dadabhai Naoroji's 1901 classic *Poverty and Un-British Rule in India*.

historical experience where in trade was viewed as 'exploitative' and 'enforced' rather than as beneficial to development and growth.[4]

Thus, in post-independence India, even as India's share of world trade declined from 2.0 per cent in 1950 to 0.5 per cent by 1980, her share of both bilateral and multilateral aid increased significantly, with India emerging as a major beneficiary of such assistance. In the period 1960s and 1970s India's share of total ODA (official development assistance) was 10 per cent, with South Asia as a whole receiving as much as the whole of Africa in ODA. In the period 1960-2003, India had a share of 5.6 per cent in the ODA of the US and Norway, ranking as the third largest recipient, next to Israel and Egypt.[5]

On FDI (foreign direct investment), India initially adopted a more open stance till the end of the 1950s, with Nehru actively soliciting FDI. What this open stance meant was that even as the share of exports in India's national income fell from over 6.0 per cent in the early 1950s to less than 4.0 per cent by the end of the 1950s, the share of imports in national income went up from around 6.0 per cent to nearly 8.0 per cent in the same period. This resulted in a sharp fall in India's Sterling reserves. It is the consequent BoP (balance of payments) crisis, of 1958-59, that altered perceptions about the role of external flows in aiding economic development. While the government's initial response to the foreign exchange shortage of the late 1950s was to in fact further open up the economy to foreign investment, India became less open to foreign investment by the end of the 1960s.[6]

All this would explain, in part, the difference in India's approach to MFIs (multilateral financial institutions), that is the IMF and WB, and to the global trading system, especially under GATT. The Indian national movement's concern with de-industrialisation and the national leadership's focus on protecting domestic industry against external competition shaped policy with respect to external trade.

4. For a classic leftwing statement of this view see Chandra (1966). For a liberal academic presentation of both sides of the debate see: Kumar et al. (1982).

5. Gupta et al. (2006).

6. Panagariya (2008).

On the other hand, the planners' desire to bridge the resources gap meant that the financing of development remained open to the possibility of external aid. India was not interested in seeking a more open trading system, hence it vacillated between indifference to and active resistance of GATT and free trade. But India faced a resources gap and was keen to seek access to low cost external financing and so remained open to IMF support and WB assistance.[7]

Differences in approach to India's relations with the world have also persisted between India's external affairs ministry and foreign policy strategists, on the one hand, and her economic ministries and economic policymakers on the other. Ironically, in the 1950s the foreign policy strategists were more internationalist in their orientation while economic policymakers were more nationalist, while by the 1980s the reverse seems to have been the case.[8] While critics of the MFIs and of recent trends in multilateralism remain dissatisfied,[9] India's approach to multilateral institutions and to multilateralism was best summed up by Prime Minister Singh in his very first address to the United Nations General Assembly in September 2004.[10] Stating that democratic principles should govern international institutions as much as they ought to govern national ones, Singh underscored the importance of what he dubbed a "culture of genuine multilateralism" adding:

> The United Nations and its specialised agencies are the only instruments available for responding effectively to the challenges we face collectively. But what is missing, is our sustained commitment to democratising the functioning of the United Nations. It is common knowledge that the UN is often unable to exert an effective influence on global economic and political issues of critical importance. This is due to what may be called as 'democracy deficit', which prevents

7. Patel (2002).

8. Possible reasons for this are discussed in Baru (2009).

9. Dubey (2004). See also Mukherjee and Malone (2011).

10. Manmohan Singh joined government service in India in 1972 as economic advisor in the ministry of commerce. He then went on to occupy every important economic policymaking office in the government of India including Chief Economic Advisor, Secretary, Economic Affairs, Governor of the Reserve Bank of India, Deputy Chairman of the Planning Commission and Finance Minister in 1991-1996.

effective multilateralism, a multilateralism that is based on a democratically evolved global consensus.[11]

He embedded India's support for UN reform within this wider context of the UN's 'democratisation. Thus, while advocating reform of multilateral institutions and seeking greater say in their functioning, India has reaffirmed her commitment to working with them. While 'idealism' still marks India's approach to multilateralism in general, 'realism' characterises her approach to multilateral economic institutions.

'Realistic Restructuring' of the Bretton Woods Institutions

British India was represented at the Bretton Woods Conference, where the IMF and the WB were created, by both British and native Indian officials. However, a key member of the Indian delegation, A.D. Shroff, complained that India had not secured its due in the shareholding structure of the Fund and the Bank. He complained to John Maynard Keynes, the head of the British delegation,who in fact thought he had fought hard to increase India's quota from $300 million to $400 million. Shroff's main complaint, which is being echoed even today, is that the United States was more accommodative of China, which was granted a higher quota share than India. It is worth quoting at length from the detailed account of the episode in Robert Skidelsky's (2000) authoritative biography of Keynes:

> Raymond Mikesell, who served under White in the US Treasury, had worked out a complicated formula for allocating 90 per cent of the available money, leaving $800mn, 'to be added to any place we wanted to'. White had told him that the formula should yield a quota of $2.5bn for the USA, about half of that for Britain and its colonies, with the Soviet Union and China assured third and fourth places. To 'cook' the results White wanted, Mikesell had to introduce data for national income. 'These last had to be approximated and their uncertainty afforded opportunities for making minor adjustments to the suggested quotas when these did not conform to political realities.' The quotas were made public for the first time at Bretton

11. Prime Minister Manmohan Singh's address to United Nations General Assembly, New York, 23 September, 200 (*http://pmindia.nic.in/speech-details.php?nodeid=18*).

> Woods, but the basis for their calculation remained secret. When the figures became known, there were explosions of affronted pride. Russia, which wanted quotas to reflect military as well as economic prowess, said it would not accept a quota smaller than Britain's. Britain said that if Russia got a larger quota, so should India. India wanted equality with China. France would accept a smaller quota than China, 'for political reasons', but insisted on a larger quota than India.[12]
>
> Keynes confined his efforts to getting the Indian quota raised from $300mn to $400mn. His success was not received with much satisfaction. 'Indian amour propre in connection with China' wrote Lionel Robbins, 'was still far from satisfied; and it was very vocal. Moreover, they are still ambitious for a permanent seat on the Executive. Keynes, who received them, lying on his couch railed them on their ingratitude and urged with much force that they now had an excellent case to present at home, which he proceeded to outline in the form of an imaginary speech which might be delivered by Mr A.D. Shroff (an Indian delegate to the conference). All this was without much visible effect.[13]

Independent India took its participation in both the United Nations system as well as MFIs seriously. It sent some of its best officials and diplomats to these institutions. While India did not always like and accept the policy advice they offered, Nehru did not shy away from tapping into the best talent available worldwide as far as economic planning and management were concerned. Thus he invited many policy advisors, including from MFIs, and from Chicago School's Milton Friedman to Poland's Michal Kalecki, a wide range of external policy advice was available, given and taken.[14]

India's relations with the Bretton Woods sisters deteriorated only after the infamous devaluation episode of 1966.[15] The unprecedented drought of 1965-66 had forced India to import food grains, thereby exerting pressure on her BoP. India approached the United States,

12. Skidelsky, 2000: 351.
13. Skidelsky, 2000.
14. Rosen (1986). See also Bhagwati (1993).
15. Chaudhry et al. (2004).

the IMF and the WB for support. A combination of bilateral US assistance and multilateral funding was offered but India was forced to devalue the Rupee and was advised to reverse its policy of import-substituting industrialisation. The political backlash in India against Prime Minister Indira Gandhi forced her to abandon the programme half way. The 1966 devaluation episode constituted a turning point in the way in which India viewed the Bretton Woods sisters. Opinion was sharply divided both politically and among economists. India became a critic of the world economic order, cemented a new relationship with the Non-Aligned Movement (NAM), created the G-77 and other developing country forums and became an advocate of the New International Economic Order, a platform that was critical of the Bretton Woods institutions and the so called "Washington Consensus"—conservative macroeconomic policies that were aimed at encouraging debtor nations to reduce fiscal and budget deficits, privatise public enterprises, liberalise external trade and open up capital markets to external flows.[16]

Wary of such policies in the 1970s, India did not approach the IMF for BoP support till 1981 when Indira Gandhi chose to seek its support once again. Returning to office in 1981 Indira Gandhi was a changed political animal. Her nuanced position on the Soviet invasion of Afghanistan in 1979, which India did not endorse, and her meeting with US President Ronald Reagan at Cancun, Mexico, in October 1981 were indicative of this change in her view of the US and, therefore, of what India perceived as 'US-led institutions'. However, in response to a renewed political attack against her by the Left Front, which targeted her decision to seek IMF assistance, she opted to give up the last installment of the loan and pre-pay the loan, making it a symbol of her independence of action.[17]

The 1981 episode is instructive. India's application for IMF lending met with initial resistance from the United States. India's case was presented starkly by her executive director on the IMF board, M. Narasimham, who told his US counterpart that if the US blocked IMF

16. See Williamson (1984).

17. Patel (2002), chapter 7.

support India would have no option but to turn to the Soviet Union for financial assistance.[18] The US chose to abstain on the vote in the IMF board thereby enabling India to get access to IMF support, while at the same time expressing her disapproval of Indian policies at the time by not actually voting in favour of the loan application.

It was only in 1991, a decade later and under very different circumstances, that India returned to the IMF for BoP support and secured this on the condition that India would put in place policies approved by the IMF and its principal shareholders, especially the US and European Union. The 'new turn' in India's economic policies and the reconfiguration of her foreign policy in the post-Cold War era mark a turning point in India's approach to the Bretton Woods institutions.

The new Indian view was that as a founder member of the IMF and WB it was entitled to financial support from these institutions and that the policies then advocated by the institutions were any way in India's own interests and reflected the thinking within the Indian government. As the then finance minister Manmohan Singh told Parliament, in his budget speech of February 1992:

> It has been alleged by some people that the reform programme has been dictated by the IMF and the World Bank. We are founder members of these two institutions and it is our right to borrow from them when we need assistance in support of our programmes. As lenders, they are required to satisfy themselves about our capacity to repay loans and this is where conditionality comes into the picture. All borrowing countries hold discussions with these institutions on the viability of the programmes for which assistance is sought. We have also held such discussions. The extent of conditionality depends on the amount and the type of assistance sought. However, I wish to state categorically that the conditions we have accepted reflect no more than the implementation of the reform programme as outlined in my letters of intent sent to the IMF and the World Bank, and are wholly consistent with our national interests. The bulk of the reform programme is based on the election manifesto of our Party. There

18. Author's interview with M. Narasimham and his executive assistant Y.V. Reddy, circa 2000.

> is no question of the Government ever compromising our national interests, not to speak of our sovereignty.[19]

This assertion of sovereignty combined with a realist approach to the institutions and to the policies being adopted has since become the leitmotif of the Indian approach to MFIs. India has not approached the IMF after 1991 and, after the Asian financial crisis of 1997-98 as well as the experience with the US and Japanese sanctions in the aftermath of the nuclear tests in May 1998, it has opted to build adequate foreign exchange reserves to insulate itself from the need to do so. This is a tactic adopted by many other Asian economies, although India also continued to assert its right to tap the Bank and other affiliates for its development funding. Today India is the Bank's biggest borrower.[20] In 2010 the Bank's lending arms, International Bank for Reconstruction and Development (IBRD) and International Development Association (IDA), lent India a sum of $9.1 billion, compared to $6.4 billion to Mexico, $3.8 billion to South Africa, $3.7 billion to Brazil and $3.0 billion to Turkey. Accordingly, the World Bank's India Country Strategy for 2009-2012 "envisages a total proposed lending program of US$14 billion, for the next three years, of which US$9.6 billion is from the IBRD and US$4.4 billion (SDR 2.982 billion equivalent at the current exchange rate) from the IDA."[21] Half of the sums lent have been allocated to four sectors, namely, agriculture, rural development, energy and public transport.[22]

Summing up India's nuanced approach to multilateral assistance and external funding early in his tenure, Prime Minister Singh told a conference in New Delhi in 2005 that:

> As a developing economy we must draw on international resources to fuel our development. We should be more open to global capital flows and better prepared to take advantage of new markets for goods and services. India is wholly committed to multilateralism in trade.

---

19. Singh (1992).
20. World Bank (n.d.).
21. Ibid.
22. See Indian Ministry of Finance website for details of fund allocation. *http://finmin.nic.in/the_ministry/dept_eco_affairs/MI/sector_wise_ongoingProj.pdf*

> But we will seek the reform and democratization of multilateral institutions.[23]

One aspect of the new 'realism' is that India has come to terms with the reality of China's larger quota, no longer complaining as Shroff did in 1944, but willing to live with a restructured IMF in which China has a much larger voting share than India. India therefore joined the BRICS—Brazil, Russia, India, China and South Africa—consensus that has sought a re-allocation of Fund quotas in favour of emerging economies. Having said this, the Indian proposal at the New Delhi BRICS Summit for the creation of a BRICS Development Bank is aimed at encouraging China to divert some of its foreign exchange surplus into a BRICS run bank in which India would have a larger say than it is likely to have in the IMF.[24]

In the interim, however, India has chosen to be pragmatic and accept the reality of Western dominance of Bretton Woods institutions. When the IMF and WB last selected new heads, some analysts adopted a revisionist view and urged India to play a more pro-active role in the selection of the heads of these institutions by putting up their own candidate for the post of managing director of the IMF and the WB president.[25] However, Prime Minister Singh took the 'realist' view that since the IMF and WB are "shareholder driven" organisations the majority shareholders will get the management of their choice as long as they remain majority shareholders. So there was no point in a marginal player like India sponsoring a candidate of her own till the shareholding structure itself was altered.[26] Thus, in seeking a restructuring of the quotas in favour of emerging economies, India adopted a 'realist' approach, accepting the existing shareholder structure as a given and going along with the 'majority'

23. Prime Minister Manmohan Singh, India Today Conclave, 25 February 2005 (*http://pmindia.nic.in/speech-details.php?nodeid=73*).

24. This observation is based on conversations with Indian ministry of finance officials who were part of the BRICS Delhi Summit preparatory work.

25. Mattoo and Subramaniam (2008).

26. As told to the author by Prime Minister Singh at the time of the selection of Dominique Strauss-Kahn as managing director of the Fund.

in supporting the candidature of the nominee of the European Union, Christine Lagarde.

India will continue to maintain such a realist view, recognising that no existing power voluntarily cedes power and any forced reallocation of quotas at this stage would benefit China more than India. India will, however, seek a 'realistic restructuring' of the shareholding of these institutions that gives emerging economies a greater say in their functioning. Till that happens India, like most other Asian countries, will seek to avoid tapping the IMF for BoP support, opting instead to maintain an adequately large foreign currency reserve. The developing country aversion to seeking IMF support is a consequence of their experience during the Asian financial crisis. It was in response to this, and the experience of other countries like Russia in the 1990s, that emerging economies chose to build up their foreign exchange reserves as an insurance against having to seek IMF support to address BoP problems.

Hedging its Bets on the Multilateral Trade Regime

India was one of the 23 contracting parties to the GATT in October 1947. Yet, unlike with the Bretton Woods sisters from whom the Indian ministry of finance had always hoped to secure financial support, even from Nehru's time, in GATT India's interest was largely defensive. A combination of export-pessimism and the strategy of ISI (import-substituting industrialisation) shaped India's trade and industrial policy, especially after the first BoP crisis of 1958. India saw its share of world trade diminish from 2.4 per cent in 1948 to less than 1.0 per cent a decade later and to a lowly 0.41 per cent by 1981.[27] Economists have debated whether the decline in trade share contributed to the export pessimism or the ISI strategy contributed to the decline. Whatever the causal factors, the consequence was a general neglect of external trade, and therefore a defensive approach to multilateralism in trade.[28] Interestingly, Prime Minister Singh's DPhil thesis at Oxford University was a critique of India's export

27. Srinivasan and Tendulkar (2003).

28. Bhagwati and Desai (1970).

pessimism and drew attention to the growth potential of foreign trade, but it was a view that was ignored by policy makers at the time.[29] India's strategy in GATT was, therefore, a defensive one aimed at minimising exposure to a more open and intrusive multilateral trade regime.

In fact, one could argue, India was adept at deploying 'diplomatic cover' and promoted developing country unity to secure a less open multilateral trading regime that enabled it to protect its own markets and promote its domestic industrialisation process. This, however, is not how Indian diplomats viewed her GATT strategy.[30] Rather, the dominant view at the time, in the 1950s and 1960s, was that India had played a leadership role in securing protection for developing countries in the GATT system. Dubey notes with pride India's robust activism in securing benefits for developing countries like the generalised system of preferences, the multi-fibre agreement, rejecting criticism that India was a 'free-rider' in GATT and claiming credit for India's activism in rule making under GATT aimed at protecting the interests of developing countries.[31]

As Mattoo and Subramaniam observe: "India's stance in the GATT/WTO has always tended to be defensive, seeking freedom to use restrictive policies, which has been one of the two prongs of the so-called special and differential (S&D) treatment embraced by developing countries as a whole."[32] Indeed, one could argue that by the 1970s and into the early 1980s India's stake in the real policy outcome in various rounds of GATT negotiations was minimal, given its low share of world trade. On the other hand, active participation and strenuous bargaining for fair outcomes may have yielded foreign policy benefits with developing countries. While this approach made eminent 'diplomatic' sense, since it gave India a leadership role among developing countries, it did not help India increase its share of world trade. Since India's economic strategy was based on import-

29. Singh (1964a).

30. See, for example, Dubey (1996).

31. Dubey (2007).

32. Mattoo and Subramaniam (1999).

substitution and export pessimism her defensive approach to GATT, her disinterest in carving out a larger share of the world market did not appear to its planners as counter-productive.

Given this diplomatic background and the economic policy approach, that lasted well into the 1980s, it is not surprising that India initially went into the Uruguay Round of GATT negotiations (from 1986 to 1994), which eventually resulted in the dissolution of GATT and the creation of a new WTO, with a plan to scuttle the round. India had strong reservations about bringing services into the GATT system. It had grave doubts about the purpose and consequence of replacing GATT with a formal institution, the WTO.[33] In the late 1980s and well into 1991, India fought hard to resist both the creation of WTO and widening the scope of the multilateral trading system. Dubey, India's foreign secretary at the time and a key negotiator with a personal interest in multilateral economic diplomacy, claims that it is only after the inclusion of a dispute settlement mechanism and the assurance that the GATT's 'special and differential treatment' for developing countries would continue with WTO that India agreed to support the creation of WTO.

India, however, remained strongly opposed to bringing in new issues like intellectual property rights and trade-related social policy issues, like labour standards, into the WTO's ambit. India's official approach to multilateral trade negotiations in the early months of the Uruguay Round was no different from its approach to previous rounds, even though by the 1980s the share of foreign trade had begun to rise in India's national income and the export pessimism of the earlier era was no longer as prevalent.[34] The non-oil imports to GDP ratio went up from around 4.0 per cent in the early 1970s to over 8.0 per cent by the early 1980s. Total foreign trade (exports plus imports) to GDP ratio went up from around 7.0 per cent in the early 1980s to over 12 per cent in the early 1980s and to over 25 per cent in the mid-1990s.[35]

33. Dubey, 2007.

34. Panagariya, 2008.

35. Panagariya, 2008, chapters 2, 3,4 and 10.

The shift in India's approach to multilateral trade negotiations and to the WTO came with her adoption of the new policy of economic liberalisation and reform in 1991. But this shift in thinking was on the part of the new team that had taken charge of economic policy making in 1991, including the then finance minister Manmohan Singh and his key economic policymaking team of Montek Singh Ahluwalia, Shankar Acharya and Rakesh Mohan.[36] The ancient regime represented by the then finance secretary S.P. Shukla, who had earlier handled the Uruguay Round negotiations as India's commerce secretary, Muchkund Dubey and Deepak Nayyar, the chief economic advisor who had earlier worked as an economic advisor in the commerce ministry, continued to advocate India's more defensive approach. By the end of the 1990s, the dispute settlement mechanism was also seen as strategically important because China had secured entry into the WTO and its trade and fiscal policies were viewed as non-transparent and therefore supportive of anti-competition practices. As Nottage notes, "Ambassador Bhatia of India recently stated that the 'WTO dispute settlement system is certainly one of the most valuable achievements of the Uruguay Round.'"[37]

The critics of the WTO in the Indian government finally fell in line, so to speak, defending their change of heart as a response to the WTO's adherence to an important principle of multilateralism, namely, the principle of "one country one vote" with decision making defined by the principle of consensus.[38] There is no doubt that this 'democratic' principle set WTO apart from the Fund and Bank, and gave 'voice' and 'vote' to developing countries. It is a different matter that in practice real power, that is real negotiations, has been

36. While Ahluwalia was an 'Oxbridge' trained economist, like many in the post-independence generation of economic policy makers in India, Rakesh Mohan and Shankar Acharya studied at US universities. All three had worked for the IMF and WB before returning home to work for the government. From their perch in the ministries of finance and industry they led the process of economic reform and liberalization in the 1990s.

37. Nottage (2009). Remarks of Ujjal Singh Bhatia, Ambassador and Permanent Representative of India to the WTO, "SettlingDisputes Among Members", Presentation at the *WTO Public Forum 2008*, Session 6, 24 September 2008, are available at: *www.wto.org/english/forums_e/public_forum08_e/programme_e.htm*.

38. Shukla (2000).

restricted to major trading economies that form part of the "Green Room" process of informal discussions that in effect define the final outcomes.[39] In fact, the core of the green room participants are the "quad"—Canada, European Union, Japan and the United States—who dominated GATT and seek to retain influence within WTO.

In the past decade the quad have been checked by the emergence of Brazil, China, India and South Africa as important developing country negotiators. With the entry of Russia as a WTO member, it is now possible that a BRICS group could seek to balance the quad in the WTO.

But the shift in India's approach to multilateralism in trade came much before these structural changes in the global economy and the consequent shift in geopolitics. The new turn in India's economic policy had three elements: first, the end of the 'Licence-Permit Raj' involving decontrol of production quotas and location and size restrictions on firms; second, fiscal stabilisation aimed at reducing government deficits including through privatisation; and, third, most importantly, opening up of the Indian economy to easier flows of external trade and FDI.[40] The sharp reduction in tariffs was something India voluntarily adopted through its budget proposals for 1991-92 and 1992-93. This enabled India to negotiate with greater conviction as the Uruguay Round came to a close and the WTO came into being.[41]

Through the 1990s, and especially after the Singapore Ministerial of the WTO in 1996 and the Seattle meeting in 1999, India became an active participant in the WTO process. There is a misplaced view in the western media and among western analysts that the high profile and critical stance of Indian trade ministers in WTO meetings, especially in the ongoing Doha Development Round is a sign of India's resistance to multilateralism in trade. This is a superficial view based on appearances and a lack of understanding of India's domestic politics. The three trade ministers of the past decade—Murasoli

39. World Trade Organisation, *Understanding the WTO* (*www.wto.org/english/thewto_e/whatis_e/tif_e/org1_e.htm*).

40. Panagariya (2008).

41. Debroy (2007).

Maran (at Doha, 2001), Arun Jaitley (in Cancun, 2003) and Kamal Nath (Geneva, 2008)—adopted postures aimed at a domestic political audience knowing full well that an impasse between the US and one or another country (on occasion the European Union or west African cotton exporters or someone else) would stall any agreement.

It would be an overstatement to suggest that Kamal Nath had wrecked the ministerial, as many in the West believed at the time.[42] It is entirely possible that Nath believed the US was not prepared for a deal months before a presidential election. Perhaps Nath rode a high horse to win accolades at home, as indeed he did for espousing the cause of the developing world![43] However, it is possible that Nath had won these plaudits at the cost of securing an admittedly sub-optimal deal. Prime Minister Singh was willing to arrive at a compromise that could have helped conclude the round. While he never said so publicly, Singh believed that as an essentially net food importing country India would benefit from cheaper imported agriculture products. However, the commerce ministry resisted yielding ground on the plea that "any 'bad' decision would 'haunt' them for having caused harm to future generations."[44]

India's stake in the multilateral trading regime has been repeatedly emphasised by Prime Minister Manmohan Singh. He has often referred to India's 'strategic stake' in the multilateral trading system. A stake that has increased with the rise in India's share in

42. Beattle (2008).

43. Lakshmi (2008).

44. This view of the commerce ministry was conveyed to the media in response to a statement that I had made speaking at the India Global Forum of the International Institute for Strategic Studies in New Delhi on 8 April, 2008. Believing at the time that I reflected the PM's thinking I had suggested India should soften its resistance to US and EU farm subsidies and help break the logjam in the Doha Round. *http://www.iiss.org/conferences/iiss-citi-india-global-forum/igf-plenary-sessions-2008/first-plenary-session-economic-and-financial-outlook/first-plenary-session-dr-sanjaya-baru/*. For a news report of the discussion see: *http://www.financialexpress.com/news/baru-calls-for-softening-of-india-s-stance-on-us-eu-farm-subsidies/299053/0*. To quote the Financial Express report: "Speaking at the IISS-Citi India Global Forum here, Baru argued that since domestic consumption of food is rising without an increase in supply, the country should welcome cheap food imports. Underlining that he was speaking in his personal capacity and not as a government spokesman, Baru said, "We may not be able to make the same argument against the US subsidies. It would be in the interest of India to favour continuation of farm subsidies by the US and the European countries so that import prices remain low."

trade in services and the WTO's embrace of services trade in the Uruguay Round.[45] In an address to foreign service officers, virtually on the eve of the 2008 Geneva WTO ministerial, he best summed up his own view on the importance of trade and the need for a multilateral regime in these words:

> When I talk about international environment, I have in mind the fact that what happens to the world trading system impinges on our capacity to grow at a faster pace. International trade particularly in the globalised world we live in has emerged as an important engine of growth of nations. And therefore we have to create an environment with which India's trade can grow, India's economy will benefit enormously if our exports are given a level playing field if we don't face barriers to increase exports of our country and therefore what happens to the multilateral trading systems, what happens to barriers to trade, barriers to commerce, is a very important indicator of what will be the pace of development of our country.[46]

Even as India has remained committed to multilateralism in trade, the continued impasse in the Doha Development Round has encouraged India to pursue, on a parallel track, a range of bilateral and regional free trade and comprehensive economic partnership (including trade and investment treaties) agreements. Apart from the South Asian Free Trade Agreement (SAFTA), India has signed FTAs (free trade agreements) with ASEAN (and separately with its member countries like Singapore and Thailand) and South Korea. It has PTAs (preferential trade agreements) with a large number of countries and is presently negotiating one with the EU.[47]

The range of FTAs that India has signed and is negotiating point to a new strategy on New Delhi's part. It has opted to engage widely, secure market access to growing Asian markets while continuing to support the multilateral trading system, especially with an eye on the WTO's dispute settlement mechanism.[48] India is willing to be part

45. Mukherjee and Malone (2011a).

46. Prime Minister Manmohan Singh's address to foreign service officers, 11 June 2008 (*http://pmindia.nic.in/speech-details.php?nodeid=666*).

47. See *http://www.india-briefing.com/news/indias-free-trade-agreements-4810.html/*.

48. Mukherjee & Malone, 2011a.

of as many plurilateral and regional groupings as necessary, building temporary coalitions when required. In climate change negotiations India chose to be part of BASIC—an alliance of Brazil, India, South Africa and China. India has become active in BRICS, has reactivated South Asian Association for Regional Cooperation, the Indian Ocean Rim Association for Regional Cooperation and has been an active member of the East Asian Summit process, signing on at the recent ASEAN-India Summit to negotiate a Regional Comprehensive Economic Partnership (RCEP) agreement that could be a precursor to the creation of an Asian Economic Community.

In pursuing these regional trade agreements Prime Minister Singh would repeatedly emphasise India's commitment to multilateralism, defending the regional trade agreements on the grounds of geo-political imperatives as much as their economic benefits. Thus, for example, defending the ASEAN-India FTA against criticism from his own party, because of pressure from producer groups that felt they would be hurt by lower tariffs, he wrote to Congress Party President Sonia Gandhi:

> Our approach to regional trade agreements in general, and FTAs in particular, has been evolved after careful consideration of our geo-political as well as economic interests. Although India has a large domestic market, our experience with earlier relatively insular policies, as also the global experience in this regard, clearly bring out the growth potential of trade and economic cooperation with the global economy.[49]

However, precisely because the WTO runs a consensus based multilateral trade regime, it has its limitations from the point of view of developed and developing economies. Hence both have sought to explore parallel networks of regional and plurilateral free trade arrangements that are, in principle, 'WTO-compatible', but in practice have sought to circumvent the multilateral system in seeking either a more or less liberal trading regime. Bhagwati has dubbed them "the termites in the trading system."[50] The so-called "noodle bowl" or

49. The Economic Times (2006).

50. Bhagwati (2011).

"alphabet soup" of FTAs and regional trade agreements has weakened the multilateral system and the WTO is now at the crossroads, seeking renewal through the completion of the Doha Development Round. While India has been actively engaged in signing FTAs and PTAs with many of its trade partners, it has a strategic stake in strengthening the WTO mainly because of the competitive pressure exerted by China's rise as a trading power.[51]

The China Syndrome

The most important 'geo-political' factor shaping India's attitude towards multilateralism in general and multilateral economic institutions in particular is the rise of China and the challenge this poses to the management of the global environment. While China continues to resist supporting India's claim for membership of the UNSC and India is critical of the P-5 nuclear powers for keeping it out of the NPT, China and India have also been able to work together, in seeking the reconstitution of multilateral economic institutions and regimes, affirming Prime Minister Singh's assertion that the bilateral relationship would be characterised by both "cooperation and competition". India's 'revisionist' stance towards existing multilateral institutions is balanced by her desire to seek a rule-based multilateral order. As a founder member of the G-20 India appreciates all the more the need to adhere to rule-based multilateralism, since the G-20 is really India's first major step forward from being a 'rule-taker' to a 'rule-maker' in multilateral institutions. For this reason, India attaches much importance to the G-20 as a plurilateral institution.[52]

Living through this transition in world affairs from being a 'rule-taker' to becoming a 'rule-maker', India seeks a restructuring of multilateral institutions while adhering to all the inherited disciplines and articles of association. This paradoxical stance is a reflection of the combination of aspiration and grievance and of idealism and realism that informs the Indian approach.

51. Bhat et al. (2006).

52. Bénassy-Quéré et al. (eds.) (2009).

References

Baru, Sanjaya (2000) "Managing Multipolarity and Globalisation in the New World" in Kamlesh Sharma (ed.), *Imagining Tomorrow: Rethinking the Global Challenge*. New York: United Nations. pp.218-25.

———. (2009). "Can Indian Think Tanks and Research Institutions Cope with the Rising Demand for Foreign and Security Policy Research?", *ISAS Working Paper*. June. *http://www.isas.nus.edu.sg/Attachments/PublisherAttachment/ISAS_working%20paper_66_21102009181035.pdf*

Beattle, Alan (2008). "India's Local Hero Evokes Mixed Emotions in World Trade Circuit", *Financial Times*, 3 December.

Bénassy-Quéré, Agnès, Rajiv Kumar, Jean Pisani-Ferry (eds.) (2009). *The G20 is Not Just a G7 With Extra Chairs*. New Delhi, Indian Council for Research in International Economic Relations

Bhagwati, Jagdish and Padma Desai (1970). *India: Planning for Industrialisation*. London: Oxford University Press.

Bhagwati, Jagdish (1993). *India in Transition*. Oxford: Clarendon Press.

———. (2011). "The Doha Round's Premature Obituary", *Project Syndicate*, 28 April. *http://www.project-syndicate.org/commentary/the-doha-round-s-premature-obituary*

Bhat, T.P., Atulan Guha and Mahua Paul (2006). *India and China in WTO: Building Complementarities and Competitiveness in the External Trade Sector*. Report of a Study Sponsored by Planning Commission, Government of India. New Delhi: Institute for Studies in Industrial Development. April. *http://planningcommission.nic.in/reports/sereport/ser/stdy_indch.pdf*

Chaudhry, Praveen K., Vijay L. Kelkar and Vikash Yadav (2004). "The Evolution of 'Homegrown Conditionality' in India: IMF Relations", *The Journal of Development Studies* 40(6): 59-81, August. *http://people.hws.edu/vyadav/publications/jods.pdf*

Chandra, Bipan (1966). *The Rise and Growth of Economic Nationalism in India: Economic Policies of Indian National Leadership*. New Delhi: People's Publishing House.

Debroy, Bibek (2007). "India's Economic Liberalisation and the WTO," in Suparna Karmarkar, Rajiv Kumar and Bibek Debroy (eds.), *India's Liberalisation Experience: Hostage to the WTO?* New Delhi: Indian Council for Research on International Economic Relations.

Dubey, Muchkund (1996). *An Unequal Treaty: World Trading Order After GATT*. New Delhi: New Age International Ltd.

———. (2004). *Multilateralism Besieged*. Geneva: The South Centre.

———. (2007). "India and the WTO", in Wolfgang Blaas and Joachim Becker (eds.), *Strategic Arena Switching in International Trade Negotiations*. London: Ashgate Publishing Ltd.

Gupta, Sanjeev, Catherine Pattillo, and Smita Wagh (2006). "Are Donor Countries Giving More or Less Aid?", *IMF Working Paper* WP/06/1. January. Accessed at: *http://www.imf.org/external/pubs/ft/wp/2006/wp0601.pdf*

Kumar, Dharma, Tapan Raychaudhuri, Irfan Habib and Meghnad Desai (eds.) (1982). *The Cambridge Economic History of India*. Vols. 1 & 2. Cambridge: Cambridge University Press.

Lakshmi, Rama (2008). "Hard Line at WTO Earns India Praise", *Washington Post*, 1 August.

Mattoo, Aditya and A. Subramaniam (1999). *India and the Multilateral Trading System after Seattle: Toward a Proactive Role*. Washington DC: World Bank.

———. (2008). "India and Bretton Woods II", *Economic and Political Weekly* XLIII(45): 62-70, November 8.

Mukherjee, Rohan and David M. Malone (2011). "From High Ground to High Table: The Evolution of Indian Multilateralism", *Global Governance* 17: 311-29.

Mukherjee, Rohan and David M. Malone (2011a). "Global Responsibilities: India's Approach", *Jindal Journal of International Affairs* 1(1): 182-203, October. *http://www.jsia.edu.in/JJIA/RMDMbstract.htm*

Nottage, Hunter (2009). "Developing Countries in the WTO Dispute Settlement System", *Global Economic Governance Programme Working Paper* 2009/47. Oxford, University College. Available at: *http://www.globaleconomicgovernance.org/wp-content/uploads/nottage-working-paper-final1.pdf*

Panagariya, Arvind (2008). *India: The Emerging Giant.* New Delhi:Oxford University Press.

Patel, I.G. (2002). *Glimpses of Indian Economic Policy: An Insider's View.* New Delhi: Oxford University Press.

Planning Commission (1950). *First Five Year Plan.* Delhi: Government of India. Chapter 1. para 44-45. *http://planningcommission.nic.in/plans/planrel/fiveyr/index9.html*

Rosen, George (1986). *Western Economists and Eastern Societies: Agents of Change in South Asia, 1960-1970.* Baltimore: Johns Hopkins University Press.

Shukla, S.P. (2000). "From GATT to WTO and Beyond", *Working Paper* No. 195. (Helsinki: UNU-WIDER. *http://www.wider.unu.edu/publications/working-papers/previous/en_GB/wp-195/_files/82530864827082831/default/wp195.pdf*

Singh, Manmohan (1964). *India's Export Trends and the Prospects for Self-sustained Growth.* Clarendon Press.

———. (1964a). *India's Export Trends.* London: Oxford University Press.

———. (1992). *Budget Speech.* New Delhi: Ministry of Finance, Government of India. 29 February (*http://indiabudget.nic.in/bspeech/bs199293.pdf*).

Srinivasan, T.N. and Suresh Tendulkar (2003). *Reintegrating India with the World Economy.* Washington DC: Peterson Institute for International Economics.

Skidelsky, Robert (2000). *John Maynard Keynes: Fighting for Britain, 1937-1946.* London: Macmillan. pp.351-52.

The Economic Times (2006). "No Disagreement on FTA: Congress", *The Economic Times*, 9 May. *http://articles.economictimes.indiatimes.com/2006-05-09/news/27437763_1_india-asean-fta-india-asean-free-trade-agreement-prime-minister.*

Williamson, John (ed.) (1984). *The Political Economy of Policy Reform.* Washington DC: Institute for International Economics.

World Bank (n.d.). *India Country Strategy 2009-12* (*http://www.worldbank.org/en/news/2010/04/06/india-country-strategy*).

7

The Influence of Business and Media on Indian Foreign Policy

> I sincerely believe that in the modern world the relationship between Governments is increasingly mediated through and influenced by the relationship between civil society and the business community. It is on the foundation of people-to-people and business-to-business relations that we in Government try to build State-to-State relations."
>
> —Prime Minister Manmohan Singh,
> Sixth India-EU Business Summit, New Delhi, 7 September 2005

Manmohan Singh was perhaps the first Indian Prime Minister to so clearly articulate the rising influence of civil society and business in the making of Indian foreign policy. Turning a 19th century aphorism on its head, the Prime Minister seemed to suggest that it is no longer trade that "follows the flag", but "the flag" that follows trade.

It is of course clear that this view of international relations is intimately related to the nature of society we are talking about. It is only in democratic societies that civil society has any significant influence on the foreign policy. Business interests could still influence foreign policy in non-democratic societies, if the regime in question has commercial, business and wider economic interests to pursue through its foreign policy. But public opinion can shape foreign policy only by influencing domestic politics. Needless to add, business and media have for long been instruments of diplomacy, but this chapter is not about diplomacy. Its purpose is to examine the influence of business and media on foreign policy.

The interaction between people, in the form of migration, and between businessmen and merchants, through trade, have always been at the centre of the relations between nations. As the Nobel

Prize economist and the guru of strategic economics, T.C. Schelling claimed, "Aside from war and preparations for war, and occasionally aside from migration, trade is the most important relationship that most countries have with each other."[1] In an influential essay entitled "Trade Policy is Foreign Policy"[2], Richard Cooper, took the view that while traditionally trade policy had dominated "high foreign policy", the Cold War had brought political issues to the fore and reduced the salience of business interests in shaping foreign policy. The end of the Cold War, the economic transformation of China, and the processes of globalisation, accelerated by the Uruguay Round of multilateral trade negotiations and the spread of regional trade blocs, have raised the profile of business and economic factors in the foreign and strategic policy considerations of most nations.

The past decade has also witnessed increased global migration and the globalisation of media, with new satellite technologies and the Internet making McLuhan's 'global village' truly global. These trends have impacted on the choices available to Governments in dealing with national and international issues and bilateral, regional and multilateral relations. This has had its inevitable impact on India, which has been transformed this past decade by its increased economic openness. This in turn has shaped India's relations with the world economy and global communities.

The Influence of Business in Foreign Policy

Indian foreign policy in the post-Independence period was shaped essentially by geo-political considerations and the priorities of nation-building. The requirements of economic development did have a direct bearing on foreign policy, as India's first Prime Minister Jawaharlal Nehru clarified in his very first speech on foreign policy in the Constituent Assembly in December 1947.[3] But the Nehruvian era

1. Schelling (1971).
2. Cooper (1973).
3. See Baru (2006). Nehru said: "Talking about foreign policies, the House must remember that these are not just empty struggles on a chessboard. Behind them lie all manner of things. Ultimately, foreign policy is the outcome of economic policy, and until India has properly evolved her economic policy, her foreign policy will be rather vague, rather inchoate, and will be groping."

in economic policy was one of central planning and the public sector occupying the "commanding heights" of the Indian economy. Hence, business-to-business relations willy-nilly became state-to-state relations. It was only in the 1980s that Indian business, especially the private corporate sector, came into its own and began to influence political thinking on foreign policy issues. Prime Minister Rajiv Gandhi was the first Indian Prime Minister to invite business leaders to join him on official visits abroad. This practice received further boost during the tenure of Prime Minister Narasimha Rao.

The liberalisation of economic policy in 1991 opened a new chapter in government-business interaction in India. Not only did business leaders accompany the Prime Minister, External Affairs Minister and Union Finance and Commerce Ministers on their visits abroad, but their views began to be better articulated through the two principle chambers of business, the Federation of Indian Chambers of Commerce and Industry (FICCI) and the Confederation of Indian Industry (CII). The CII's Partnership Summit in fact became a major diplomatic event with foreign leaders invited to it. FICCI's efforts through the South Asian Business Forum was another such effort in the SAARC region.

In the immediate post-Independence period, Indian business had little influence in shaping political thinking on foreign policy issues. Jawaharlal Nehru's dominating personality, India's immediate concerns with its geo-political neighbourhood and the larger dynamics of decolonisation, post-colonial development and Cold War shaped India's foreign policy options. To be sure, national economic interests did play an important role in shaping foreign policy, as already mentioned.

Contrary to more recent thinking, Nehru did not adopt a hostile view either towards the West or towards western business. On his first visit to the United States as Prime Minister in 1945, Nehru sought out US business and sought greater US economic engagement with India. It was the United States that spurned Nehru largely because the US was focused on post-war reconstruction in East Asia and Western Europe and also because it was not enthusiastic about Nehru's plan for public sector-led industrialisation in India.

In subsequent years, India's inward-oriented industrialisation strategy meant that even Indian business was more focused on the domestic market and was satisfied with protectionist policies. This ensured that the normal synergy one expects between the interests of business and foreign policy choices democratic governments make was weak. India's non-alignment policy did not yield any significant economic benefits for Indian business, perhaps also because Indian business was not outward-oriented and did not seek markets and investment opportunities in developing countries. India's friendship with the Soviet Union had spin-offs in defence and strategic industries which were all in the public sector. The only important private sector beneficiaries of India's relations with the Soviet Union were tobacco growers in Andhra Pradesh (many of whom liberally funded the local communist parties!) and a few traders who dipped into the rupee based trading opportunities.

It was only in the 1980s, when Indian business began to look at market opportunities abroad, especially during the term of Prime Minister Rajiv Gandhi, that the external economic and business interests of Indian business began to shape official thinking on foreign policy. The CII became actively involved in projecting Indian interests abroad and in pursuing Track-II Diplomacy at home and abroad.[4]

The real turning point, however, was 1991. Several factors contributed to increased business engagement in Indian diplomacy, which are discussed in detail below:

The Economic Crisis of 1990-91 and the End of the Cold War

The timing of India's external payments crisis in 1990-91 was significant. It occurred almost in parallel with the collapse of the Soviet Union. Facing for the first time the prospect of external debt rescheduling, Government of India tried hard to secure multilateral and bilateral support. It found great difficulty in securing such support without adopting policies that would open up the Indian economy to greater play of market forces. It also found it had very few friends in G-7 capitals. Hence, the policy of economic liberalisation

4. For a discussion of trends in economic diplomacy and the role of economics in bilateral diplomacy see Khosla (2006 and Rana (2002).

was launched in part to address the problem of India's economic isolation in the context of the post-Cold War world.

The factors driving external economic liberalisation were independent of the felt and expressed need of domestic enterprise. Domestic enterprise was keen on internal liberalisation but was not very enthusiastic about external liberalisation. In fact, as tariffs came down and quantitative restrictions on imports were removed, domestic business enterprise became restive. While the Chambers of Commerce officially welcomed these initiatives, some leading business groups mobilised themselves to campaign against what they called the wrong sequencing of reform. The "Bombay Club", a group of businessmen who met in Bombay to draw a charter of demands laced with protest against the Government's external liberalisation policies, argued that the latter should wait till internal liberalisation had been completed and Indian business had secured "a level playing field" vis-à-vis global multinationals.

The negative middle class reaction to such "trade unionism of business elites", forced Indian business to rethink its strategy and encouraged them to back off. Such middle class reaction was increasingly shaped in the 1990s by the global success of Indian professionals, especially in the field of information technology.[5] Consequently, the three Chambers of Commerce—CII, FICCI and the Associated Chambers of Commerce (ASSOCHAM)—began to offer compromise formulas that would combine the interests of domestic business with the imperatives of economic liberalisation. They understood the imperatives of BoP (balance of payments) management, which where mollified by a liberalised exchange rate mechanism, easing of foreign exchange controls, greater access to external finance and the trade-offs secured on internal economic policies. They also understood the imperatives of the post-Cold War world and India's need to seek new external relationships.

In fact, the CII embraced enthusiastically India's new "Look East Policy", inviting Singapore's Prime Minister Goh Chok Tong as the

5. See Baru (2006), chapter "Sizing up the competition", Ch.37: "IT and the e-Economy: The Ballast for India-US Relations"; and chapter 63: "An India of Narayana Murthy or Sudarshan?"

Chief Guest to its Centenary Celebrations in Calcutta in January 1995. India's "Look East Policy", of engaging the ASEAN economies and also Japan and South Korea was a direct outcome of the end of the Cold War and India's outward-economic orientation. As the key architect of the reforms of 1991, the then finance minister Dr Manmohan Singh openly acknowledged the experience of South Korea and ASEAN in reorienting Indian economic policies. This gained for India new access to Asian capitals. India got on to the fast track in being invited to be a partner country of ASEAN by the late 1990s.[6]

The Change in India's Negotiating Stance at the World Trade Organization (WTO)

Almost on a parallel track with these policy changes was the change in India's negotiating stance at the WTO. Till 1990, India firmly opposed a new round of multilateral trade negotiations under the General Agreement on Trade and Tariffs (GATT). Even after the Uruguay Round was launched India opposed new areas like trade in services and trade-related intellectual property rights from being brought into trade negotiations. Indian industry played an important role in campaigning against the new agenda being promoted by the developed economies. Sector specific lobby groups were set up by Indian businessmen to campaign against trade liberalisation through the multilateral route.

After 1991 India changed course. Interestingly, Indian industry changed course too! Rather than block the Uruguay Round, both Indian government and industry opted to negotiate and secure an outcome favourable to India. This marked a new phase in Indian business's diplomatic engagement. The CII and FICCI actively canvassed support for the Indian point of view in various world capitals. They invited foreign dignitaries to well-organised and well-attended gala events of Indian business organisations in New Delhi and Bombay and sought to win them over to their point of view. The message was clear—don't destroy the Indian private sector, we can be your allies in the spread of market capitalism in this part of

6. See Baru (2008).

the world. By projecting private Indian business as an ally in the onward march of market economies in the post-Cold War world, Indian business established new relationships for India in developed industrial economies.

India was not wholly satisfied with the outcome of the Uruguay Round, but the process marked a fundamental shift in India's trade diplomacy. Not only did India emerge as an active participant in the WTO process, it was also able to establish itself simultaneously as a champion of the interests of developing economies and as a willing negotiator with developed economies. This "bridge power" status in multilateral negotiations was new for India, having been a long time leader of the non-aligned and on the wrong side of the Cold War divide. Indian industry played a crucial role in facilitating this transition. The experience gathered in the Uruguay Round negotiations helped Indian business to take a more pro-active role in the Doha Development Round process. Indian business chambers took the initiative, for the first time, and played a pro-active role in trade diplomacy. Rather than wait for Government to take the lead, business chambers began crafting their own strategy for the Doha Round. FICCI constituted a trade policy group in 1999, drafting the services of an officer of the Indian Administrative Services (on secondment from Government to FICCI), that outlined broad parameters for the Doha Round negotiating strategy.

The investment CII and FICCI made in trade diplomacy was of great use for Indian business and for the Indian government. Indian business also emerged as an important participant in "track two" diplomacy on the trade front. The CII set up an office in Geneva and representatives of Indian business accompanied the Indian commerce minister on important travels abroad related to trade diplomacy. Abandoning the 'protectionist' rhetoric of the 'Bombay Club' of the early 1990s, both CII and FICCI adopted a pro-active negotiating stance.

Trade liberalisation in the 1990s and the increased exposure of Indian business to external competition forced Indian business to adopt a pro-active role in Indian trade diplomacy. This then became an important route through which business associations began to influence Indian foreign policy options. Since "trade policy is foreign policy", and since in the era of globalisation trade policy has strategic consequences, the growing involvement of Indian business in crafting Indian trade policy options gave them a new profile in influencing foreign policy outcomes.

Another important factor that contributed to a greater engagement of business with foreign policy was the rise of China, as a business rival. China's entry into the WTO opened a new chapter in India-China trade relations. By year 2000, Indian business became worried about dumping of cheaper Chinese goods.[7] While China has emerged as India's biggest bilateral trade partner, over-taking the United States (though still lagging behind the European Union), fear of China grips Indian business. It has begun to shape business thinking on relations with other Asian economies, including the strategic importance of the India-ASEAN Free Trade Agreement. Like in so many other countries, business pro-activism in foreign policy has been greatly influenced by the rise of China as a trading power.

The Outward Orientation of Large Indian Companies Though Only Towards the End of the 1990s

A third factor, a more recent one, that has contributed to the increased involvement of business in foreign policy has been the growing interest of Indian business groups in overseas investment. Major Indian business groups began investing abroad in the 1980s. However, it is only in the past five years that there has been a quantum increase in foreign investment.[8] The main stimulus for this was the policy of the National Democtatic Alliance (NDA government to increase capital outflows as part of its strategy to manage a surge in capital inflows since the early 2000s. Outward investment by Indian

7. At the *Financial Express*, where I was Chief Editor at the time, we were constantly bombarded by information from Indian business about "unfair" trade competition from China. The FE ran a series of news reports under the banner "Enter The Dragon", drawing attention to the "China threat" in the Indian market. Soon China began increasing its imports from India. This created a business lobby in India that saw a "China opportunity". At the *Financial Express* we began a new series, in 2002, called "Beyond The Great Wall".
8. Ramamurti and Singh (2009) discusses in some detail the phenomenon of Indian multinational enterprise.

entities increased sharply from around US$2.0 billion in 2003-04 to US$14.4 billion in 2006-07.[9]

Outward investment by Indian firms has a wide geographical spread, including UK (where Indian investors top the charts on inward investment into UK), US, China, Russia, South-East, and South Asia and Africa. In each of these bilateral equations the role of prominent business leaders, in particular, and of business interests, in general, has increased considerably. Business leaders increasingly 'facilitate' meetings between officials and politicians of countries, they influence the bilateral agenda, and they contribute funds to political parties or leaders when asked to.

The rising interest of Indian firms, both in the services and manufacturing sector, in foreign trade and foreign investment has increased their interest in shaping India's diplomatic initiatives with respect to various regional forums and specific countries. Indian business delegations now routinely accompany the Prime Minister when he travels abroad. The Prime Minister meets accompanying business leaders before he goes in for a bilateral meeting with the host Head of Government to understand their concerns with respect to the country being visited. Regional forums like SAARC, BIMSTEC, ASEAN and EU invite Indian business leaders to participate in parallel meetings along with the Prime Minister.

It would be incorrect to dismiss such travel as mere diplomatic and business tourism. The views of business leaders are discussed even within closed door meetings between high officials, and issues like market access, investment opportunities, visa regimes, are increasingly focused on business perspectives. High profile global acquisitions by business leaders like Lakshmi Mittal (steel) and Ratan Tata (steel and auto), high profile global contracting out by major Indian companies like Reliance and India's energy diplomacy have given such business leaders great influence in bilateral relations.

Perhaps one must make a distinction between the diplomatic influence and interest of non-resident and largely globalised business leaders of Indian origin, like the Hindujas and Mittals, and the

9. Ministry of Finance (2008).

more nascent business diplomacy of increasingly globalising Indian business leaders like the Tatas and the Ambani brothers.

The Hinduja Brothers, for example, have been known to be influential in various capitals of the world for many years. The legendary 'continuity' in their influence in Iran, from the days of the Shah to those of the Ayatollahs, has earned them a special place in the business lobbyists hall of fame. However, they are no longer unique. Several other businessmen have emerged with similar 'bipartisan' influence in the corridors of power in various capitals. They lubricate the system and help Indian diplomats and politicians secure access and strike deals. The Hindujas have been 'diplomatically active' in a wide range of countries including the United States and the UK. They played a helpful role in the political lobbying associated with India's civil nuclear cooperation agreement with various member countries of the Nuclear Suppliers Group.

Similarly, Lakshmi Mittal has been diplomatically active in Central Asia and Europe. The lower profile of business leaders of Indian origin in South-east Asia, as compared to their Chinese-origin counterparts, may have meant that Indian business played a less important role in shaping India's relations with the region, though even here wider business interests have without doubt shaped India's strategic relations.[10]

Track Two Diplomacy

An important consequence of this is the willingness of Indian business groups to invest in 'track two' diplomacy and in shaping foreign policy perspectives. One of India's largest business houses has funded a think tank focused on strategic policy and foreign affairs, with several former diplomats hired as faculty. This is the Observer Research Foundation (ORF), funded by Mukesh Ambani's Reliance Industries. While Mukesh Ambani has directly funded a foreign policy research institute, other Indian companies have funded 'track two' diplomatic initiatives through the CII and FICCI.

10. See Baru (2008).

The CII runs several 'track two' dialogues funded by various member companies. The countries covered so far include the US, Japan, Singapore and Malaysia. Business leaders with country specific interests invest in these dialogues and also participate in them. Thus, Ratan Tata has consistently funded, and often participated in, the CII-Aspen Strategy Group dialogue on India-US relations. Launched in 1999, partly to contain the diplomatic damage of the Pokhran II nuclear tests and build bridges between Indian and the US opinion makers, business leaders and legislators, the India-US Dialogue has been sustained over 8 years, with two meetings every year, one in the US and another in India.

Other business leaders like Sunil Mittal, Sunil Munjal, Harpal Singh and Gautam Thapar have invested and participated in these and other such dialogues. FICCI has also initiated a similar effort with the Woodrow Wilcon Center and the Heritage Foundation. An important initiative of FICCI has been the Forum of Parliamentarians set up to engage elected representatives from India and their counterparts in the US, the UK, Germany, EU, Singapore, Japan and Pakistan. According to FICCI's Secretary-General, Dr Amit Mitra:

> The IUFP, constituted six years ago along the lines of the "India Caucus" and "Senate Friends of India" Group in the US Congress, provides an important platform to the Indian Parliamentarians to develop and strengthen India-US relations through Track II initiatives. Encompassing all aspects of bilateral relations, the forum makes an earnest effort to facilitate wider exchange of views, dialogue and discussions on bilateral and global issues between Indian parliamentarians and their counterparts in the US, senior Administration officials, business leaders, opinion-makers and the Indian-American community, thereby adding an important parliamentary dimension to bilateral ties.[11]

FICCI has also recently launched similar forums with Commonwealth of Independent States (CIS), Russia, China and Italy. The India-US Forum played an important role in shaping thinking of young Parliamentarians on the issue of India-US civil nuclear cooperation agreement, and in providing a forum for newly

11. Interview to author, September 2008.

elected Parliamentarians from Pakistan to interact with their Indian counterparts.

The Forums of Parliamentarians is a multiparty body of seven Forums with 130 members belonging to various political shades of India with many of its members serving on important parliamentary committees. The Forums with the US, the UK, Germany, EU, Singapore, Japan and Pakistan launched consecutively since the formation of the India-US Forum of Parliamentarians (IUFP) in March 2002, have played a significant role in promoting inter-parliamentary exchange and dialogue with its counterparts in these countries. The Forums have gone beyond and facilitated dialogue with senior government officials, leading think tanks experts, business leaders and civil society at large, in these countries on several issues of bilateral and global concerns.[12]

In 2007, FICCI's India-US Forum of Parliamentarians took the initiative to launch "The India-Yale Parliamentary Leadership Programme", a first of its kind for Indian parliamentarians. This programme gives Parliamentarians an opportunity to spend time at Yale University to reflect on a wide range of issue they deal with as members of Parliament. The Second India-Yale Parliamentary Leadership Programme, conducted in June 2008, covered topics like, "The Economics of Mitigating Climate Change and Sustainable Development"; "Global Economic Risks and the New Financial Order"; "Three Decades of Reform, Rule of Law and Governance Challenges in China"; "Poverty and Economic Development"; "Religion and Politics"; "Reform of Higher Education in India"; "2008 US Presidential Election: Predictions and Realities"; "India and Globalisation"; "Effective and Strategic Political Communications"; and so on.

There has always also been a 'below the radar' role for business in diplomacy. This is normally confined to a few influential business leaders who may provide 'facilitation' for unofficial contacts between diplomats and political leaders. A business leader could act as a 'conduit' for 'backroom' and unofficial discussion and pre-meeting negotiation between Heads of Government. As Indian businessmen

12. This information was provided by Dr Amit Mitra, Secretary-General, FICCI and Mr Ramesh Chandran, FICCI.

globalise and become part of the global 'cocktail and golf circuits', and fund politicians and political parties in other countries they are also able to shape relations between India and other countries. This 'below the radar' role of business leaders is on the rise and can be seen in South Asia, in rest of Asia, in Africa, in large parts of Europe and in India's relations with major powers like US, Russia and China.

Another form of 'below the radar' influence for business is their funding of politicians, lobbies and interest groups in foreign countries. While some of this activity would normally be regarded as 'illegal gratification' of policy makers, some countries permit public funding of lobbying efforts, ranging from payment to advertisements in the media to sponsoring interest and focus groups, supporting 'track two' diplomacy and other public diplomacy efforts, including support for university chairs and research centres.

Indian business leaders are increasingly investing funds in think tanks and influential educational institutions in the US and other countries to influence people and win friends. Membership of the Boards of presitigious 'ivy league' institutions and US think tanks enables them to contribute to the bilateral relationship while getting their business done. Among recent high profile initiatives are Nandan Nilekani's funding of a chair at Yale University, and Sunil Mittal joining the Board of Trustees of the Carnegie Endowment.[13]

India's Success in Software and the Globalisation of Indian IT and Software Business

The Indian information technology, software and business process outsourcing industry has without doubt changed India's global profile. Its impact on Brand India is well known. Visiting Heads of State and Government now routinely add Bangalore and Hyderabad to their itinerary. A visit to the Infosys or Wipro campus or to Cyberabad is a high profile part of India's economic diplomacy. India's success in these areas, as well as in the entertainment sector,

---

13. "Initiative to Transform Yale University's Engagement with India", Available at: *http://opa.yale.edu/news/article.aspx?id=6223;* "Sunil Mittal Joins Carnegie Endowment Board of Trustees," Available at: *http://www.carnegieendowment.org/publications/index.cfm?fa=view&id=22901&prog=zgp&proj=zsa*

has contributed to enhancing India's 'soft power'. Indian IT and software capabilities now open doors for Indian diplomats abroad in the corridors of power.

This has given business leaders in these sectors high level access both within India and in other world capitals. More importantly, the economic importance of software and BPO business for the Indian economy has ensured that such business interests can no longer be ignored by Indian foreign policymakers. In fact, the promotion of Indian capabilities and business interests in these areas is intrinsic to the projection of Indian 'soft power', both in developed and developing countries.

All this cannot be dismissed as mere diplomacy. It is having a palpable influence on foreign policy as well. Today India cannot ignore the business interests of its burgeoning IT, knowledge and data processing sectors in crafting its foreign policy options. Indeed, India's relations with the US, in particular, and with the 'English-speaking' world, in general, has increasingly been influenced by the enormous pull of business and professional interests involved in this sector. Billions of dollars are now at stake for Indian software, data and business processing companies in western markets. The sharp decline in India-Russia economic relations in the 1990s, as compared to a similarly dramatic increase in India-China trade and the importance of US and Asian markets for Indian business have become important determinants of India's foreign policy options.

Clearly, Indian business is increasingly willing to invest time and money in promoting economic diplomacy and wider foreign policy objectives for a wide variety of reasons. These could range from the promotion of specific corporate interests to wider objectives of securing influence and proximity to political leaders.

At least one powerful influence of influence-peddling available to corporate leaders is the media. Both through direct financial investments in the media, and indirect investment in the form of advertisement revenue, businesses do acquire influence in the media. This influence is used both to promote corporate interests and wider policy objectives, including in the realm of foreign policy.

The Influence of Media in Foreign Policy

The media has an obvious and independent role in shaping public opinion on foreign policy issues in a democracy. However, the influence of media on foreign policy is shaped by two important factors: first, the extent of domestic political disagreement or consensus on foreign policy issues; second, the relationship between the Government of the day and the media.

Indian foreign policy was marked by a high degree of domestic political consensus in the initial years after Independence. Few in the national press questioned Jawaharlal Nehru's overall foreign policy orientation. During the Cold War there was a weakening of this consensus in the press, with some favouring a closer relationship with the West and the others favouring a stronger 'anti-imperialist' stance. The mainstream public and political opinion in India favoured Nehru's path of 'non-alignment' in the Cold War. Contrary to popular western, especially the US, view of 'non-alignment' as an 'ideological anti-West and pro-Soviet' stance, Nehru's non-alignment was essentially a pragmatic and nationalist assertion of India's independent and autonomous stance in international affairs. Nehru was in favour of good relations with the West as well as with Soviet Union, but sought for India an 'independent' voice in world affairs. This stance had broad national support and the media of the time went along with this stance.

Given the political dominance of the Congress Party and a high degree of consensus among mainstream political parties the media had at best a marginal role to play. There is no doubt, however, that the Cold War played itself out through the columns of the Indian media but the moot point is that this did not influence official thinking in any significant way.[14]

14. There is continuing controversy in the Indian media and on the internet about allegations made in the papers of the "Mitrokhin Archives" regarding KGB funding of Indian journalists. Similar allegations have been made about CIA funding of media personalities. More recently there have been allegations that countries like China, Iran and Pakistan have been active in winning friends and influencing people in the Indian media. But all these remain unsubstantiated charges and rumours. *http://www.southasiaanalysis.org/%5Cpapers16%5Cpaper1549.html*

Given the high degree of freedom that Indian media enjoys, foreign Governments have, from time to time, tried to win friends and influence opinion in the media. The Indian Government also seeks to do this. However, it's approach is to 'win' over the media to its point of view, rather then be influenced by any independent thinking within the media. The media is viewed as an instrument for promoting the Government's view point, not as the 'Fourth Estate' whose 'independent' voice must be heard! During the Cold War period, the Governments of the day were fairly successful in securing broad media support for their foreign policy.

The Ministry of External Affairs has traditionally maintained a close connection with influential editors and columnists to ensure, what a high ranking Indian diplomat has dubbed, a "cosy relationship".[15] While some journalists view this with deep suspicion and may even refuse to accept Government hospitality as a way of defending media freedom, one must not exaggerate the success that Government's have in winning over the media to their viewpoint.[16] In India's increasingly fractious political environment and given rising budgets of private media organisations, Government freebies and

15. The cosy relationship at the time between the foreign policy establishment and the media was best summed up by the current Spokesperson of the Ministry of External Affairs: "In the comfortable old days—again, we need to look no further than 15 years ago—the world of diplomacy in India was covered by a set of about 20 erudite, polite gentlemen of the press and the dutiful Doordarshan and All India Radio. Briefings were comfortable, friendly and somewhat leisurely affairs, full of intellectual wit and repartee. The media persons would gather what they could before turning to the chai, samosa and gulab jamun and thereafter find, their way back to their offices to type out the stories for the rest of the evening. Today, we have to deal with not only a hugely expanded print media but also more than 30 24-hour TV news channels, several news agencies and even on-line journals." Sarna (2007).

16. See for example, Rajdeep Sardesai's comment: "The other ministry which equally effectively manipulates the media is the Ministry of External Affairs. When they take you on a summit being attended by Atal Behari Vajpayee, they ply you with the choicest whisky and caviar on the flight and in turn it is expected that you will follow, hook, line and sinker what the ministry is saying. For instance, if the prime minister's recent visit to China is a success or if the Ministry of External Affairs feels it is a success, then you have to say that it is one. If you choose then to interpret that somewhere down the line there has been a compromise on Tibet, you are not supposed to use the word, "compromise" because the overarching philosophy is that since they paid for you to come to China, how can you now write that the prime minister has sold out on Tibet? ...because the media does not have the means of resisting the pressures from them (the reason being that sources of information will be completely cut off) it often toes the line." Sardesai (2006).

junkets have declining influence in shaping media thinking on major policy issues.

Ironically, a substantial part of the work of the External Publicity Division of the Ministry of External Affairs has in fact been in dealing with domestic media rather than international media. The Division is more often engaged in seeking internal publicity for external policy rather than external publicity for internal policy![17] It is difficult to point to any important example where the Indian Government shaped thinking on Indian policies in any significant way in any foreign media.

Equally, it is difficult to offer any example where the Government of the day has altered its policy in foreign affairs or bilateral relations due to pressure from the media. In fact, Indian diplomats often take pride in claiming that they can 'get the media they want'! This is, without doubt, changing with the breakdown of the domestic political consensus on foreign policy issues, and the pervasive influence of 24x7 television news channels.

The electronic media, like Parliament, has become an arena in which party political differences on foreign policy do get articulated more forcefully because of the nature of the medium. In fact, TV news channels may have contributed to increased public discord on foreign policy by deliberately strait-jacketing all 'discussions' into binary, conflictual 'for-and-against' debates. Rather than facilitate a consensus such 'argumentative' debates foster divergence. While television resorts to this practice to increase viewer attention and make news more 'entertaining', this has increased the role of the media in shaping political thinking on foreign policy issues.[18]

The last decade, therefore, marks a turning point in the role of the media in shaping foreign policy. This is on account of three very different factors: (1) the gradual erosion of the domestic political

17. Sarna's essay on "Media and Diplomacy", published in a major official publication of the Ministry of External Affairs and proclaimed as an authoritative and comprehensive survey of Indian foreign policy is almost entirely focused on the domestic media, with only a passing reference to foreign media!

18. The pro-active role of Indian media on human rights abuses in Tibet is a good recent example of media activism exerting pressure on Government.

consensus on foreign policy, giving the media the role of an arbiter and an independent analyst of contending political views; (2) the media revolution and expansion, with the rise of television and business journalism and the growing importance of private corporate advertisement revenues, as opposed to government support for media, in influencing media economics; (3) finally, the increasing influence of the middle class and the business class in the media has also influenced media thinking on foreign policy.

An early example of the media playing an important role in shaping public opinion and government policy with respect to a foreign and strategic policy issue, in the context of domestic political discord, was the role played by the *Times of India* in 1996 on the issue of India signing up on the Comprehensive Test Ban Treaty (CTBT) agreement.[19] Indian political parties were divided on the issue of India's stance on CTBT, since India had for a long time advocated such a test ban and had in fact sponsored the CTBT. However, when CTBT got linked to NPT renewal and India felt it was being discriminated against on the question of its nuclear status, the view gained ground that India should not sign CTBT. A major debate took place in the columns of Indian newspapers in which the *Times of India* editorially called for India rejecting CTBT in the form in which it was then being proposed. India can be a signatory only as an acknowledged nuclear weapons power and not as a non-weapon State. This finally became the official Indian position.

The entire mainstream media has been a strong and consistent supporter of the India-US agreement on cooperation in civil nuclear energy. Overwhelming media support for the civil nuclear agreement, with the exception of *The Hindu*, under the pro-CPM editorship of N. Ram and *The Asian Age*, during the editorship of M.J. Akbar, strengthened the Government's hand in politically defending its' case

19. See Uday Bhaskar (2004). Bhaskar (p.55) observes: "Through seminars, workshops, lectures and his steady stream of newspaper articles, K. Subrahmanyam (KS) shaped the Indian response to the nettlesome nuclear issue and the media became a contested domain. .... The TOI's op-ed page became a veritable battle-field. Sanjaya Baru, the editorial page editor, played a central role in shaping the Indian debate and from my modest perch at the time, I would aver that KS through his searing columns helped steer the debate over the CTBT so that the government of the day could take a firm decision in the matter".

at home, against political criticism from Left and Right opposition. More than print, television played an extremely influential role in generating public support for the nuclear accord. No major TV news channel campaigned against the agreement, while many of them took a strong supportive stance.

Some critics of the media may dismiss its role as peripheral given the limited reach of media in an educationally backward society. To be sure, foreign policy always engages the elite much more than the masses. Hence, it is rarely a subject for mass politics, except perhaps in the case of India-Pakistan relations, and that too in northern India.[20] However, the fact remains that with the decline of large pan-Indian national political parties and the emergence of fractured coalitions, difference between political parties on national policy issues, including foreign policy, is bound to grow. With such diversity of opinion in the political arena, the national media can secure for itself an influential autonomous role provided it is able to articulate a national policy that will find wide public acceptability and will stand the test of professional scrutiny.

The objective basis for such independent and informed view on foreign policy options within the media exists, even if in actual fact nothing is done to tap into that potential. Large media groups no longer look to Government alone for their survival. The phenomenal growth in the advertisement budgets of private corporates has increased the autonomy of the media with respect to Government, even if this has resulted in growing corporate influence on the media. In the context of our discussion what this means is that media can adopt a stance independent of Government, perhaps reflecting the interests of business and the professional classes, on foreign policy issues. News coverage of countries in the Indian media is increasingly influenced by revenue considerations.[21] But this in turn does not have any significant impact on Government policy, as yet.

---

20. Pattanaik (2004).

21. One must not exaggerate the significance of this factor. Despite high business interest in Africa, Indian media's coverage of Africa is abysmal. On the other hand, the large presence of Indians in the Middle East and Persian Gulf has contributed to high media coverage of the region, including in the regional media in States like Kerala, which is home of a large proportion of migrant labour to that region.

This increased relevance of business and middle class preferences for media policy implies that their world view will count for more in shaping media thinking on foreign policy. This is demonstrated by the near-unanimous support for the India-US nuclear agreement in the business and English-language media. The policy preferences of these two segments of the media in the foreign policy arena do tend to influence Indian language media also. However, perceptions on foreign policy in Indian language media wary, due to local political, social and cultural factors. For example, the national media is less interested in India's policy towards Sri Lanka than the Tamil language media. Similarly, there is much less coverage on developments in the Islamic world in the national media as compared to the Urdu language media, that caters largely to a Muslim readership.

The thinking of these categories of readers, who may be politically influential in specific regions and constituencies, do not always get reflected in the national media, including television. It is the views of the more articulate English-speaking middle classes that gets a greater play in national and mass media. What this means, of course, is that any news about the US or Pakistan is almost always front page and headline stuff, while news about most other developing countries makes no waves. The visit of the US President, for example, secures saturation coverage in the Indian media, but the India-Africa Summit meeting in 2008 was not even reported on the front pages of most papers!

Such preferential bias in the national media's treatment of different regions, countries and international issues may influence public opinion and even the thinking of politicians. But, in the corridors of decision-making, especially when it comes to the permanent civil service, contrarian thinking in the media and disagreeable media coverage is at best a nuisance to be tolerated, not a viewpoint to be taken account of in formulating policy!

Finally, we do believe that the national media does not as yet view itself as an active player in foreign policy, even if some newspapers give more coverage to foreign affairs than others. One important reason for this is that Indian media has not found a business plan to justify greater foreign coverage and the posting of foreign correspondents. Among the world's 'major powers' Indian media has the least number of foreign correspondents. Only a handful of print and TV organisations have correspondents posted in major world capitals and in neighbouring countries. There has in fact been a scaling down of foreign correspondents, with most Indian media drawing on news put out by foreign news agencies and foreign media partners. While China has emerged as India's largest trade partner and is India's biggest neighbour, only 3 media organisations (one subsidised by Government) have correspondents stationed in China!

Conclusion

In this chapter we have defined 'media' in its normal limited sense of news media, and that too national news media. We have largely ignored the role of 'regional' and Indian language media. This is mainly because regional media by and large takes its cue on foreign policy issues from the national media. With the exception of specific instances, like the Tamil media's special interest in India's Sri Lanka policy, or the Urdu media's special interest in Pakistan and the Islamic world, regional media does not take an independent view on larger strategic and foreign policy issues at variance with the Delhi-based national media.

This chapter also does not examine the role of the entertainment media, especially Indian cinema, and the 'soft power' dimension to media and foreign policy. One could argue that in a wider sense Indian media is helping project India globally. But there is little proof as yet of Indian 'soft power' shaping 'foreign policy' of other countries towards India, or India's policy towards others. The 'soft power' of Indian media is at best an adjunct to foreign and strategic policy, if that, and not an active component of such policy.

India's economic globalisation and the rise of the globalised professional middle class have raised the profile of business and media in Indian foreign policy making. International trade and capital flows, as well as the economic importance of Indian migrants abroad have increased the importance of people-to-people and business-to-business relations in India's state-to-state relations with other countries. In turn, these factors are beginning to shape Indian foreign policy thinking and will perhaps count for more in years to come.

References

Baru, Sanjaya (2006). "The Economic Dimension of India's Foreign Policy", in *Strategic Consequences of India's Economic Performance.* Chapter2. New Delhi: Academic Foundation, London: Routledge, New York: Francis & Taylor and Beijing: Citic Press.

———. (2008). "India and the World—Economics and Politics of the Manmohan Singh Doctrine in Foreign Policy", *ISAS Working Paper* No. 53, November. *http://www.isasnus.org/events/workingpapers/52.pdf*

Cooper, R.N. (1973). "Trade Policy is Foreign Policy", *Foreign Policy* 9, Winter, 1972-73.

Khosla, I.P. (ed.) (2006). *Economic Diplomacy.* Delhi: Konark Publishers Pvt Ltd.

Ministry of Finance (2008). *Economic Survey, 2007-08.* New Delhi: Govt of India.

Pattanaik, Smruti S. (2004). *Elite Perceptions in Foreign Policy : Role of Print Media in Influencing India-Pakistan Relations, 1989-1999.* New Delhi: Manohar.

Ramamurti, Ravi and Jitendra V. Singh (eds.) (2009). *Emerging Multinationals from Emerging Economies.* Cambridge University Press

Rana, Kishan S. (2002). *Bilateral Diplomacy.* Delhi: Manas Publications.

Sardesai, Rajdeep (2006). "Manipulations and Bias in News," in Uday Sahay (ed.), *Making News: Handbook of the Media in Contemporary India* Oxford University Press. pp. 166-171.

Sarna, Navtej (2007). "Media and Diplomacy", in Atish Sinha (ed.), *Indian Foreign Policy: Challenges and Opportunities.* New Delhi: Academic Foundation & Foreign Service Institute.

Schelling, Thomas C. (1971). *Report of the US Congress Commission on National Security Considerations Affecting Trade Policy.* Washington DC.

Uday Bhaskar, C. (2004). "KS: Vamana of Indian Nuclear Theology?" in C. Uday Bhaskar (ed.), *A Boquet of Tributes to K Subrahmanyam at 75.* New Delhi

8

India's Economic Rise and South Asian Integration

The member nations of the South Asian Association for Regional Cooperation (SAARC) have been engaged for a long time in securing a reintegration of the sub-continental economy through a regional free trade agreement (SAFTA) and move towards a South Asian Economic Union (SAEU). In pursuing this shared regional agenda the member countries of SAARC will only be reintegrating a geographically and historically constituted regional economy that has benefitted from centuries of free flow of goods, capital flows, people and ideas. South Asia, as it is known today, is nothing more than the 'Indian sub-continent' that the world has been familiar with for centuries. The Indian sub-continent was both an integrated economic entity as well as the 'crossroads' of inter-regional trade flows across the Eurasian land mass and the Indian Ocean littoral.

Indian Sub-continent as an Integrated Economic System

An 'Economic Union' implies the integration of markets, the ease of travel and trade, efficient connectivity and cultural interaction. All these attributes have increasingly come to characterise interaction within the region called South Asia. South Asia is the modern term for what geographers have for long called the 'Indian sub-continent'. With the end of British rule in India in 1947, the political landscape of the sub-continent changed once again, as it had through the centuries, with the creation of new nations. The Republics of India and Pakistan came into being. The two, along with the Kingdoms of Nepal and Bhutan and the Republic of Sri Lanka defined the broad contours of the new 'South Asia'.

South Asia's integrated economic and ecological system got broken up into compartmentalised political entities due to the emergence of independent States in the region. In seeking to reestablish a 'SAEU', it is important to remember that the 'political' division of the region created artificial discontinuities that are now being sought to be removed through institutions of regional cooperation and integration.

South Asia—Island or Crossroads?

There are some economic historians and geo-economists who have viewed South Asia as a 'self-contained' unit, bounded by natural boundaries and barriers that have limited the region's interaction with the Eurasian land mass and the Indian Ocean littoral. Thus, for example, geopolitical analyst George Friedman (2008) put forward the view that the sub-continent was an 'island':

> The geopolitics of India must be considered in the geographical context of the Indian subcontinent—a self-contained region that includes India, Pakistan, Bangladesh and, depending how one defines it, Nepal and Bhutan. We call the subcontinent "self-contained" because it is a region that is isolated on all sides by difficult terrain or by ocean. In geopolitical terms it is, in effect, an island.
>
> This "island" is surrounded on the southeast, south and southwest by the Bay of Bengal, the Indian Ocean and the Arabian Sea. To the west, it is isolated by mountains that rise from the Arabian Sea and run through Pakistan's Baluchistan province, stretching northward and rising higher and higher to the northwestern corner of Pakistan. There, at the Hindu Kush, the mountain chain swings east, connecting with the Pamir and Karakoram ranges. These finally become the Himalayas, which sweep south east some 2,000 miles to the border of Myanmar, where the Rakhine Mountains emerge, and from there south to India's border with Bangladesh and to the Bay of Bengal.

As opposed to this 'isolationist' view of the region stands its exact opposite, the view that South Asia was indeed the 'crossroads' of Asia, integrated with the land-based and sea-based trade and flow of people across Asia. Historian K.M. Pannikar's (1945) classic treatise, "India and the Indian Ocean" offers a comprehensive account of the ancient and more recent maritime links between South Asia and the Persian Gulf and Arab peoples, on the western side, and South-east Asia and the peoples of Indo-China, on the eastern side.

As historian Fernand Braudel (1988) observed in his three volume account of the rise of the global economy:

> The far East taken as a whole, consisted of three gigantic world economies—Islam, overlooking the Indian Ocean from the Red Sea and the persian Gulf, and controlling the endless chain of deserts stretching across Asia from Arabia to China; India, whose influence extended throughout the Indian Ocean, both East and West of Cape Comorin; and China, at once a great territorial power—striking deep into the heart of Asia—and a maritime force, controlling the seas and countries bordering the pacific. And so it had been for many hundreds of years.

It is important to appreciate this historical context. The South Asian region was not only internally integrated through history, but it was an integral part of the larger Asian and Indian Ocean economies that linked the Arabs of West Asia, the varied ethnic groups of Central Asia and the peoples of the Indo-China region (now South-east Asia). More recently, during the colonial era, the industrial economies of the region were also integrated across current political boundaries.[1]

SAEUin the 21st century will, therefore, enable the region to reconnect 'internally', thereby re-establishing economic links that existed even till the middle of the 20th century, as well as 'externally' with Asia to its West, North-west, East and South-east, reintegrating much older economic and cultural links that had once created the world's most prosperous continental economy.[2]

South Asia is not merely a geographical or a geopolitical entity, it is also a civilisational entity. This latter notion would be rejected by many in each of the countries of the region since each one of them is seeking to establish not just their individual national identity, but also a distinct cultural identity. Unlike in Europe, where the effort has

1. Bagchi (1972).
2. Braudel (1988).

been to emphasise the civilisational oneness of the region, in South Asia nascent State formation has meant that each country has sought to focus on what differentiates one nation from another, rather than the common roots of their contemporary identity. However, the fact is that racial and cultural similarities are threads that run through the fabric of the region.

What geography proposes, history disposes. Despite the ties that bind South Asia, post-colonial nation building, the geopolitics of the Cold War and unsettled political and territorial disputes have hobbled regional cooperation. As part of its own nation-building project Pakistan sought to 'look west' to the Islamic nations of West and Central Asia. In due course India, Nepal, Bhutan and Sri Lanka began looking East. It is in the face of such hurdles that a regional association for cooperation was sought to be formed.

The creation of the SAARC was, therefore, an act of faith. It is the most important framework for regional cooperation in South Asia, though other sub-regional groups have come into being aimed at speeding up the process of regional integration.[3]

Regional Cooperation and Institution Building in South Asia: P2P, B2B and G2G

There are three distinct dimensions to bilateral and regional integration: G2G (government-to-government) relations, B2B (business-to-business) relations and P2P (people-to-people) relations. All regional groups, be it the European Union (EU) or the Association of South-east Asian Nations (ASEAN) or any other such regional entities have entailed cooperation/integration across all three dimensions.

Measured against these criterion, South Asia has seen considerable economic integration. Contrary to a widespread feeling that South Asia has been a laggard in RCI (regional cooperation/integration), the facts on the ground suggest a high level of G2G, B2B and P2P interaction within the region.[4] As Baru (2010) observed, "there are good reasons to believe that a variety of local and global

3. Baru (2010).
4. Baru (2010)

factors will increasingly push the countries of the region in the direction of increased regional cooperation." Among these factors are:

1) shared concerns about low level of human development, mass poverty and the consequent problems of social and political instability and violence, migration, disease and such like;
2) recognition of new synergies in industrialisation and growth of services economy;
3) shared platforms in dealing with multilateral trade negotiations; and
4) shared concerns regarding climate change and multilateral regimes pertaining to environmental standards.

There is growing recognition in the sub-continent that their shared historical and socio-economic legacies have imposed a shared burden in terms of inadequate human development and poverty alleviation. The Late Dr Mahbub ul Haq, an eminent Pakistani economist and initiator of the UNDP Human Development Reports (HDRs), took the initiative to publish an annual South Asian HDR focusing on such issues. The SAARC's Social Charter and agendas for poverty eradication and eradication of illiteracy and disease takes some of these ideas forward. The region can benefit collectively from shared programmes of population control, women's education and empowerment given the complex religio-cultural barriers to change.

In the field of industrial development, earlier fears of a regional free trade agreement being a zero-sum game in favour of India are being replaced by growing recognition that this could be a win-win process.[5]

Finally, the region has collectively benefited from working together at the World Trade Organization (WTO) and other such multilateral economic forums and organisations. Even at the International Monetary Fund (IMF) and World Bank, and at the Asian Development Bank (ADB) south Asian governments resist 'beggar-thy-neighbour' approaches and try to work together on regional and national issues.

---

5. The success of the India-Sri Lanka FTA in benefitting both partners, especially Sri Lanka, has added to this understanding. Also see Burki (2006) on Pakistani attitudes to SAFTA.

Apart from such shared concerns, regional cooperation would be pushed forward by the need of the sub-continental neighbours, India, Pakistan, Bangladesh, Nepal and Bhutan to arrive at consensual frameworks for river water utilisation. All these countries are critically dependent on snow-fed rivers originating in the upper Himalayas and flowing through the Tibetan peninsula. The sub-continental countries will have to work together to ensure that China does not curtail their access to these waters and, at the same time, ensure that they arrive at equitable and practical agreements for river water sharing. Till now India has had bilateral water-sharing agreements with its neighbours. It is possible that in future countries may seek regional solutions involving all riparian States.

These issues have come to the fore in the on-going discussions on climate change. There is a recognition, especially after recent earthquakes and the tsunami that the region has a shared geography that necessitates not just working together on natural disaster management but also on larger issues of environmental change. South Asia could well adopt a consensual position in the negotiations on climate change and carbon emission norms.

Finally, shared security concerns, especially the threat of terrorism, is forcing the Governments of the region to work more closely together, especially in the field of intelligence sharing.

Despite the slow progress of regional institution building in South Asia, a growing realisation that the region faces common natural, economic and political challenges is forcing the pace of regional cooperation in South Asia. This could, in turn, contribute to better institution building.

South Asian Regionalism

Three factors have shaped the formation of 'regional cooperative institutions' in the post-War period. First, what may be termed as 'state' driven factors, namely, the dynamics of the Cold War and its resultant alliance formations; second, 'market' based factors, namely, the globalisation of business and the dynamics of cross-border investment and trade flows; third, 'civil society' and 'political' factors, namely national security and economic interests of member-nations.

Unlike in other regions, most importantly western Europe and south-east Asia, none of these factors played an important role in driving the process of regional cooperation in South Asia. There are few 'shared security concerns' and hardly any shared security threat to bring the nations of South Asia together, at least till recently. In fact, the Cold War divided the region than unite it, unlike in western Europe and south-east Asia. The roots of both the EU and the ASEAN lie in the Cold War era when shared security concerns brought the nations of these regions together. Nor indeed did cross-border mergers and the 'Flying Geese' factor play a role in South Asia, given the relatively low levels of foreign direct investment in the region, compared to Europe and South-east Asia.

As Gowher Rizvi (1993: 153), a perceptive analyst of Bangladeshi origin, has observed:

> Even though the compulsion towards regional cooperation in South Asia is enormous, the process of the establishment of an organisation has been slow, hesitant and uncertain. Not only have the economic linkages with the metropolis, Indo-Pakistan rivalry and the fear of India acted as brakes on cooperation, but South Asia also lacks some of the preconditions which have facilitated cooperation in other regions. There is no perception of external or internal threat common to all the States of South Asia. The threat to security is perceived to come from each other, not from an external enemy.

Against the background of internal political differences, SAARC chose to stay away from bilateral political issues and focus on opportunities for regional economic and civil society cooperation. The launch of a South Asian Free Trade Agreement (SAFTA) and other South Asian projects and programmes, both inter-governmental and non-governmental have imparted further momentum to the association. Thus, institution building in SAARC has largely been around opportunities for economic cooperation with the initiative remaining largely with governments.[6] While there is considerable P2P movement across borders, especially between India, Sri Lanka, Nepal

6. For detailed history of South Asian regionalism and the evolution of SAARC see, among others, Bhargava et al. (1995); Dash (1996; 2008); Gonsalves and Jetley (1999); Mendis (1991); Muni and Muni (1984); and Rizvi (1993).

and Bangladesh, the virtual absence of cross-border supply chain and logistics networks has meant limited B2B interaction. However, G2G interface has remained high and often robust.

SAARC as G2G: Institutions and Iconic Projects/Programmes

Regional associations have two characteristics—first is geographical proximity, if not necessarily contingiuty, and the second is shared economic, cultural and other characteristics of a community. Thus 'neighbourhood' and 'community' are two dimensions of a regional association. There is, however, a difference between 'neighbourhood' and 'community'. The former is a purely geographical concept. The latter entails social, cultural and economic commonalities. SAARC has both characteristics. It is a geographically well-defined 'neighbourhood' and a 'community' with several shared characteristics. Hence, it is only natural that SAARC has been able to emerge as an active association of nations, despite its slow start and persistent bilateral problems between some members.

There are two ways of assessing SAARC. First, its 'institutional capacity' and second its 'regional activities'. While SAARC's institutional capacity is limited by the absence of a strong, well staffed and well funded Secretariat, it has been able to create a large number of regional institutions and activities that have created a 'sense of community' within the region.[7] While the SAARC Charter does not define the role of the Secretariat but a Memorandum of Understanding on the Establishment of the Secretariat, November 1986, states that the "role of the Secretariat shall be to co-ordinate and monitor the implementation of SAARC activities and to service the meetings of the Association."[8]

Apart from being the administrative head of a Secretariat whose main function is to implement the resolutions of the SAARC Summit and decisions taken by the Council of Ministers and the Standing Committee (Foreign Secretaries of member countries, and assist

7. Baru (2010).
8. Ibid.

in organising various ministerial and official meetings, the SAARC Secretary-General is expected to:

> Act as the channel of communication and linkage, when so empowered by the Standing Committee, between SAARC and other international organisations on matters of mutual interest. In doing so, the Secretary-General shall be guided by the decision of the Council of Ministers that initiatives for collaboration with external agencies should stem from SAARC itself based on its own determination of priorities and keeping in mind the relevant provisions of the SAARC Charter.

We have argued elsewhere that as a first step towards the creation of a SAEU, the SAARC Secretariat would have to be strengthened, with funds and professional staff. Apart from diplomats representing member country governments, the Secretariat will have to employ subject and technical experts who can guide SAARC in the implementation of programmes and projects.

Regional groupings of nations have always thrived on iconic projects and programmes. The creation of the EU 'Single Market' had huge symbolism for the EU, apart from practical relevance for the unification project. SAARC took a long time to define such an iconic regional project or even programme. It launched a series of 'regional' institutions' but few have had any significant regional impact. At last count, SAARC had established as many as 13 regional institutions covering a wide range of activities. These include: SAARC Agricultural Information Centre (Bangladesh), SAARC Tuberculosis and HIV/AIDS Centre (Nepal), SAARC Human Resources Development Centre (Pakistan), SAARC Documentation Centre (India), SAARC Energy Centre (Pakistan), SAARC Coastal Zone Management Centre (Maldives), SAARC Meteorological Research Centre (Bangladesh), SAARC Forestry Centre (Bhutan), the SAARC Audio Visual Exchange Committee (Nepal) and more recently the South Asian University (SAU) (India) and SAARC Disaster Management Centre (India). The SAARC Secretariat is responsible for reporting to the Summit on the activities of these institutions. The activities of these centres are approved by the Programme Committee and SAARC summits, while the implementation responsibility vests with host country government.

SAARC has created a number of Technical Committees (TC) and Working Groups (WG) that bring together a range of subject experts from member countries. These institutions enable closer interaction between professionals and institutions in member countries. The TC and WG span a wide range of subjects including infrastructure, science and technology, biotechnology, tourism, energy, human development, and agriculture and rural development. The establishment of a SAU is an important step forward both in SAARC's institutional development and in the promotion of greater civil society interaction. This institution could emerge as an 'iconic' SAARC project, like the Food Bank. SAARC desperately needs such iconic projects that make wider civil society impact for regional cooperation to acquire popular appeal. Though its initial development leaves much to be desired!

The Regional Centres have not been able to make that impact, despite there being numerous such centres. Poor funding and inability to attract good talent could be one reason for these regional centres not making a regional impact. If the SAU has to make an impact and emerge as an iconic project it would need adequate funding and high profile and high quality leadership.

SAARC has created a large number of governmental 'umbrella organisations' and is supporting even larger numbers of 'non-government' initiatives and institutions that have already helped create a sense of 'community' within the region.[9]

Building Blocks of B2B and P2P Cooperation

An important next step paving the way for the creation of a SAEU would be the strengthening of existing regional institutions and initiatives. In his comprehensive account of the current status of regional cooperation in South Asia, Nguyen (2010: 34) draws attention to the already existing high degree of regional cooperation and integration in South Asia and concludes:

> Regional economic integration in South Asia and Southeast Asia is driven by strong production networks and development of vertical

9. Recent ADB Papers on SAARC: Srinivasan (2010); Moinuddin (2010); Ghate (2010); Bhaskaran (2010); Kardar (2010); Nguyen (2010); Desai (2010).

specialization. Southeast Asia is the most active region in Asia in facilitating vertical specialization. South Asia is indeed ranked second after Southeast Asia in vertical specialization, especially in the sectors of textiles, food processing and services. But the two regions still have to continue to remove obstacles to encourage greater fragmentation of production networks and higher degree of specialization among countries.

These existing institutions and programmes constitute the building blocks of G2G, P2P and B2B cooperation in South Asia. This paper on a "road map for SAEU" assumes that these existing institutions and programmes will be progressively strengthened to facilitate the maturation of a South Asia 'community'. Having taken the 'first step' of strengthening SAARC Secretariat and the 'second' step of sustaining these initiatives, SAARC will have to take the next, 'third' step of facilitating greater economic and financial integration in the region.

This will require: First, a shared regional economic policy framework beginning with the early implementation of the SAARC free trade agreement (SAFTA), creation of regional financial and regulatory institutions to enable smoother functioning of all factor markets, including capital markets. Second, modern and efficient regional connectivity—including road, rail, air, telecom and maritime infrastructure. Third, integration of energy, water and food security systems to enable region wise response to energy security, water security and food security and, finally, disaster management response. Fourth, greater cultural connectivity in terms of access to media and entertainment, books and other publications, and educational opportunities. This requires a liberal visa regime and development of tourism and tourism infrastructure, regional educational and employment opportunities.

SAFTA

Early and full implementation of SAFTA must take precedence. As Kardar (2010: 10) observes:

> Presently, the distinguishing features of the South Asian Free Trade Agreement (SAFTA), which make the pact ineffectual in many

> respects, continue to be substantial negative lists, tariff concessions restricted to a relatively narrow range of products, high non-tariff barriers, complicated and stringent product specific rules of origin and the exclusion of services, capital mobility and movement of at least skilled labour to levels prevailing in other regional groupings, from the ambit of this accord. These factors and fears about asymmetry in gains have influenced the existing configuration of trade and prevented the region from realizing its potential for inclusive growth over an extended period offered by the vertical integration of production structures. The pattern of industrialisation can be changed with countries specializing through the sub-division of production processes, using modern technology and the opportunities for trade provided by lower transportation costs and improved communication physical infrastructure and systems.

Trade integration is a step in the direction of greater economic integration. This involves integration of capital and financial markets, liberalisation of cross border investment and the creation of regional supply chain networks, facilitated by multinational investment.

There is now adequate literature substantiating the claim that regional economic integration will accelerate the pace of economic growth and development in South Asia. The literature is emphatic in underscoring the economic benefits to both large economies, like India, and the smaller economies in the region. The ADB has lent its imprimatur to this body of intellectual opinion with its wide-ranging analysis of regional cooperation and integration.[10]

Regional trade is an important instrument of regional cooperation, but it is not an end in itself. Trade facilitates cross-border investment and is in turn facilitated by it. Intra-regional cross-border investment is still insignificant in South Asia. The literature on South-east Asian economic integration demonstrated the central role of cross-border investment and the establishment of regional supply chains (ADB, 2008).

An important step taking South Asia closer to the creation of an economic union would be to adopt policies that facilitate the establishment of such regional supply chain networks, involving both

10. See ADB (2008); Burki (2006); Bhaskaran (2010) and Ahmad and Ghani (2007).

regional and global corporations. Improved physical connectivity, supportive financial systems that facilitate cross-border business activity and regional integration of markets would facilitate this process.

Connectivity

Regional connectivity is a key challenge for South Asia. Physical connectivity must accompany economic policies that facilitate greater interaction between the peoples and businesses in the region. There are four dimensions to connectivity: (a) transport and the facilitation of movement of goods and people; (b) financial integration and the movement of capital; (c) infrastructure and policies for the movement of energy, water and food; finally, (d) telecommunication, information flow and the movement of entertainment, publications and cultural products.

Transport

An ADB (2006) report on building a regional multimodal transport system in South Asia observed:

> The globalisation of economies is now a universal phenomena that resulted in the integration of national economies at both regional and sub regional levels. The international production system is being increasingly characterized by a new division of labour that often involves break down of the production process into sub activities that are spread across national boundaries. This is making production increasingly multi-national in character and isolated economies are becoming increasingly dependant on and linked with each other. A more liberalized regime of trade and transport coupled with advances in international logistics, information technology, electronic documentation, cross border facilitation measures, streamlined customs procedures and other such developments have greatly expanded the scope for international trade in goods and services with consequent increased demand for movement both within and across national boundaries.

In a highly competitive world economy transport cost is a significant determinant of competitiveness and an integrated and efficient transport network is an essential element of regional development. This has been recognised at the Heads of Government (HoG) level at the SAARC summits (Islamabad, 2004 and Thimpu, 2010). The SAARC Regional Multimodal Transport Study (SMRTS) identifies a variety of steps that governments in the region must take to reduce the cost of poor connectivity in improving the competitiveness of SAARC economies.

Surface transport remains the dominant mode of transport in South Asia. Road transport accounts for 65-70 per cent of the freight movement in the mainland countries in SAARC. Restrictions on movement of goods, services and people, as well as the absence of good infrastructure have come in the way of greater regional integration. The most comprehensive study of regional transport connectivity was undertaken by ADB for the SAARC secretariat. The SRMTS, published in June 2006, has identified several existing road connectivity points for the region, and has identified the hurdles to improved road connectivity that have to be removed. These are:

1) Absence of a common regional road transport and motor vehicles act.
2) Poor infrastructure at border posts.
3) Complex documentation and checking systems.

In the case of rail transport the problems identified are:

1) Lack of through-transport agreement and infrastructure for rail wagons. The lack of standardisation of infrastructure and rolling stock makes through-transport impossible. Also, there is a lack of through-transport agreements between the countries concerned to allow rail wagons from one country to traverse to the other. The technical incompatibility between the tracks, with narrow gauge and broad gauge tracks meeting at the border, reinforces the problem.
2) While passenger train links have been established between India and Pakistan, freight train infrastructure is not yet in place. The Munabao station (on the Indian side) had been commissioned as the main inter-change point, equipped with facilities to handle passenger traffic including Customs, Security and Immigration facilities. However, infrastructure for handling goods trains including yard lines, goods sheds

and customs check points are non-existent. Rail connectivity will once again become a major form of transportation of both goods and people in the years to come. South Asia has to revive erstwhile links and create new ones.

Inland waterways remain even less developed as a mode of transport both within countries and between countries in South Asia. While the infrastructure for maritime connectivity is improving, with the modernisations of ports, it also remains under-developed as a mode of transport of both goods and people. Inland waterways traffic has been curtailed by poor maintenance of canals and rivers, siltage, erosion and the drying up of rivers and canals. Yet, water-based connectivity has been an important means of transport of people and goods in South Asia and is set to regain importance. Apart from infrastructure and environmental hurdles, water and sea transport within SAARC is constrained by the same problems that land based connectivity encounters, in terms of the cumbersome procedures for transportation, of both people and goods, and poor infrastructure and logistics support.

Surprisingly, air connectivity too is weak and inadequate in South Asia. It is easier, and even cheaper, to fly from Colombo to Dhaka or Kathmandu via Bangkok rather than New Delhi or Kolkata. Inadequate direct flights between important cities in the regions also acts as a constraint on air transport connectivity.

At present there are 21 airports in the SAARC region from which there are flights to other regional destinations. SAARC region's share of international passengers is only 1.9 per cent while that of its regional passengers is even lower at 0.5 per cent, and most of the latter is made up of tourists and those originally from SAARC countries who are now expatriated and residents in other parts of the world. Thus, travel undertaken by residents of SAARC would actually be lower than 0.5 per cent. Given SAARC's low level of per capita income one should expect South Asia to lag behind other regions in air transportation, but the numbers suggest that South Asia lags behind other regions by a wide margin in terms of intra-regional air traffic.

In keeping with our view that South Asia must not be viewed as an 'island' but as the 'crossroads' of Asia, it is necessary for SAARC to view intra-regional surface transport connectivity as part of wider trans-continental connectivity. The proposed Trans-Asian Railways Network[11] can revive land links between Eurasia and South Asia as well as with South-east Asia. The threat of climate change and the rising cost of crude oil could make land transport more economical in the 21st century. Putting the infrastructure in place would, therefore, be the priority for the creation of not just an SAEU, but also an Asian Economic Union/Community.

Energy, Water and Food Security

South Asia shares a common problem of being resource deficient in per capita terms. Given the adverse man/land ratio, the relatively low deposits of hydrocarbons in the region and the shortage of water and arable land, relative to population, South Asia requires a regional strategy to facilitate the movement of energy, food and water from other regions. Improved cross-border transport connectivity will be a key game changer. This apart, SAARC needs investment in infrastructure to draw energy and other natural resources from Central Asia and South-east Asia to South Asia. This requires long-term capital that the ADB can provide. It also needs rational economic policies, especially with respect to energy, water and food pricing, that would facilitate long term investment as well as rationalise the consumption of these scarce resources.

The SAARC Summit at Dhaka (2005) approved the creation of a SAARC Energy Centre with an objective to establish an 'Energy Ring' in South Asia. Currently, a number of bilateral energy trade agreements exist among the SAARC member states (SMS) as well as with neighbours Iran and Central Asia. These agreements are focused on hydro power, electricity and petroleum products. Significant amount of electricity trade is going on between India-Bhutan and India–Nepal. Afghanistan has various agreements in place with its Central Asian neighbours and Iran for energy supply.

11. Refer to *http://www.unescap.org/sites/default/files/TAR%20map_GIS.pdf* for the Trans-Asian Railways Network

Of all the proposals on the table the one that has progressed most till now and holds promise for the western region is the Turkmenistan-Afghanistan-Pakistan-India (TAPI) Gas Pipeline project. It aims to bring natural gas from Dauletabad and adjacent gas fields in Turkmenistan to India through Afghanistan and Pakistan. The ADB is the lead developer and coordinator for the project. TAPI faces significant hurdles in terms of security concerns—in addition to the fact that the pipeline will pass through regions of Afghanistan and Pakistan that are strife torn, there are doubts about the adequacy of Turkmenistan natural gas supplies to meet its proposed export commitment in the TAPI pipeline project (Cole, 2008). The project was expected to start in 2010 and reach completion over the next five years. Turkmenistan claims that it had total gas reserves of 8 tcm but Pakistan and India want certification about the gas reserves before further moving ahead towards TAPI gas pipeline project (Obaidullah, 2010).

An important project on the eastern side is the Myanmar-Bangladesh-India (MBI) Gas Pipeline Project. Plans exist for a Trans Myanmar Natural Gas Pipeline Project from off-shore gas fields of Myanmar coast to West Bengal in India across Bangladesh linking of the gas fields of Tripura, India. The estimated project cost was about US$ 300 million of which US$ 150 million would be spent to implement Bangladesh segment of the proposed pipeline. The proposal indicated supply of natural gas to the state of West Bengal and other northern states of India such as Meghalaya, Mizoram, Assam. In the south, both onshore and offshore territories of Myanmar, gas has been discovered and developments of gas fields are currently progressing. In the state of Tripura, gas has been found adjacent to the structures of Titas and Bakhrabad gas fields of Bangladesh. A preliminary routing proposal was included and it was stated to conduct a detail survey for a final route proposal for approval of the respective governments.

In electricity generation and distribution as well as river water sharing, South Asia has several bilateral agreements in place and most of these have worked well. The India-Bhutan and India-Nepal agreements on electricity trade, the India-Pakistan and India-Bangladesh treaties on river water sharing are examples of successful bilateral cooperation. The Indus Water Treaty is a good example of a successful bilateral agreement on water sharing.[12] A regional energy and water security treaty would be an important element of the SAEU, with bilateral treaties offering a template for a regional agreement on river water and energy sharing.

The SAARC Food Bank is the first step towards a regional food security initiative. Given the sensitive nature of energy, food and water security issues, these milestones will have to be reached after the initial building blocks of regional cooperation in the fields of trade and connectivity have been put in place.

Culture

South Asia has been a continuum of cultural interaction since millennia. Freer flow of cultural products, including books, films, television programming and media content should be the final milestone of regional economic integration. Already there is considerable cross-border flow of cultural products. However, a large part of such interaction is still illegal under existing, highly restrictive regimes. A South Asian regional framework for cultural, academic and media interaction is necessary. The setting up of the SAU is the first step in this direction, though the project has not got off to a good start and requires special attention for a re-launch. India must pay special attention to ensure that 'regional' institutions in fact grow and develop as truly pan-regional institutions and retain that character. This is not an easy task, as we have seen with SAU. By willy-nilly allowing SAU to become a mediocre Indian institution, rather than develop as a regional centre of excellence India may have missed an opportunity in his vital field of regional cooperation and institution building.

There are several non-governmental initiatives in place. However, official rules and regulations continue to restrict the movement of peoples, ideas, entertainment and other cultural products. IPR (intellectual property rights) protection is an important requirement of greater regional integration. A South Asian IPR protection regime

12. Varghese (1996)

will be necessary for confidence building and ensuring that there are no copyright violations or cross-border stealing of intellectual property. Regional institutions for IPR protection and assurance of competitive market conditions are vital to the development of the services, knowledge and entertainment businesses. The free cross border flow of entertainment products will only help divert existing business away from the underground market to legal trading activity, especially between India and Pakistan.

India as an Opportunity

South Asia's two decade old institutional attempt to reintegrate its markets and infrastructure has yielded some results for all and, therefore, arrived at a decisive stage when India should take the initiative to impart greater momentum to the process. The Indian 'sub-continent' has been a 'natural' region of inter-connected development since millennia. Even in the early 20th century, as the regional industrialised, natural economic links were built up that got disrupted by the political restructuring of the region. After more than a half century of development, the region has acquired adequate political maturity, even with unresolved bilateral political differences, to re-integrate the region economically for the benefit of all.

Towards this endeavour, India must take a more pro-active role, enabling increased cross-border economic transactions as well as intra-regional economic integration. SAARC member nations must establish regular channels for policy communication on trade, monetary and fiscal policy, infrastructure development and policies pertaining to regulatory institutions, IPR protection and the smooth functioning of factor markets.

The acceleration of economic growth in India has not only imparted self-confidence to India to enable her to play the role of a regional engine of growth, but it has also enabled her neighbours to view India as a land of opportunity. Notwithstanding the recent deceleration of economic growth, India is on a long term trajectory of around 8.0 per cent growth in the medium term. Sustaining this growth process will further bolster India's role as a regional engine of growth.

Being the region's biggest economy, India's economic growth must be viewed as a source of opportunity for all her neighbours, certainly for the less developed and smaller ones. Regional re-integration spanning the sub-continent will in fact facilitate pan-Asian re-integration of the sub-continent as a whole with Asia to its west, north-west and south-east. The Indian sub-continent will then once again become the crossroads of Asia and the Indian Ocean region.

A Summing Up

History weighs heavily in South Asia. Unlike the EU and ASEAN, SAARC is a unique association of hitherto integrated regions that have since been politically separated. India's Prime Minister Manmohan Singh put it very pithily when he said:

> I dream of a day, while retaining our respective national identities, one can have breakfast in Amritsar, lunch in Lahore and dinner in Kabul. That is how my forefathers lived. That is how I want our grandchildren to live.[13]

This vision of free movement of people, recapturing the lost continuities of South Asia informs the search for a SAEU. The integration of markets through liberalisation of trade, investment and capital flows is only the first step in this journey. Efficient connectivity is the next step. Regional structures for energy and food security is a third step. Greater cultural connectivity, that is P2P interaction, is the final step.

There are many policy initiatives governments can take at the G2G level. The challenge lies in creating a policy environment that will facilitate increased B2B and P2P interaction. It is not always easy to quantify the gains from trade and regional economic integration, much less the distribution of gains. However, in the case of South Asia the re-establishment of regional economic connectivity is only one way, albeit an important way, in which the economies of the region can reconnect and rediscover long standing economic and social links.

---

13. Manmohan Singh, Address to FICCI Annual General Meeting, New Delhi, 8 January 2007. *http://pmindia.nic.in/speech/content.asp?id=486*

References

Ahmed, Sadiq and Ejaz Ghani (2007). *South Asia: Growth and Regional Integration.* World Bank and Macmillan.

Ahluwalia, Isher Judge, Jasjit Singh, Dipankar Banerjee, Sanjaya Baru and Muchkund Dubey (1998). *Peace, Security and Economic Cooperation: India and South Asia in the 21st Century.* New Delhi: ICRIER.

Asian Development Bank (2006). "SAARC Regional Multimodal Transport Study". (*mimeo*).

———. (2008). *Emerging Asian Regionalism: A Partnership for Shared Prosperity.* Manila.

Bagchi, A.K. (1972). *Private Investment in India 1900-1939.* Cambridge University Press.

Banerjee, D. and N. Manoharan (2008). *SAARC Towards Greater Connectivity.* New Delhi: Konrad Adenauer Stiftung.

Baru, Sanjaya (2006). *The Strategic Consequences of India's Economic Performance.* New Delhi: Academic Foundation and New York: Routledge.

———. (2008). "India and the World: Economics and Politics of the Manmohan Singh Doctrine in Foreign Policy", *ISAS Working Paper*, November. At: *http://www.isasnus.org/events/workingpapers/52.pdf*

———. (2010). "Early Steps Towards Regionalism in South Asia: SAARC & Other Arrangments", *Background Paper for ADB Flagship Study on Institutions for Regionalism.* Asian Development Bank.

Batra, Amita (2008). *Preferential Trading Agreements in Asia: Towards an Asian Economic Community.* New Delhi: Academic Foundation.

Bhargava, K.K., H. Bongartz and F. Sobhan (eds.) (1995). *Shaping South Asia's Future: Role of Regional Cooperation.* New Delhi: Vikas Publishing House.

Bhargava, K.K., I.N. Mukherjee, Bimal Prasad and C.D. Wadhwa (1994). *South Asia: Towards Dynamism and Cooperation.* Delhi: Popular Prakashan.

Bhaskaran, Manu (2010). *Can Regional Cooperation Thrive in a Challenging Political/ Security Environment in South Asia.* ADB. April.

Braudel, Fernand (1988). *Civilization and Capitalism, Volume 3: 15th-18th Century: Perspective of the World.* Collins/ Fontana Press. p.484.

Burki, J. Shahid (2006). *Facilitating Freer Trade Under SAFTA: Issues in Pakistan, India and Afghanistan.* Washington DC: USAID. May.

Chanda, Rupa and G. Sasidharan (2008). "Understanding India's Regional Initiatives within Asia", , *ISAS Working Paper.*

Chandra, Ramesh and Rajiv Kumar (2008). *Emerging Asian Regionalism: Ten Years after the Asian Financial Crisis: South Asian Integration Prospects and Lessons from East Asia.* ICRIER.

Chaturvedi, S.K., S.K. Sharma and Madhurendra Kumar (2006). *Encyclopaedia of SAARC.* Delhi: Pragun Publications.

Dash, Kishore C. (1996). "The Political Economy of Regional Cooperation in South Asia", *Pacific Affairs* 69(2).

———. (2008). *Regionalism in South Asia: Negotiating Cooperation, Institutional Structures.* New York: Routledge.

Desai, V.V. (2010). *The Political Economy of Regional Cooperation in South Asia.* ADB.

Francois, J., Pradumna B. Rana and G. Wignaraja (2009). *Pan-Asian Integration: Linking East and South Asia.* Asian Development Bank.

Francois, Joseph F. and Ganeshan Wignaraja (2008). "Economic Implications of Asian Integration", *Global Economy Journal* 8(3).

Friedman, George (2008). *The Geopolitics of India: A Shifting, Self-contained World*. December. Available at: *www.stratfor.com*

Ghate, Prabhu (2010). *The Institutions of Regionalism in South Asia: Do Institutions Matter?* ADB, April.

Gonsalves, Eric and Nancy Jetly (eds.) (1999). *The Dynamics of South Asia: Regional Cooperation and SAARC*. New Delhi: Sage Publications.

Gupta, Sisir (1964). *India and Regional Integration in Asia*. Asia Publishing House.

Hafiz, M. Abdul and Iftekharuzzaman (eds.) (1985). *South Asian Regional Cooperation: A Socio-economic Approach to Peace and Stability*. Dhaka: Bangladesh Institute of International & Strategic Studies.

Heo, Uk and Shale Horowitz (ed.) (2003). *Conflict in Asia: Korea, China-Taiwan, and India-Pakistan*. Westport: Praeger.

Kalegama, Saman (2004). "SAFTA: A Critique", *South Asia Journal*.

Kalam, Abul (2001). *Sub-regionalism in Asia: ASEAN and SAARC Experiences*. Delhi: UBS Publishers & Distributors Ltd.

Kardar, Shahid (2010). *South Asia-Intra Regional Cooperation: The Way Forward*. 8 June.

Khatri, Sridhar (1987). *Regional Security in South Asia*. Kathmandu: Centre for Nepal and Asian Studies, Tribhuvan University.

Kumar, Debendra (ed.) (1992). *SAARC: Regional Co-operation and Development: Perspectives, Problems, Policies*. Delhi: Deep & Deep Publications.

Lama, Mahendra (1999). *Integrated Programme of Action in SAARC: Genesis, Evaluation, Constraints, and Rationale for Revamping*. New Delhi: Research and Information System for the Non-Aligned and Other Developing Countries.

Moinuddin, K. (2010). *The Provision of Regional Public Goods in South Asia*. ADB. February.

Muni, S.D. and Anuradha Muni (1984). *Regional Cooperation in South Asia*. Delhi: National Publishing House.

Muni, S.D. (1996). *Post-Cold War Regionalism in Asia: With Special Reference to the SAARC Sub-Region*. Tokyo: Institute of Developing Economies.

Naqvi, Syed Nawab Haider and Syed Abdus Samad (1992). *SAARC Link: An Econometric Approach*. New Delhi: Oxford & IBH Pub. Co.

Nguyen, Cuong Minh (2010). *South Asia is not too far behind South-east Asia in Regional Cooperation and Integration*. ADB. November.

Nirmala Devi (ed.) (2007). *India and Bay of Bengal community, the BIMSTEC Experiment: Bangladesh-India-Myanmar-Sri Lanka-Thailand Economic Cooperation*. Gyan Publishing House.

Obaidullah, A.N.M. (2010). *Integrated Energy Potential of South Asia*. SAARC Energy Centre. September. Available at: *www.saarcenergy.org/PDF%20Files/IEPSA_Vision2020-Obaid.pdf*

Pannikar, K.M. (1945). *India and the Indian Ocean*. London: George, Allen & Unwin.

Prasad, Bimal (ed.) (1989). *Regional Cooperation in South Asia: Problems & Prospects*. Delhi: Vikas Publishing House.

Reed, Ananya Mukherjee (1997). "Regionalism in South Asia: Theory and Praxis", *Pacific Affairs* 70(2).

Rizvi, Gowher (1993). *South Asia in a Changing International Order*. New Delhi: Sage Publications.

Sabur, A.K.M. Abdus and Mohd. Humayun Kabir (2000). *Conflict Management and Sub-regional Co-operation in ASEAN: Relevance for SAARC*. Dhaka: Academic Press and Publishers Limited.

Sawhney, Aparna and Nisha Taneja (n.d.). *Revitalizing SAARC Trade*. ICRIER.

Singh, Hernaikh and Jayan Jose Thomas (eds.) (2005). *Engaging South Asia: Challenges and Opportunities—International Conference on South Asia 2005*. Institute of South Asian Studies.

Siddiqui, Anjum (2007). *India And South Asia: Economic Developments in the Age of Globalization*. New York: M.E. Sharpe.

Sridharan, Kripa (2007). *Regional Cooperation in South Asia and Southeast Asia*. Singapore: Institute of Southeast Asian Studies.

Srinivasan,P.V. (2010). *Regional Cooperation and Integration Through Cross-Border Infrastructure Development in South Asia: Impact on Poverty*. ADB. February.

Sudhakar E. (1994). *SAARC: Origin, Growth, and Future*. Delhi: Gyan Publishing House.

Taneja, Nisha (1999). *Informal Trade in the SAARC Region*. ICRIER.

Tandon, Rameshwar (2007). *New Institutions: Asian Monetary Fund, SAFTA, ASEAN, APEC—A New Funeral for New Regionalism in this New Century?* Sydney: Macquarie University.

Verghese, B.G. (1996). *Water Conflicts in South Asia: Studies in Conflicts and Terrorism*.

Vernon, L.B. Mendis (1991). *SAARC: Origins, Organisation & Prospects*. Perth: Indian Ocean Centre for Peace Studies.

Wadhwa, Charan D. and Mukul G. Asher (eds.) (1985). *ASEAN: South Asia Economic Relations*. Singapore: Institute of South-East Asian Studies, New Delhi: ICRIER and Colombo: Marga Institute.

Wadhwa, Charan, S.A. Reza, Hafiz Siddiqui, Zafar Mahmood, S. Sureshwaran and Yvonne Schokman (1987). *Regional Economic Cooperation in Asia: Bangladesh, India, Pakistan and Sri Lanka*. Delhi: Allied Publishers.

Wickramasinghe, Upali (2006). *Operationalising SAFTA: Issues and Options*. Available at: *www.centad.org/download/Ch11_PDF4_final_March1.pdf*

Wriggins, Howard, Gregory Gause, Terence P. Lyons and Evelyn Colbert (1992). *Dynamics of Regional Politics: Four Systems on the Indian Ocean Rim*. New York: Columbia University Press.

Others:

IDC Japan Reports:

(i) *Schemes of Regional Economic Cooperation Aimed at Fostering Economic Growth in South Asia: The Role of Japan: India Study Report*. National Council of Applied Economic Research, New Delhi, 1996.

(ii) Mahmood, Zafar (1996). *Schemes of Regional Economic Cooperation Aimed at Fostering Economic Growth In South Asia: The Role Of Japan: Pakistan Study Report*, 1996

(iii) Weerakoon, Dushi (1996). *Schemes of Regional Economic Cooperation Aimed at Fostering Economic Growth in South Asia: The Role of Japan: Sri Lanka Study Report*. Colombo: Institute of Policy Studies.

(iv) *Schemes of Regional Economic Cooperation Aimed at Fostering Economic Growth in South Asia: The Role of Japan: Bangladesh Study Report*. Dhaka, 1996.

(v) *Schemes of Regional Economic Cooperation Aimed at Fostering Economic Growth in South Asia: The Role of Japan: Final Report*. Prepared for the SAARC-Japan Special Fund by International Development Center of Japan, Tokyo, 1996.

9

China and India

Bilateral Economic Relations and the Global Economy

The movement of people, ideas, and goods are the most important forms of interaction between nations. Asia's biggest neighbours and two of the oldest living civilisations, China and India, have had such contact for centuries. Yet, bilateral economic relations as understood in the modern world are a relatively recent phenomenon. By 2014, China has become India's biggest trade partner.[1] However, this rapidly growing trade is skewed, with India mainly exporting raw materials to China and importing manufactured goods. The political dissonance that the burgeoning trade deficit has caused needs to be addressed. China and India have been able to find common cause on a variety of international issues and are likely to be equally concerned about regionalism in world trade, with the United States seeking to establish a trans-Pacific and trans-Atlantic free trade area that would exclude both countries. China-India economic relations will be characterised by, according to Prime Minister Manmohan Singh, elements of "coordination, cooperation and competition."[2] It is easy to see why the economic relationship between the two continental neighbours has been limited and sporadic over the centuries and till recently. It is equally easy to predict that the recent spurt in this relationship will continue in the foreseeable future. However, the two countries will have to address new challenges that have come up at the bilateral, regional, and global level.

1. The Times of India (2014).
2. The China Post (2013).

Historical Background

As the world's dominant economic entities till well into the 16th century, China and India accounted for almost half of the world's GDP (gross domestic product) in 1500, but their bilateral trade was largely confined to cross-border trade, both across land borders and across maritime regions.[3] Border trade through the Nathu La pass in the eastern Himalayas was one of the many arms of the so-called 'Silk Route' that connected ancient China with Europe, Central and West Asia, and India. For centuries, both countries also carried on sea borne trade.

While Fernand Braudel (1985) drew attention to the dominating presence of China and India, along with Arab traders, in the Indian Ocean region and through the Straits of Malacca, bilateral trade between Chinese and Indian traders was limited. In his masterly and majestic survey of world history, Braudel (1985a) refers to India and East Asia as the "greatest of all the world economies" of the pre-industrial, pre-capitalist era.

Braudel (1985a: 485-535) defines the Far East as comprising "three gigantic world-economies":

> Islam, overlooking the Indian Ocean from the Red Sea and the Persian Gulf, and controlling the endless chain of deserts stretching across Asia from Arabia to China; India, whose influence extended throughout the Indian Ocean, both east and west of Cape Comorin; and China, at once a great territorial power—striking deep into the heart of Asia—and a maritime force, controlling the seas and countries bordering the Pacific. And so it had been for many hundreds of years.

Braudel (1985a: 484) also says that:

> The relationship between these huge areas was the result of a series of pendulum movements of greater or lesser strength, either side of the centrally positioned Indian subcontinent. The swing might benefit first the East and then the West, redistributing functions, power and political or economic advance. Through all these vicissitudes however, India maintained her central position: her merchants in Gujarat and on the Malabar and Coromandel coasts prevailed for centuries against

3. Maddison, 2001; 2007.

> their many competitors—the Arab traders of the Red Sea, the Persian merchants of the Gulf, or the Chinese merchants familiar with the Indonesian seas to which their junks were now regular visitors.

Historian Ashin Das Gupta notes how Chinese and Indian traders exchanged goods at Malacca, with neither venturing much across the waters in each other's direction, but both making their presence felt in the Indo-China region. "There can be no doubt," says Das Gupta (2001: 61), "that the emergence of Malacca as an entrepot where the Indian, Chinese and Javanese met to exchange their wares was the most important development in the history of the Indian Ocean during the fifteenth century." Das Gupta (2001) concludes that "the main aim of both the Indians and the Chinese was to buy spices from the Indonesians, but some trade took place between them as well... It does not seem that trade between India and China at Malacca was considerable." Indian traders imported Chinese porcelain and silk and exchanged these for opium, sandalwood, and pepper.

An important constraint on Chinese maritime trading activity was the official policy of the Ming emperors to withdraw from the seas and remain a land-based power. While cross-border trade across land continued, especially across the eastern Himalayas, and a sizeable Chinese trading community became resident in Calcutta, the arrival of European trading powers in Asia further reduced China-India trade until the export of opium from India by the British. Through the entire colonial period, maritime trade was dominated by European merchants with direct China-India contact being restricted to cross-border trade. Calcutta remained an important outlet for Chinese goods from southwestern China and to that extent some bilateral trade continued. By the time India and China became sovereign republics, in 1947 and 1949 respectively, their bilateral trade was insignificant.

From Inward to Outward Orientation

In the 1950s, there was considerable interest in reviving bilateral economic relations, though India's attention was focused more on its immediate Asian neighbourhood, on the Soviet Union, and the

United States. China was not seen as a major trading or economic partner even though the bilateral relationship was good.[4]

In subsequent decades, the disruption of the bilateral relationship due to the border conflict in 1962 and the pursuit of inward-oriented and import-substituting industrialisation by both countries meant that neither side paid much attention to the potential for bilateral trade and investment relations. It is helpful to recall, however, that even through this period of import-substituting industrialisation China was a bigger trading nation, with foreign trade (goods and services) accounting for 8 per cent of GDP in China in 1973, as opposed to 4 per cent in India.[5]

China's opening up to world trade, around 1980, began a decade before India's in 1991. In 1980 both countries had less than 1 per cent share each in world trade. China's vigorous pursuit of trade-oriented industrialisation in the 1980s sharply increased her share of world trade and the share of trade in national income. Thus, by 1990, China's share of world trade had increased to 1.7 per cent compared to India's lowly 0.5 per cent. By 2000, China's share of world trade was 3.6 per cent, while India's share remained below 1.0 per cent. As shares of national income, by the early 2000s, trade accounted for 30 per cent of China's national income and 15 per cent of India's.[6] Equally important, China emerged both as an exporting and an importing nation, importing both raw materials and machinery and components.

An important geoeconomic dimension to China's rise as an exporting and importing power was its growing trade relationship with other Asian economies. In South Asia, while India traditionally had a larger share of the foreign trade of its immediate neighbours, barring Myanmar and Pakistan, by 1997 China overtook India in the trade share of all South Asian economies, except Sri Lanka and Bhutan.[7]

4. Mansingh (1994).

5. Garver (2001).

6. Panagariya (2006).

7. Baru (2006).

India's 'Look East Policy', launched by the government of P.V. Narasimha Rao in 1992, was aimed at restoring India's traditional political and economic links with Southeast Asian countries that had been disrupted by the geopolitics of the Cold War era. An important consequence of India's renewed focus on the countries to its east, especially after India had itself opened up its economy to increased flows of trade and investment, was to increase the share of the Southeast Asian economies in India's external trade. However, here too, India came up against the competitive pressure exerted by China. China's mercantilist trade policy, to gain access to new markets, and non-transparent fiscal and industrial policy towards this end, became a subject of contention.[8]

Fully aware of the emergent competitive pressure from an export-oriented China pursuing a mercantilist trade policy, India nevertheless supported China's accession to the World Trade Organization (WTO).[9] India was wary of China's entry into the WTO, but her support for China's membership was defined both by an interest in strengthening the voice of the developing world within the multilateral trading regime and in seeking to bring China into the discipline of a multilateral regime, aimed at making Chinese policy more transparent and bringing China within the ambit of the WTO's dispute settlement mechanism.

The main reason for India's wariness was on account of the competition India knew it would face from increased Chinese exports in developed country markets. While China's trade liberalisation measures undertaken to qualify for WTO membership proved very helpful in boosting bilateral trade between the two countries, the rapid improvement in China's competitiveness posed a threat to other developing country exporters who found their developed country markets taken away from them by a more competitive China. Bhat et al. (2006: xvii) note the implications of China's WTO membership for India in a study commissioned by the Indian Planning Commission:

8. For an early critique of Chinese trade policy, see Bhalla (1998).

9. Bhat et al. (2006).

> Main gainers [from China's WTO entry] are developed countries, newly industrializing Asian economies such as South Korea, and Singapore and least developed countries. Because of the similar resources endowments, South Asian and South East Asian countries like Thailand, Malaysia, Indonesia and the Philippines may face keener competition in labor-intensive and low priced products. Low wages are the main source of China's comparative advantage. China has developed a strong comparative advantage in the assembly stage of technology/ capital intensive products and processing trade for a number of products. Further, it has improved its capacity in the production of components. The supply of skilled labour is high in China, which increases its potential to produce skill-intensive products. The developing countries that export labor-intensive products and assembly operations will be subjected to more of "competition effects" of China than "complementarities effects". On this basis, South Asia, Africa and Latin America may suffer from [the] competition effects of China.

The New Bilateral Economic Relationship

The normalisation of bilateral political relations in the late 1980s and India's own economic liberalisation programme launched in 1991 helped revive the bilateral economic relationship. India and China officially resumed trade in 1978, and in 1984 they signed the Most Favoured Nation Agreement. Border trade picked up after the Nathu La pass was reopened in July 1992, after a hiatus of more than 30 years, and consulates were re-opened in Mumbai and Shanghai in December 1992. By 1994, several agreements were signed in the areas of science and technology, civil aviation, and banking, and simplified procedures were adopted for granting visas. India's information technology and software revolution and role in handling the global Y2K problem enabled the country to register its presence in global services trade. India's emergence as a software services provider alerted China to the prospect of a synergy between the IT sectors of the two economies. As Chinese premier Zhu Rongji put it, during his 2002 visit to India: "You are the first in software, and we are the first in hardware. When we put these two together, we can become the world's number one."[10]

10. Quoted in Ahmad (2008).

China followed up Zhu's policy by inviting Indian software companies to set up shop in China. Tata Consultancy Services (TCS), Infosys, Wipro, and Satyam started operations and training bases in China, and NIIT and Zensar set up learning centres that offered software services training to thousands of Chinese students.[11]

Despite such a promising beginning, the bilateral trade relationship was fraught. Indian companies, especially in the manufacturing sector and in food processing and pharmaceuticals, complain of a lack of policy transparency and 'unfair' competition from 'subsidised' Chinese goods. As editor of *The Financial Express*, I ran a series of news reports in 2001 on the 'dumping' of Chinese goods in the Indian market and the use of unfair trade practices by Chinese companies. These were news reports based on interviews with Indian companies that had been hurt by Chinese imports. However, by 2003, there were enough positive stories about Indian companies entering the Chinese market that enabled me to run a new series titled "Beyond the Great Wall".

It is a measure of how rapidly both countries responded to opportunities presented by the other that the US$ 10 billion bilateral trade target referenced during Chinese Prime Minister Zhu Rongji's 2002 visit to India was easily reached. A new target of US$20 billion was set during the visit of Prime Minister Wen Jiabao in April 2005. That too was met by 2008. In November 2006, during the visit of President Hu Jintao, the revised target was US$40 billion, and this was reached by 2009. By 2010, China emerged as India's biggest trading partner, overtaking the United States. A series of bilateral agreements were signed to encourage trade and business between the two countries.[12] In 2012, India became China's 15th largest trading partner and its 19th largest exporter, with a share of 2.03 per cent in China's overall foreign trade and a share of 1.1 per cent in imports

11. "In January 2004, the government of the Shenzhen Special Economic Zone signed an agreement with an Indian software company, Zensar Technologies Ltd, to train 1000 Chinese software managers in India. Besides, a large software training company, NIIT, has set up 106 learning centres in China, training more than 25,000 Chinese software students." Quoted in Bhat et al. (2006: 234).

12. For a review of the rapid growth of China-India trade relations, see Srinivasan (2006); Panagariya (2007).

into China.[13] India was China's 7th largest export destination, with a share of 2.33 per cent of total Chinese exports to the world.[14] In 2010, the two countries identified a trade target of US$ 100 billion for the year 2015. However, in 2013-14 total bilateral trade was estimated to be S$ 66 billion (Table 9.1). The mounting trade deficit against India has in part, and among other factors, forced a slowdown of growth.

Table 9.1

China-India Bilateral Trade (US$ billon)

Year	*India's Exports to China*	*China's Exports to India*	*Total Trade*	*Trade Balance * (for India)*
2000-01	0.8	1.5	2.3	- 0.7
2001-02	1.0	2.0	3.0	-1.0
2002-03	2.0	2.8	4.8	-0.8
2003-04	3.0	4.1	7.0	-1.1
2004-05	5.6	7.1	12.7	-1.5
2005-06	6.8	10.9	17.6	-4.1
2006-07	8.3	17.5	25.8	-9.2
2007-08	10.9	27.1	38.0	-16.3
2008-09	9.4	32.5	41.9	-23.1
2009-10	11.6	30.8	42.4	-19.2
2010-11	14.2	43.5	57.6	-29.3
2011-12	18.1	55.3	73.4	-37.2
2012-13	13.5	52.2	65.8	-38.7
2013-14	14.8	51.0	65.9	-36.2

* *Note*: The trade deficit has increased further since 2014 and in 2016 was over US$50 billion.

Source: Department of Commerce, Government of India, "Export Import Data Bank", *http://commerce.nic.in/eidb/default.asp.*

While the overall numbers are impressive, the structure of the trade has been less than encouraging, with India exporting mainly raw materials to China, and Indian manufactures and agri-exports facing the problem of market access. In 2012, India's major exports to China

13. Ministry of External Affairs, Government of India, India-China Relations, *http://www.mea.gov.in/Portal/ForeignRelation/India-China_Relations.pdf.*

14. Ibid.

included ores, slag and ash (iron, chromium and zinc ore), cotton yarn (not carded/combed cotton), organic chemicals (cyclic alcohols), precious stones, and metals and iron and steel.[15] India's major imports from China were electrical machinery (with line telephony accounting for a major share), machinery (steam generating boilers and other types of boilers, steam turbines, office machine parts, cranes, air conditioning machinery, converters, ladles, ingot moulds, and casting machines, and so on), organic chemicals (antibiotics and heterocyclic compounds), and iron and steel products.[16]

Apart from the skewed structure of trade, market access issues continue to come up in official and ministerial level meetings.[17] Both governments have blamed each other for continuing non-tariff barriers to trade, but given the huge trade deficit in China's favour India believes that it is up to the Chinese government to address these issues first. Formal consultative structures have been created, including a Strategic Economic Dialogue (SED) between the two governments. For India and China to cooperate at the regional and global level, it is essential that these bilateral issues be resolved. This has gained greater urgency given the deceleration of growth in both countries.

In the case of China, the trade deficit and market access issues are viewed not merely as economic problems but also as political problems mainly because of the lack of transparency in Chinese policy. For this reason, more than any other, the trade deficit problem has been consistently raised by Indian officials and business

15. Embassy of India, Beijing, "Trade and Commercial Relations," *http://www.indianembassy.org.cn/DynamicContent.aspx?MenuId=3&SubMenuId=0.*

16. Ibid.

17. As India's ambassador in Beijing recently put it: "If overall there is a diversity of views on our ties with China, trade is perhaps the sector that is most polarized. While there is no denying that sourcing from China has created efficiencies and lowered costs in many sectors, advantages Chinese companies enjoy at home have also hurt many of their competitors in India. Reconciling the costs and benefits of our expanding trade with China is a real challenge that continues to be hotly debated. Discussions are focused around the growing trade imbalance, market access challenges faced by Indian companies in China, trade investigations, and occasionally, even national security concerns. While the Indian economy has been largely open to goods from China, our companies exporting to that country find themselves hampered by duty structures, non-tariff barriers, quotas, local production requirements, closed vendor loops and restricted Government buying." Quoted in Jaishankar (2013).

associations with their Chinese counterparts.[18] More recently, India's commerce minister Anand Sharma and external affairs minister Salman Khurshid have both drawn attention to the trade deficit during their visits to Beijing, and pointed especially to market access problems faced in China by Indian exporters of pharmaceuticals, agricultural products, buffalo meat, and information technology services.[19]

The recent ballooning of India's overall trade deficit and the current account deficit, which has increased from an average of less than 2 per cent of GDP in the decade before 2008 to over 4 per cent by 2012 and sharply higher in 2013, has raised the spectre of an external payments crisis.[20] Under the circumstances, India has had to adopt import compression measures. The need to address the China-India trade deficit has, therefore, gained even greater urgency. While India's recent decision to resume the export of iron ore may help reduce the trade deficit with China, the structure of trade would then only revert to the earlier pattern in which India exported raw materials to China and imported finished products from China.

The only way this structure can be altered is if China's rising cost of manufacturing, especially on account of rising wage costs, helps make Indian manufactured exports more competitive, or if China invests in the manufacturing sector in India. The FDI (foreign direct investment) route has the potential to reduce the trade gap and the current account deficit as well as change the structure of bilateral trade. While China has to address the issue of market access, India's decision to be more welcoming of FDI from China is one important

18. "India cannot be an exporter of raw materials and commodities to China all the time," says Nirupama Rao, the Indian Ambassador to China, flagging the rising concern over a situation she says is "unsustainable in the long run." The ambassador adds that a "deficit [with China] is tolerable only for a finite period, beyond which we risk seeing a 'positive' of the relationship assuming negative tones." Quoted in Aiyar (2007).
In 2008, India's Commerce Minister Kamal Nath raised the issue in Beijing: "Commerce Minister Kamal Nath talked tough at his meeting with the newly appointed Chinese Commerce Minister Chen Deming, a day ahead of Prime Minister Manmohan Singh's visit to Beijing. I told the [Chinese] Minister that we [India and China] have substantial trade but that this is sustainable only if there is no large deficit." Quoted in Aiyar (2008).

19. Roche (2013).

20. Kapur and Mohan (2014).

way in which the trade deficit can be addressed, if such FDI is import-substituting or export-promoting in nature.[21]

Here, again, there are two problems. First, India has had a problem with Chinese FDI in sensitive sectors like telecommunications, primarily for security reasons. While China's telecom giant Huawei has established an Indian presence, it continues to face cyber security concerns in India, as indeed in many other countries.[22] Other Chinese companies like Lenovo and Haier have had a better record of investment in India. While the JV (joint venture) route has traditionally been the preferred option for new foreign entrants into India, anecdotal evidence suggests that Indian firms are still wary of entering into JVs with Chinese counterparts. One reason offered is that Chinese counterparts do not share technology, and indeed may even steal technology.[23]

The sectors where Chinese FDI would be welcomed into India are industries like steel and infrastructure, especially construction. The roads and the real estate sectors are expected to attract massive Chinese investment.[24] The challenge going forward for both China and India is to convert the trade relationship into an investment relationship, so that capital flows from China to India can help reduce the trade deficit. However, even this route can be a challenging one if there is a lack of trust between Indian and Chinese counterparts.

Trade Deficit and Trust Deficit

Given these trends and concerns, where are India-China trade relations headed, and how can the problem of the trade deficit be tackled? First, it is important to recognise that the mounting trade deficit has become political mainly on account of persisting concerns about lack of transparency in China's domestic policies and the larger problem of a trust deficit between the two countries. Absence of

21. The Economic Times (2013).
22. DNA India (2011); Phneah (2013).
23. This complaint was made to this writer by two prominent Indian business leaders, who wish to remain anonymous, who tried the JV route with Chinese companies and ended the relationship deeply unhappy with the experience.
24. Banerjee (2013); The Times of India (2012).

credible data enables critics to speculate about intentions, including charges that China is out to 'subvert' India's manufacturing sector.[25] In fact, both China and India have levelled anti-dumping charges against each other. According to the Indian Ministry of Commerce, out of a total of 290 anti-dumping investigations initiated by the Directorate General of Anti-Dumping and Allied Duties between 1992, when the WTO system came into being, and 2013, as many as 159 cases involved imports from China.[26] Hence, China must address the issue at a political and administrative level to gain India's trust. Establishing trust is the first major challenge.

Second, Indian exporters must do more to win brand recognition and the trust of Chinese consumers. India's overall image has to improve before ordinary consumer resistance can be overcome. China has been trying to overcome such consumer resistance around the world, including in India. If a select number of Indian brands emulate Lenovo's strategy in India, they may be able to overcome consumer resistance and widen the market for Indian goods in China.[27]

Finally, China will have to graduate from exporting products to India to making India a part of its global supply chain and manufacturing some of these products in India. This is the only way in which the problem of the trade deficit can be tackled.

Managing Competition and Cooperation

Prime Minister Manmohan Singh best captured the reality of the China-India bilateral economic relationship when he said that it would be defined both by 'competition' and 'cooperation'. On the eve of his visit to Tokyo in December 2006, Prime Minister Singh told the Japanese newspaper *Yomiuri Shimbun*:

> My own view is that the world is large enough to accommodate the development ambitions of both countries (China and India). And, therefore, there is immense scope for us to cooperate with one another. There will be certain fields where we will also be competing,

25. Chaudhury (2010).
26. The Economic Times (2013a).
27. Lenovo (2013).

as is inevitable, so there is a policy of competition as well as of cooperation.[28]

In order for both countries to manage their larger bilateral relationship, it would be useful for them to identify and manage these elements so that the natural 'competition' between two 'emerging economies' and 'rising powers'—for markets, for resources, and for investment opportunities—does not result in 'conflict', and the avenues available for 'cooperation' can build trust and confidence. China and India will compete for market access in countries around the world. They will compete for access to resources including oil and gas, minerals, and food. They will compete for investment opportunities in third countries. It would be short-sighted not to recognise the potential for competition between the two economies.

However, both countries will also have opportunities to cooperate in building a global order that would be conducive to and supportive of their individual growth ambitions. Thus, they have a shared interest in creating a multilateral trading and financial regime that is supportive of their individual growth as well as the growth of other developing economies, just as they have a shared agenda with respect to the emergent regime to deal with the threat of global warming and climate change. New Delhi and Beijing would seek to ensure that the developed industrial economies eschew protectionism and continue to offer market access.

In short, in their attempt to avoid conflict on bilateral economic issues pertaining to market access, and in order to manage the competition they would engage in to secure access to third markets and resources, China and India will have to identify areas of cooperation at the regional and global level.

It would seem that has been the approach of the two governments. Their cooperation on climate change and global economic governance are obvious examples. In trade, while Indian companies have serious complaints about 'unfair trade' practices on the part of Chinese exporters, India and China have sought to work together in the WTO and have also decided to pursue a new regional trading initiative

28. China Daily (2006).

in the Indo-Pacific region, namely, the Regional Comprehensive Economic Partnership (RCEP) launched in 2012.

Opportunities for Regional Cooperation

The dynamics of regional economic integration in the 'Indo-Pacific' region have been complex and changing. Early initiatives towards regional integration were in fact taken by the smaller economies of the region, the members of the Association of Southeast Asian Nations (ASEAN). Japan, China, and India remained outside this process until Malaysia, with Japan's blessing, proposed the idea of an East Asian Economic Caucus/Group (EAEC/EAEG) in the early 1990s. However, this proposal did not find favour in the ASEAN region and even with the US.[29] Malaysian Prime Minister Mahathir's EAEG was then resurrected as ASEAN's 'ASEAN+3' (China, Japan and South Korea) group in the aftermath of the Asian financial crisis in 1997-98.[30] ASEAN took the lead to bring together China, Japan, South Korea, India, Australia, and New Zealand into an ASEAN+3 and later an ASEAN+6 grouping. China reluctantly went along with the ASEAN+6 initiative, even though its main interest was in making the ASEAN+3 group the fulcrum of East Asian regionalism. On the other hand, China quickly endorsed the RCEP idea.[31]

India also responded with alacrity to the RCEP initiative. Finding itself excluded from earlier attempts at regional cooperation like the Asia Pacific Economic Cooperation (APEC) and the ASEAN+3 (China, Japan, and South Korea) initiatives, India has been careful not to exclude itself from any new initiatives for regional economic integration in the Asia-Pacific region. Even though the RCEP is viewed as an ASEAN-China response to the US-inspired Trans-Pacific Partnership (TPP), India signed on to RCEP on the side-lines of the 2012 East Asia Summit (EAS) in Cambodia in November 2012. Welcoming this initiative and explaining India's decision, Prime Minister Singh said:

---

29. Yoshida (2004).
30. Ibid.: 7
31. Sheng (2011).

> Concerted effort and collective action on the part of the countries gathered in this room can strengthen mutual understanding and help us address shared challenges. For this, it would be necessary to develop a common set of principles, establish cooperative mechanisms and deepen regional economic integration.[32]

India viewed China's initial diplomacy in the Asian community building process as aimed at keeping India out of the region, while Chinese commentators have viewed India's 'Look East Policy' as aimed at 'encircling China'.[33] However, given ASEAN's enthusiastic endorsement of India's participation in the "ASEAN plus" processes, China has had to relent and modify its stance on India's desire to seek greater economic integration with Southeast and East Asia.[34] An important factor driving China and India closer on the issue of the regional economic, if not security, architecture in Asia is the US decision to follow up its 'Asian pivot', which India welcomes, with the TPP initiative.

The exclusion of both China and India from the TPP, it would seem, imparted momentum to ASEAN's RCEP initiative.[35] More important, China and India's shared concerns about the TPP's objectives, given its attempt to go beyond existing WTO 'rules of the game' in multilateral trade, may encourage China and India to cooperate in making RCEP a success.[36]

The trend towards regionalism in global trade, however, benefits neither China nor India, nor indeed the global economy. As an emerging and developing economy, India would be hurt by the regionalisation of trade. This concern is heightened by the fact that apart from RCEP, India is not a member of any other major regional trade arrangements and was even kept out of APEC. The new process of economic regionalisation is fraught with problems not just for India but also for all developing economies, especially if one

---

32. Press Information Bureau (2012).
33. The Times of India (2010).
34. Yuanying (2012).
35. Das (2013).
36. Das (2013); Dogra and Woo (2013).

consequence is a weakening of the multilateral trading system under the aegis of the WTO.

As the biggest developing economies,China and India have a stake in revitalising the multilateral trading regime and reversing the current process of regionalisation of free trade arrangements. They therefore have the opportunity to work together and with other like-minded countries to revitalise the WTO rather than allow new regional blocs to marginalise the WTO. It remains to be seen if the European Union will also drift away from the WTO process and join hands with the US in promoting the regionalisation of trade regimes by signing up to the proposed Transatlantic Trade and Investment Partnership (T-TIP).

The Multilateral System

China and India recognise that the regionalisation of trade arrangements and a weakening of the multilateral system are as hurtful to their future growth as the attempt by the developed industrial economies to relate free trade to a variety of social, environmental, and other factors. Greater transparency in domestic policy will, of course, go a long way in bolstering their case. Given that the regionalisation of trade and financial systems over the past decade is not necessarily in the interests of China or India, nor indeed of developed industrial economies, rule-based access to markets around the world is a goal that both China and India should pursue. It ought to be acknowledged that the mushrooming of regional, preferential, and plurilateral trade agreements in Asia, Europe, and the Americas is not a healthy trend. The WTO Ministerial Conference in Bali, Indonesia, held in December 2013, offered an opportunity to revitalise the multilateral system.

While India has vigorously pursued FTAs with ASEAN, Japan, South Korea, and other countries to ensure market access in response to the regionalisation of trade around the world, it is in India's strategic interest that the multilateral regime is strengthened, albeit in keeping with the principles enshrined in the WTO of providing developing countries adequate space for development. The Doha

Round was in fact named the Doha Development Round with a view to preserving these principles.

Both China and India are concerned that the US and the EU, seeking to overcome the consequences of the trans-Atlantic financial crisis and economic slowdown, may be walking away from the post-Cold War multilateral trading system established under the WTO in favour of regional and plurilateral arrangements. China and India may be able to work together, and with the US, EU, Japan, Brazil, and other major trading economies, to revive the multilateral process and contain the current wave of regionalism. This would be a good shared agenda for cooperation between the two countries that can have positive externalities for the global economy.

Given the size of their markets, if China and India join forces on strengthening the multilateral trading regime under the aegis of the WTO, rather than allow themselves to be overtaken by the dynamic of TPP/T-TIP, they have the potential to modify the behaviour of the US and EU given the size of their markets. In other words, a coming together of emerging economies, especially China and India, in favour of multilateralism and against regionalism can help preserve the gains of the WTO process and thwart the threat of trade regionalisation through the TPP/T-TIP route.

China and India should also work with the US, EU, Russia, and other emerging economies to strengthen the G20 as an institution and as a process. The emerging tensions between the G7 and the BRICS within the G20 should not be allowed to grow and disrupt the G20. Both the G7 countries and the BRICS countries have a stake in the successful management of global economic challenges by the G20. Unfortunately, Russia, a member of the G-8 and of BRICS, could have but has not yet been able to play a bridging role between these two blocs.[37] Global political developments in the run up to the G20 Summit in Russia in September 2013, including the conflict in Syria and growing US-Russia tensions, as well as Moscow's belligerence during the on-going Ukraine crisis, have only further reduced the prospect of Moscow playing this bridging role. Perhaps China and

37. Baru and Charap (2012).

India can play that role by working together with the US. A US-China-India trilateral partnership may help stabilise the global economy and address other global challenges, including those of climate change and energy security.

Finally, historically India has always been supportive of China's proper representation in international institutions. Thus, India supported China's membership of the UN Security Council, multilateral financial institutions, and the World Trade Organization. China should reciprocate by supporting India's proper representation in all such international and multilateral institutions.

Conclusion

While it is true that, as Indian Prime Minister Manmohan Singh put it, "the world has enough space for the growth ambitions of both countries,"[38] the jury is still out on Dr Singh's other hopeful assertion—that of positive externalities flowing from the rise of China and India for the rest of the world, from the new opportunities for development they would offer to the international community, especially other developing countries. If the two Asian neighbours can translate their own rise into new opportunities for others, resolving their differences in the process, then their individual growth and bilateral cooperation will have global benefits. Both countries seem to recognise this challenge.[39]

President Xi Jinping has outlined 'five principles' for bilateral China-India relations, under which the two countries should:

> Harness each other's comparative strengths and expand win-win cooperation in infrastructure, mutual investment and other areas...strengthen cultural ties and increase mutual understanding and friendship between our peoples...expand coordination and collaboration in multilateral affairs to jointly safeguard the legitimate rights and interests of developing countries and tackle global challenges.

38. The Indian Express (2010); Baru (2013).

39. President Xi Jinping Gives Joint Interview To Media from BRICS Countries, Ministry of Foreign Affairs of the People's Republic of China, 19 March 2013, Available at: *http://www.fmprc.gov.cn/mfa_eng/wjdt_665385/zyjh_665391/t1023070.shtml*

These principles have also been echoed by Prime Minister Singh in his own way.[40] If these principles are honoured, then the two countries would be able to address global challenges and provide both regional and global leadership. If not, their bilateral differences will keep them tied down and restrain and constrain them, individually and collectively.

References

Ahmad, Aqueil (2008). "India and China: Conflict, Competition and Cooperation in the Age of Globalization," *Share the World's Resources (STWR)*, 21 February, *www.stwr.org/india-china-asia/india-and-china-conflict-competition-and-cooperation-in-the-age-of-globalization.html*

Aiyar, Pallavi (2007). "Sino-Indian Trade: Growing Concern", *The Hindu*, 28 August. Available at: *http://www.hindu.com/2007/08/28/stories/2007082855521000.htm*

————. (2008). "Kamal Nath Asks China to Address Trade Deficit", *The Hindu*, 13 January. Available at: *http://www.hindu.com/2008/01/13/stories/2008011359630800.htm*

Banerjee, Ronojoy (2013). "Government Looks to Attract FDI in Roads from China; Seeks MoU," *Moneycontrol.com*, 26 August. Available at: *http://www.moneycontrol.com/news/cnbc-tv18-comments/govt-looks-to-attract-fdiroadschina-seeks-mou_940906.html*

Baru, Sanjaya (2006). *Strategic Consequences of India's Economic Performance.* Chapter 38. New Delhi: Academic Foundation. p.337.

————. (2013). "India's Five Thoughts on China," *Project Syndicate*, 24 March. Available at: *http://www.project-syndicate.org/commentary/india-and-china-at-the-brics-summit-by-sanjaya-baru*

Baru, Sanjaya and Samuel Charap (2012). "Russia and the G20," Conference Papers: *Prospects for the Russian Chairmanship of the G20.* New York: Council on Foreign Relations. December. pp.28-31.

Bhalla, Surjit (1998). "Chinese Mercantilism: Currency Wars and How the East was Lost", *Working Paper* 45. New Delhi: Indian Council for Research on International Economic Relations. July. Available at: *http://www.icrier.org/pdf/SurjeetB.pdf*

Bhat, T.P., Atulan Guha and Mahua Paul (2006). *India and China in WTO: Building Complementarities and Competitiveness in the External Trade Sector.* New Delhi: Institute for Studies in Industrial Development. April. *http://planningcommission.nic.in/reports/sereport/ser/stdy_indch.pdf*

Braudel, Fernand (1985). *Civilization and Capitalism, 15th-18th Century: Volume II—The Wheels of Commerce.* London: Fontana Press.

————. (1985a). *Civilization and Capitalism, 15th-18th Century: Volume III—The Perspective of the World*, Chapter 5. London: Fontana Press. pp.484.

Chaudhury, Arup (2010). "China Posing Threat to India's Manufacturing Sector", *Machinst360*, 5 February. Available at: *http://www.machinist360.com/article/48/20100205201002051043447 77757f22c6/China-posing-threat-to-India%E2%80%99s-manufacturing-sector.html*

China Daily (2006). "Enough Room for India and China—India PM Singh," *China Daily*, 5 December. Available at: *http://www.chinadaily.com.cn/china/2006-12/05/content_751323.htm*

40. Baru (2013).

Das, Sanchita Basu (2013). "RCEP and TPP: Comparisons and Concerns", *ISEAS Perspective* #02. Singapore: Institute of South East Asian Studies. 7 January. Available at: *http://www.iseas.edu.sg/documents/publication/ISEAS%20Perspective%202013_2.pdf*

Das Gupta, Ashin (2001). *The World of the Indian Ocean Merchant, 1500-1800*, New Delhi: Oxford University Press. p.61.

DNA India (2011). "Huawei Deal: We are not Compromising India's Security, says Kapil Sibal," *DNA India*, 30 June. Available at: *http://www.dnaindia.com/india/1560793/report-huawei-deal-we-are-not-compromising-india-s-security-says-kapil-sibal*

Dogra, Suvi and Jun Jie Woo (2013). "Where Does India Stand Amid Changing Asia-Pacific Trade Dynamics?", *The Financial Express*, 4 April. Available at: *http://www.financialexpress.com/news/where-does-india-stand-amid-changing-asiapacific-trade-dynamics-/1097246/0*

Garver, John W. (2001). *Protracted Contest: Sino-Indian Rivalry in the Twentieth Century*. New Delhi: Oxford University Press.

Jaishankar, S. (2013). *India and China: Perceptions and Reality*. Distinguished Alumni Lecture. New Delhi: Jawaharlal Nehru University. 14 March.

Kapur, Muneesh and Rakesh Mohan (2014). "India's Recent Macroeconomic Performance: An Assessment and Way Forward", *IMF Working Papers* 14/68. p.26.

Lenovo (2013). "Lenovo Remains Bullish on its India Business", *Press Note*. 30 January. Available at: *http://www.lenovo.com/news/in/en/2013/01/press-note.html*

Maddison, Angus (2001). *The World Economy: A Millennial Perspective*. Paris: Organisation for Economic Co-operation and Development (OECD).

————. (2007). *Chinese Economic Performance in the Long Run, 960–2030 AD*. Paris: OECD.

Mansingh, Surjit (1994). "India-China Relations in the Post-Cold War Era," *Asian Survey* 34(3): 285-300, March.

Panagariya, Arvind (2006). "India and China: Trade and Foreign Investment", *Working paper* 302. Stanford: Stanford Center for International Development. November. Available at: *http://www.stanford.edu/group/siepr/cgi-bin/siepr/?q=system/files/shared/pubs/papers/pdf/SCID302.pdf*

————. (2007). *India and China: Past Trade Liberalisation and Future Challenges*. 4 February. Available at: *http://www.nomurafoundation.or.jp/app_list/hdd/2006120607_Arvind_Panagariya.pdf*

Phneah, Ellyn (2013). "Huawei, ZTE under Probe by Indian Government," *ZDNet*, 10 May. Available at: *http://www.zdnet.com/in/huawei-zte-under-probe-by-indian-government-7000015185/*

Press Information Bureau (2012). *Statement by the Prime Minister at Plenary Session of 7th East Asia Summit*. Government of India. 20 November. Available at: *http://pib.nic.in/newsite/erelease.aspx?relid=89132*

Roche, Elizabeth (2013). "India, China Discuss Reducing Trade Gap, Peace Along Borders," *LiveMint*, 20 August. Available at: *http://www.livemint.com/Politics/JZZDDEinFFSAVpiEZoIxTM/India-China-discuss-reducing-trade-gap-peace-along-borders.html*

Sheng, Zhong (2011). "Asean Plus Three Cooperation is the Driving Force for East Asia,"People's *Daily Online*, 16 August. Available at: *http://english.peopledaily.com.cn/90780/91343/7571027.html.*

Srinivasan, T.N. (2006). "China, India and the World Economy", *Working Paper* 286, Stanford: Stanford Centre for International Development. July. Available at: *www.stanford.edu/group/siepr/cgi-bin/siepr/?q=system/files/shared/pubs/papers/pdf/SCID286.pdf*

The China Post (2013). "Is World Big Enough for India, China?" *The China Post*, 10 April. *http://www.chinapost.com.tw/commentary/the-china-post/frank-ching/2013/04/10/375571/Is-world.htm*

The Economic Times (2013). "India Invites Chinese Foreign Direct Investment," *The Economic Times*, 27 February. Available at: *http://articles.economictimes.indiatimes.com/2013-02-27/news/37331014_1_chinese-companies-china-s-jaishankar-mutual-investment*

———. (2013a). "India Initiated 159 Anti-dumping Cases against China," *The Economic Times*, 12 August. Available at: *http://articles.economictimes.indiatimes.com/2013-08-12/news/41332741_1_anti-dumping-probe-trade-deficit-product-and-country*

The Indian Express (2010). "World has Enough Space for India and China to Grow: PM," *The Indian Express*, 27 October. Available at: *http://archive.indianexpress.com/news/world-has-enough-space-for-india-and-china-to-grow-pm/703293/*

The Times of India (2010). "India's Look East Policy Shouldn't Mean 'Encircle China': People's Daily," *The Times of India*, 28 October. Available at: *http://articles.timesofindia.indiatimes.com/2010-10-28/china/28237805_1_largest-trade-partner-east-china-sea-wen-jiabao*

———. (2012). "Anil Ambani Teams up with China's Wanda," *The Times of India*, 14 December. Available at: *http://timesofindia.indiatimes.com/business/india-business/Anil-Ambani-teams-up-with-Chinas-Wanda/articleshow/17606754.cms*

———. (2014). "China Emerges as India's Top Trading Partner: Study," *The Times of India*, 2 March. *http://timesofindia.indiatimes.com/business/india-business/China-emerges-as-Indias-top-trading-partner-Study/articleshow/31268526.cms.*

Yoshida, Tadahiro (2004). "East Asian Regionalism and Japan", *Working Paper* 03/04: 9. IDE APEC Study Center. March. Available at: *http://www.ide.go.jp/English/Publish/Download/Apec/pdf/2003_09.pdf*

Yuanying, Pei (2012). "India's 'Look East Policy'," *People's Daily Online*, 6 April. Available at: *http://english.peopledaily.com.cn/90780/91343/7778951.html*

10

The Geoeconomics of the GCC and Asia

The Changing Global Economy

At the turn of the century, the Organisation for Economic Cooperation and Development (OECD) commissioned historian Angus Maddison to extend his statistical work estimating world income in the period 1820 to 1992 and offer a millennial perspective on global economic trends. Maddison's classic two-volume study, *The World Economy* (2007) offered the most comprehensive statistical account of the shift of world income from the trans-Atlantic economies of western Europe and north America to Asia's 'newly industrialising economies' (Table 10.1).

The share of Western Europe in world GDP (gross domestic product) reached a peak of 33.6 per cent in 1870 and declined to 26.3 per cent in 1950 at the end of the Second World War and the beginning of the era of decolonisation. By the end of the century, this share was down to 20.6 per cent. The United States of America (US) and the English-speaking countries of Canada, Australia and New Zealand together saw their shares decline from a peak of 30.6 per cent in 1950 to 25.1 per cent by 1998.

By contrast, the share of Asia (including Japan) which stood at 59.2 per cent in 1820 and was reduced to 24.5 per cent by 1913 (mainly on account of the sharp decline of the shares of China and India), stood at 18.5 per cent in 1950. Japan's post-War recovery helped it to more than double its share of world GDP by 1973. The newly industrialising economies of East and South-east Asia, followed by China and then India, managed to improve their share of world GDP by the end of the century, with Asia (excluding Japan) accounting for 29.5 per cent of world GDP in 1998.

Table 10.1

Trends in Per Capita GDP (A) and Share of World GDP (B)

Region	*1000*		*1500*		*1820*		*1870*		*1913*		*1950*		*1973*		*1998*	
	A	*B*	*A*	*B*	*A*	*B*	*A*	*B*	*A*	*B*	*A*	*B*	*A*	*B*	*A*	*B*
Western Europe	400	8.7	774	17.9	1232	23.6	1974	33.6	3473	33.5	4594	26.3	11534	25.7	17921	20.6
Western Offshoots	400	0.7	400	0.5	1201	1.9	2431	10.2	5257	21.7	9288	30.6	16172	25.3	26146	25.1
Japan	425	2.7	500	3.1	669	3.0	737	2.3	1387	2.6	1926	3.0	11439	7.7	20413	7.7
Asia (excl Japan)	450	67.6	572	62.1	575	56.2	543	36.0	640	21.9	635	15.5	1231	16.4	2936	29.5
Latin America	400	3.9	416	2.9	665	2.0	698	2.5	1511	4.5	2554	7.9	4531	8.7	5795	8.7
Eastern Europe & Former USSR	400	4.6	483	5.9	667	8.8	917	11.7	1501	13.1	2601	13.1	5729	12.9	4354	5.3
Africa	416	11.8	400	7.4	418	4.5	444	3.7	585	2.7	852	3.6	1365	3.3	1368	3.1
WORLD	435	100	565	100	667	100	867	100	1510	100	2114	100	4104	100	5709	100

Note: Per capita GDP (A) is estimated in 1990 US Dollars & Column B represents percentage shares. ('Western Offshoots' refers to United States, Canada, Australia and New Zealand.)

Source: Maddison (2 007: 126-27): Tables 2 & 3.

China's share of world GDP, estimated in PPP (purchasing power parity) terms, increased sharply over the past decade and was estimated to be 13.3 per cent in 2010. Over the next two decades Asian economies are expected to increase their share of world GDP, led by high growth economies of Asia, especially China, India and some South-east Asian economies (See Table 10.2).

Table 10.2

Income Growth Projections, 2010-2030

Country/ Group	*GDP Growth Rate (PPP Dollars)*	*Per Capita Income Growth Rate (PPP Dollars)*
United States	2.5	1.7
European Union	2.0	1.9
China	5.9	5.5
India	7.6	6.5
Middle East	5.2	3.2
Africa	7.4	5.3
BRICs (Brazil, Russia, India & China)	6.1	5.3
Indonesia	6.3	5.5
Asia minus Japan	6.3	5.4

Source: Subramanian (2011): Table 4.2.

The trans-Atlantic financial crisis of 2008 and the Great Recession that followed and the continuing economic crisis in Europe and the US has further accentuated this underlying trend, with the trans-Atlantic economies and Japan continuing to grow slowly and many Asian economies, especially China and India, posting robust growth (See Table 10.3)[1] Bear in mind, however, that the facile assumptions about a 'de-coupling' of 'emerging markets' from 'developed industrial economies', because of Asian growth, have been shown to be false, and Asian economies have slowed down too.[2]

1. For a discussion of the geo-political implications of the trans-Atlantic financial crisis of 2008 see Baru (2009).
2. D. Subbarao, Intervention at IMF Annual Meetings, Washington DC, 23 September 2011. Accessed at: *http://rbi.org.in/scripts/BS_SpeechesView.aspx?Id=601*

However, the global economy has been characterised over the past few years by the emergence of what could be called 'multiple cycles of growth' with, as the International Monetary Fund's (2011: 7) *World Economic Outlook* noted recently, the "expansionary forces" offsetting the impact of "contractionary forces" on world economic growth.

Table 10.3

World Output Growth after the Trans-Atlantic Financial Crisis

Region/Country	*2007*	*2008*	*2009*	*2010*	*2011*	*2011**
Developed Countries	2.6	0.3	-3.6	2.5	1.8	1.6
United States	2.1	0.4	-2.6	2.9	2.3	1.5
Japan	2.4	-1.2	-6.3	2.9	2.3	-0.5
European Union	3.0	0.5	-4.2	1.8	1.9	1.7
Russia	8.5	5.6	-7.9	4.0	4.4	4.3
Developing Countries	8.0	5.4	2.5	7.4	6.3	6.4
Africa	5.9	5.4	1.8	4.4	3.5	5.21
Latin America & the Caribbean	5.6	4.0	-2.2	5.9	4.7	4.5
Brazil	6.1	5.2	-0.6	7.5	4.0	3.8
China	14.2	9.6	9.1	10.3	9.4	9.5
India	9.6	5.1	7.0	8.6	8.1	7.8
South-east Asia	6.6	4.2	1.0	7.8	5.0	5.32
West Asia	5.2	4.8	-0.8	6.0	6.4	-0.23
WORLD	4.0	1.7	-2.1	3.9	3.1	4.0

Notes: 1. Sub-Saharan Africa; 2. ASEAN-5; 3. Middle East & North Africa.
Source: Cols. 2-6: UNCTAD (2011); Col. 7: International Monetary Fund (2011).

The structural shift underway in the world economy, with Asia making up for the lost dynamism of the trans-Atlantic economies, is altering the geography of development. Consequently, investors around the world have been reassessing their investment strategies, forecasts regarding demand for energy, commodities, goods and services. Asia, says a recent report of the Asian Development Bank (ADB, 2011), "is in the midst of a truly historic transformation. If it continues to grow on its recent trajectory, it could, by 2050, account for more than half of global GDP, trade and investment, and enjoy widespread influence," returning the continent to the status it enjoyed 300 years ago. In the immediate future, however, sustaining global growth and ensuring stability of oil and commodity prices is critical both for global growth and for Asia's own growth.

The ADB lists demographic change, urbanisation, rise of a new middle class, reduced transportation costs, and the communications revolution as driving the shift of manufacturing and services, and consequently incomes, from the trans-Atlantic economies to, what the ADB (2011: 2) calls, "the seven engines of Asia's re-emergence", namely, China, India, Indonesia, Japan, Korea, Malaysia and Thailand. These economies will matter for more for the Gulf, as sources of demand for energy and supply of goods and services.

Asia's rising income share has already contributed to a rise in its share of world trade, investment and consumption. As observed by Anderson and Strutt (2011):

> Asia's share of global merchandise trade has doubled since 1973, to just over 30 per cent, with its exports growing at three times the rate for the rest of the world over the past decade; and the People's Republic of China is now the world's largest exporter (followed by Germany and the United States). In the 1960s barely one third of the trade of Asia and Australasia was with other countries in the region, whereas in recent years that share has been more than one half—with less than one quarter with North America and Western Europe (WTO, 2010).

Anderson and Strutt project a sharp increase in the share of Asian economies in world exports and imports over the next two decades (Table 10.4).

Various factors are driving these changing structures of global income and trade. The most important of these is the process of 'catch up' as poorer economies become more productive. A second factor is demography, with Asian population growth generating young people needed both within Asia and in other developed economies that are facing manpower shortages. Third, the shift of both manufacturing and low cost services to China, India and other Asian economies. Finally, as a consequence of all these factors, the two driving social tendencies of the early 21st century in Asia, namely, urbanisation and the rise of a middle class.

Rising per capita consumption in the world's most populous nations, China and India, is driving the rising demand for commodities, especially energy. This is the most important geo-economic phenomenon shaping new trade and investment relationships within Asia, between the 'newly industrialising economies' of East, South-east and South Asia and the energy rich regions of West Asia and Central Asia.[3]

Table 10.4

Shares of World Trade of All Goods and Services

Region	*Exports*		*Imports*	
	2004	*2030*	*2004*	*2030*
Western Europe	42.3	26.3	42.5	31.0
Eastern Europe	3.6	3.9	3.2	3.7
US & Canada	13.7	10.8	18.8	18.0
Australia & New Zealand	1.3	1.3	1.4	1.5
Japan	6.1	2.5	5.1	4.4
China	6.7	19.6	5.7	12.1
ASEAN	6.0	8.2	5.2	6.8
Rest of East Asia & Pacific	6.4	7.0	5.3	5.8
South Asia	1.4	4.4	1.7	3.9
Central Asia	0.4	0.6	0.4	0.5
Latin America	5.4	6.6	4.7	5.4
Middle East & Africa	6.8	8.8	5.8	7.1
High Income Economies	67.0	45.0	71.0	59.0
Developing Economies	33.0	55.0	29.0	41.0
Of which Asia	21.0	40.0	18.0	29.0
Total	100.0	100.0	100.0	100.0

Source: Anderson and Strutt (2011)

The so-called 'new silk road', presently a 'maritime' route linking West and Central Asia to East and South-east Asia through the Indian Ocean, and a precursor to greater 'South-South' trade and capital

3. ADB (2011: 23): "The emerging middle class will become a key driver of Asia's economic growth because of the demand for goods and services and because the middle class is the source of savings and entrepreneurship that drives new products and processes."

flows, is emerging as a major 'highway' of energy, investment, goods and services and people flows.[4] Says King (2011: 6):

> With the formation of new trade and capital market connections between the nations of Asia and the Southern hemisphere, South-South trade growth is about to become turbocharged... supported by rapid urbanisation, an infrastructure revolution and a fundamental change in the political and financial landscape.... With trade between Asia and Latin America set to rise ten-fold in the years ahead and southern capital flows heading ever-higher, we are witnessing the creation of a Southern Silk Road.

The shifting geo-economics of the 21st century is defined by these anticipated structural shifts in the world economy, as the centre of gravity of the global economy moves from the Atlantic to the Asian landmass, sweeping from West Asia to East Asia, across India and South-east Asia. The present chapter will examine the implications of this global shift for the Gulf, mainly the Arab states, and their relations with Asia, in general, and with China and India in particular.

The Gulf and Asia

Past

What does this geo-economic shift of income to Asia mean for West Asia in general and the Gulf in particular? To be sure, the transformation of the Gulf is very much a part of the 'rise of Asia' and there are bound to be economic, social and geo-political consequences of the unfolding transformation of the continent. More specifically, the 're-emergence' of China and India and the rise of the economies of East and South-east Asia have already altered the flow of energy out of the Gulf, the trade flows between the Gulf and Asia and the movement of capital and people between the regions. This rapidly developing transformation is reviving traditional, 'pre-colonial' links between the Gulf and Asia.

Historian Fernand Braudel (1984: 484) described the 'pre-colonial' economies of what he called the "Far East" thus:

> The Far East taken as a whole, consisted of the three gigantic world economies—Islam, overlooking the Indian Ocean from the Red Sea

4. King (2011).

> and the Persian Gulf, and controlling the endless chain of deserts stretching across Asia from Arabia to China; India, whose influence extended throughout the Indian Ocean, both East and West of Cape Comorin; and China, at once a great territorial power—striking deep into the heart of Asia—and a maritime force, controlling the seas and countries bordering the Pacific. And so it had been for many hundreds of years. The relationship between these huge areas was the result of a series of pendulum movements of greater or lesser strength, either side of the centrally positioned Indian sub-continent. The swing might benefit first the East then the West, redistributing functions, power and political or economic advance. Through all these vicissitudes, however, India maintained her central position—her merchants in Gujarat and on the Malabar or Coromandel coasts prevailed for centuries on end against their many competitors—the Arab traders of the Red Sea, the Persian merchants of the Gulf or the Chinese merchants familiar with the Indonesian seas.

The enduring links of Arab traders to the economics of pre-colonial Indian Ocean and Arabian Sea trade, and their links to the Indian sub-continent and beyond, reaching deep into East and South-east Asia, disrupted by the violent entry of the Portuguese into these waters, is well documented by economic historians.[5] In the 20th century the Gulf was drawn into geo-political and geo-economic equations revolving around the trans-Atlantic powers, with a bulk of the demand for oil coming from industrial economies of the West and a bulk of oil surpluses invested in US and European currencies in western banks and financial institutions. Japan was the first Asian industrial economy to build links with the Gulf region, given its growing demand for oil through the 20th century. She was followed by the 'Asian Tigers' (Korea, Taiwan, Hong Kong and Singapore) as they industrialised and urbanised. The more recent engagement of China with the Gulf follows a familiar pattern set by Asia's industrialising economies.

Present

Since oil has fuelled the engines of growth in the industrial era, the Gulf has mirrored all the structural changes in the global

---

5. See McPherson (1993), Arasaratnam (1994), Furber (2004) and Chakravarti (2001).

economy in the industrial and post-industrial era. The Gulf has been at the epicentre of geo-political and geo-economic changes in the 20th century, and will continue to be so for the foreseeable future. In its relations with the rest of Asia, the Gulf has distinct histories and politics linking it to the five major regions of Asia, namely, West Asia, South Asia, Central Asia, East Asia and South-east Asia.

While the politics of the Muslim world defines the Gulf's equations with its West Asian neighbours, the interaction with Central Asian 'stans' is limited, both in political and economic terms. The Gulf's larger economic links have been, and will continue to be, with the 'NICs' (newly industrialising economies) of South, South-east and East Asia, re-discovering the Arab world's maritime links to Asia and shaping the geo-politics and geo-economics of a rising Asia.

In its immediate West Asian neighbourhood, the most important geo-political factor that marked a turning point for the Gulf states towards the end of the last century was the end of the Cold War. The power balance in the region altered with the collapse of the Soviet Union. After a phase of intense regional rivalry between Iran and Iraq and heightened tension over Israel, new political equations, including the spread of social unrest are altering the region's relations within itself and with the outside world. The global war against terrorism and extremism has also impacted on the region and its relations with both the West and the rest of Asia.

In the East, South and South-east region the more important factor that has shaped the relationship with the Gulf, has been the rise of the NICs. To begin with Japan and South Korea, subsequently other 'Asian Tigers', namely Hong Kong, Singapore and Taiwan, followed by Malaysia and Indonesia, and more recently China and India, which are both overtaking South-east Asia in terms of energy demand and wider economic links with the Gulf.

The extant economic links between the Gulf and Asia revolve around: a) energy; b) migration and remittances; c) capital flows; d) trade (food, consumer goods and services); and e) education and tourism.

Over the past two decades China and India and other South-east Asian economies have increased their share of Gulf energy. Most assessments of demand for oil point to the growing importance of the Asian market, which is expected to grow at the average rate of close to 4.0 per cent per annum over the next decade.[6] Alterman and Garver (2008) believe that:

> China and India represent the single most important drivers for future energy demand growth in the world. With a combined population of 2.5 billion and expected average growth rates to be the highest in the world through 2030, it should come as no surprise that "Chindia" will account for more than a quarter of world energy consumption by 2030 (28%, according to the U.S. Energy Information Administration). In contrast, the U.S. share of world energy consumption will fall from about 21 per cent in 2006 to 17 percent in 2030.

But it is not energy alone that has shaped the Gulf's relations with Asia to its east. Equally important, from the point of view of the Gulf states, have been the flow of migrant labour, that have fuelled the construction boom and manned the services sectors of the region, and, the opportunities offered in Asia for long-term investment of Gulf oil surpluses.

Beginning with the post-1974 oil shock boom the Gulf attracted large numbers of labour migrants from South and South-east Asia, with such labour accounting for 90 per cent of all private sector jobs in the Gulf Cooperation Council (GCC) region (Martin, 2008: 13). Pradhan (2010: 78) estimates that in 2010 around 6.5 million South Asians lived in the GCC countries:

> Making them the single largest expatriate community (17% of the total resident population). The South Asian expatriate community could be categorised into four broad groups, *viz.*, (a) unskilled workers, employed in construction companies, municipalities, agricultural farms and as domestic workers; (b) skilled and semi-skilled workers; (c) professionals, such as doctors, engineers, accountants, employed in government and private sectors; and (d) businessmen.

The other side of the coin of Asian migration to the Gulf is the vital role of Gulf remittances for BoP (balance of payments)

---

6. Cordesmann(2002).

management by developing countries in Asia. India's central bank, the Reserve Bank of India (RBI), has estimated the rising importance of the GCC countries in inward foreign exchange remittances to India, with the GCC overtaking the US as the most important source in 2007 (Table 10.5). While total foreign remittances may constitute a relatively small per cent of the GDP of large countries like India (4%) and China (1%), these could constitute important source of foreign exchange for smaller Asian economies like Philippines and Bangladesh.

Table 10.5

Region-wise Distribution of Private Transfers Inflows to India

(US$ million)								
Period	*Gulf Countries*	*North America*	*South America*	*Europe*	*Africa*	*East Asia*	*Others*	*Total*
2006-07	9,012	10,022	1,264	5,239	690	1,749	2,859	30,835
2007-08	12,670	14,242	1,800	7,357	971	2,488	3,979	43,508
2008-09	14,430	13,790	1,891	9,163	1,503	1,952	4,174	46,903
2008 (Apr-Sept)	8,079	7,832	1,080	5,137	851	1,106	2,287	26,371
2009 (Apr-Sep)	8,428	8,174	1,127	5,359	888	1,154	2,384	27,515

Source: RBI, 2010.

Next to energy and remittances, the third most important economic link between Asia and the Gulf is the outward investment from the Gulf, especially in infrastructure and services sector. Gulf-based SWFs (sovereign wealth funds) have become major funding sources for long-term investment in roads, housing, other construction, telecommunications, hotels and the financial sector in several Asian economies. While the size of Gulf-based SWFs would be a function of the price of oil and the nature of domestic demand for investment, GCC SWFs have acquired considerable importance as sources of investment in many Asian economies. Since few GCC SWFs insist on managerial control of their overseas assets, mainly due to non-availability of home country talent, they often constitute an attractive source of 'passive' investment for several Asian companies in search of funds but unwilling to give up ownership control.[7] While SWFs are likely to be risk averse in the immediate future, due to persistent global uncertainties, this may not impact as much on investments into Asia. One recent study makes the point that GCC investors are likely to reduce their exposure to the US, where they have had high investments, and increase their exposure to Asian economies.[8]

GCC foreign assets are estimated to have exceeded $900 billion in the five years ending June 2008, with US-based assets (equities, debt and deposits) accounting for more than one-third of Gulf investment. But an estimated $60 billion worth of GCC investment went into Asia, and that is likely to increase.[9]

Asia's 'demand' from the Gulf region is for energy, employment and remittances and investment, on the other hand, Asia 'supplies' labour, food and technology to Gulf states.

The GCC countries import 80 per cent of their food requirements and food imports have increased sharply in recent years, rising from US$17 billion in 2006 to $24 billion in 2008, and expected to rise to $48 billion by 2020.[10] While Latin America is the most important source of food imports into the GCC region, Africa and Asia are also important sources of food. South Asia is an important source of basmati rice, sugar, wheat and poultry.[11] Asia is expected to become an increasingly important source of import of consumer goods, with East and South-east Asia being a major source of manufactured goods.

Trade, in energy, manufactured goods and food, migration of labour, and capital flows have increasingly brought the Gulf closer to Asia's emerging and 're-emerging' economies and powers. This engagement is bound to grow as both Asian giants continue to grow and matter for more.

7. EIU (2009).
8. Pradhan (2010).
9. Pradhan (2010: 75). Also see EIU (2009).
10. EIU (2009: 3).
11. Pradhan (2010).

China, India and Indonesia account for more than half of GCC's trade with Asia.[12] However, other Asian economies, especially Japan, Republic of Korea and the ASEAN member countries will also matter for more as Gulf's economic partners.[13] The 'seven engines of Asian re-emergence', as the ADB put it in its study of Asia 2050, namely China, India, Indonesia, Japan, South Korea, Malaysia and Thailand will be increasingly important markets for Gulf energy and other exports, and investment, as well as source of imports and labour. Asia's urban population is expected to double by 2050, from 1.65 billion to 3.25 billion, creating a huge market for energy and services.[14]

Future

The 'newly industrialising economies' of South-East Asia, followed by China and then India have fundamentally altered the Gulf's balance of economic interest in favour of Asia, establishing new B2B (business-to-business) and G2G (government-to-government) relations between the two regions of Asia. The new Asian demand for energy and capital is balanced, as it were, by Gulf's own demand for labour and services, reviving traditional 'P2P' (people-to-people) links between the Gulf and the Indian sub-continent in particular.

There are four dimensions to the growing relationship—trade (in energy, manufactured goods and food); investment & finance (including the growing interest of Gulf-based sovereign wealth funds in Asian equities and of Chinese funds in Gulf equities), and insurance and retail banking; movement of natural persons (skilled and unskilled labour, professionals and managers and tourists); and, the services sector (including aviation, maritime, hotels, retail trade and telecommuniation).

The most obvious emerging link between the Gulf and Asia is through the latter's rising consumption of energy. Asia, mainly East, South and South-east, accounted for 20 per cent of world's energy

12. EIU (2011).

13. ADB, 2011.

14. Ibid.: 4.

consumption in 2000, and is forecast to double its share to 40 per cent by 2050, with 90 per cent of this being imported.[15] This rising dependence on imported energy will impact on regional security and the security of energy supplies. According to the Economist Intelligence Unit (2011: 4):

> Asia will be the most important emerging-market region for the GCC. This is partly a story about rising demand for oil: we forecast that oil consumption in Asia will grow by 4.4% per year on average over the next five years, while the OECD's demand is expected to plateau. But it is not just an energy story. Growth in China and India is now moving into a new phase, from being focused on exports to a greater focus on domestic demand. Rising consumption in Asia, fuelled partly by an expanding middle class, will produce a host of new opportunities for trade. Tourism, one of the GCC's competitive strengths, is already benefiting from the growing Chinese middle class. Most of our interviewees expressed certainty that China would be the GCC's most important economic partner by 2020, although India's historical and cultural links with the region will also stand it in good stead. Nonetheless, South Korea, Singapore, Malaysia and India will remain important as providers of technology and know-how for the GCC states.

The structural shift in the world economy, that we have referred to earlier (Section I), is expected to further accentuate in coming decades with China and India together accounting for at least a quarter of world GDP by 2030. To be sure, the US and Europe, as well as Japan and other East Asian economies, will remain important markets for Gulf energy. While their share in world demand can be expected to decline, both on account of a decline in their share of world GDP as well as their concerted effort to switch to new and renewable sources of energy, they will still continue to remain important markets for Gulf energy. Further, the Gulf's relations with Africa and Latin America will also require attention as the region becomes more dependent on them for food and other natural resources.

This means, even as China and India emerge as important markets, perhaps even as the more important markets for Gulf

15. ADB, 2011: 71.

energy, the economies of the West and the South will continue to remain important partners for the Gulf. This will entail a 'rebalancing' of the Gulf's relations with the West and Asia, rather than a 'shift' in the Gulf's focus away from the West to the East. While neither China nor India are anywhere near the US and Europe in terms of strategic influence and reach in the region, they may be expected to devote more resources in this direction, given their growing dependence on the Gulf for energy.

By the end of 2010, China's accumulated direct investment in the 22 member countries of the League of Arab States was estimated to have touched US$ 15 billion. This included non-financial investment worth US$ 4.2 billion. China's total contracted projects in the region, an important means by which China has engaged its partners given the size and competitiveness of its construction industry, were valued at US$ 116.9 billion, while Chinese FDI (foreign direct investment) has been mainly focused on the energy, light industry, textiles, automobile and chemical sectors. China has a large volume of investment in energy in Sudan, Egypt and Algeria. For their part, Arab nations have also invested heavily in China, with total investment estimated to be US$ 2.15 billion in mid-2010, mainly in real estate, chemical and food sectors. The Arab League nations are the eighth-largest trading partner for China. In 2010, Sino-Arab trade reached US$150 billion.[16] Trade stood at US$ 107.4 billion in 2009[17] and US$ 132.8 billion in 2008.[18] This compares with a trade level of US$ 5.8 billion in 1996.[19]

India too is an increasingly important trade partner for the Gulf, with its trade (exports plus imports) with West Asian and North African (WANA) economies estimated to be US$120.7 billion in 2009-10, with crude oil accounting for a large part of the trade. While exports to WANA markets accounted for 22 per cent of total Indian exports, imports from WANA was estimated to be 28 per cent of

16. *http://www.chinadaily.com.cn/business/2011-04/09/content_12297375.htm*
17. *http://english.peopledaily.com.cn/90001/90778/90861/7153067.html*
18. *http://www.gov.cn/english/2010-09/26/content_1709995.htm*
19. *http://www.chinadaily.com.cn/china/2010-09/26/content_11350326.htm*

total Indian imports. Interestingly, the Government of India's official *Economic Survey 2010-11* reported earlier this year that the United Arab Emirates had overtaken the US and China to become India's number one trading partner in 2009 (Government of India, 2011: 169):

> The UAE has displaced the USA as the topmost destination of India's exports in 2008-09 and 2009-10 with an export share of 13.2 per cent and 13.4 per cent respectively.

The share of India-UAE total trade in India's total trade was 9.3 per cent in 2009-10, compared to a share of 9.1 per cent for China and 7.8 per cent for the US. India's fourth largest trade partner was Saudi Arabia with a share of 4.5 per cent. Taken together the WANA countries had a larger share of India's total trade than the European Union (See Table 10.6).

Apart from merchandise trade, services sector trade has become increasingly important for India. In 2008-09, prior to the trans-Atlantic financial crisis, services exports reached a peak of US$ 106 billion, declining to US$ 95.8 billion in 2009-10. Next to software services, mainly aimed at the US and other Anglo-saxon markets, services exports to West Asia remain an important part of India's total services exports.

Both China and India will continue to increase their trade with WANA as they consume more energy and other resources, and as the WANA region seeks more manufactured goods, food and labour services. Analysts talk about a "new silk road" connecting China to the Gulf and beyond (King, 2011). While this would be a land-based 'road' link for China, and hence the importance of closer relations between China's western provinces and the Muslim world, for India the 'new silk route' would be a maritime route, linking the Gulf to India across the Arabian Sea.

The maritime link is important for China too, given its dependence on world trade and the import of crude oil by sea. China has the largest number of container ports in the world (Table 10.7) and it will remain a sea-oriented economy, placing great emphasis on sea power and the safety of sea lanes of communication rather than depend only on land-based links to West Asia and the Gulf.

Table 10.6

Shares of India's Major Trade Partners in India's Total Trade, 2009-10

Country	*Percentage Share*
UAE	9.3
China	9.1
USA	7.8
Saudi Arabia	4.5
Germany	3.4
Singapore	3.0
Iran	2.9
Hong Kong	2.7
South Korea	2.6
Indonesia	2.5
UK	2.3
Japan	2.2
World Total	100

Source: GoI, 2011: 169.

Apart from energy and economics, there is a political dimension to the relations of both China and India, and indeed some ASEAN countries, with West and Central Asia. This is related to the Islamic dimension to both China and India's relations with West Asia. Saudi Arabia's pivotal role in the Islamic world adds a dimension to its bilateral relations with the Muslim world that countries with a majority Muslim population or even a large Muslim minority (as in India), or a strategically located minority (as in China) cannot ignore.

It is not surprising that China pays special attention to the relations between its far west Muslim regions and the Gulf. The development of a *halal* meat exporting industry and the launch of a China- Arab States Economics and Trade Forum, which had its second meeting in September 2011 and has a special focus on China's food exports to Arab markets, is an indicator of the importance of this relationship.[20] The growing importance of trade between China and the Gulf also mirrors increasing political engagement between China's

20. Official website of this forum (*http://www.cas-expo.org/atf/it/default.htm)*

Muslim provinces, the Ningxia Hui Autonomous Region in this case, and the Islamic world. Emile Hokayem (2011: 41) notes that:

> The fate of the Muslim Uighur community in China has received Arab media attention during the Xinjiang unrest of 2009 in which Beijing countered through quiet outreach to Arab Gulf leaders.

Table 10.7

World's Largest Container Ports

Port	*1989 mTEU*	*Port*	*2009 mTEU*
Hong Kong	4.5	Singapore	25.8
Singapore	4.4	Shanghai	25.0
Rotterdam	3.9	Hong Kong	20.9
Kaohsiung (Taiwan)	3.4	Shenzen (China)	18.2
Kobe (Japan)	2.5	Busan (S Korea)	11.9
Busan (S.Korea)	2.2	Guangzhou (China)	11.2
Los Angeles	2.1	Dubai (UAE)	11.1
New York/New Jersey	2.0	Ningbo (China)	10.5
Keelung (Taiwan)	1.8	Qingdao (China)	10.2
Hamburg	1.7	Rotterdam	9.7
Long Beach USA	1.5	Tianjin (China)	8.7
Yokohama Japan	1.5	Kaohsiung (Taiwan)	8.5

Note: mTEU= Million twenty-foot equivalent units.
Source: Containerisation International, The Economist.

Thus, China's growing political relationship with West Asia has come to be widely commented upon.[21] India has had a long standing relationship with countries of the region, including the Arab States and Iran. Iran occupies an important share of the political mind space of the Indian sub-continent, apart from being a source of energy and a land bridge for India into Central Asia. With Asia's rising demand for energy and the growing B2B and P2P relations between the Gulf and Asia, the strategic dimension will gain salience too. As Molavi (2011: 53) concludes,

> This West Asia-East Asia economic corridor will not only shape the future of both regions, but can strengthen regional stability, and

21. Wakefield and Levenstein (2011).

> contribute to global growth. In much the same way that the Old Silk Road converged culture and commerce, this New Silk Road has brought West and East Asia closer together, drawing a new commercial geography of the Middle East and Asia.

The new 'commercial geography' and the emerging 'geo-economics' will, without doubt, shape the new geo-politics of Asia. The Gulf will look both East and West in search of both markets and security and stability. The region's 'western' orientation of the 20th century will give way to a more balanced East-West orientation.

Gulf Regional and Maritime Security: Role of Asian Powers

The 'rising' powers of mainland Asia—China and India—that are focused on their own economic development, while remaining cognizant of the special profile of the region for their Muslim minorities, will adopt increasingly 'pragmatic' policies with respect to their relations with the Gulf.[22] This should suit the region that is presently undergoing an internal transition as well. Asia's rising powers would seem to be willing to work with western powers to seek and preserve stability and security in the Gulf, even if their relations with Israel and Iran will throw up problems from time to time.[23]

"China's Gulf policy" says Wu Bing Bing (2011: 10-11 & 13), "is subordinate to its overall foreign strategy. Before China embarked on reforms to open up its economy in 1979, China's Gulf policy shifted from an ideological orientation to pragmatism. Before that, however, ideology and geopolitical interest both played a role in Beijing's calculations...... China's economic, trade, and energy interests became more and more prominent in the Gulf region, while ideological interests were abandoned".

Alterman (2008: 34) expresses the hope that,

> To a great extent, Middle Eastern countries continue to look westward. The United States remains the most powerful and most agile fighting force in the region, and it brings potent tools to the table in governments' struggle against both international and

22. For a discussion of Asia's response to the rise of China and India see Tellis et al. (2011).
23. See Bingbing (2011)

> domestic terrorism. U.S. technology in everything from weaponry to software to oil recovery is the best in the world, and U.S. organisational practice—in business, government, and the military—is a consistent force multiplier in addressing problems.

To be sure, the US will continue to enjoy unparalleled influence in the Gulf also because China is unlikely to challenge it, even as it may seek to subvert US interests, and India would be quite happy to work with the US, even if India's own independent relations with Iran and the Gulf at times require her to adopt positions at variance with the US.

India's long-standing and wide-ranging relations with the Gulf states have now acquired a wider Indian Ocean dimension, with concerns about terrorism, sea piracy and the safety and security of energy supplies. India's maritime presence in the waters around the Gulf will increase, but India would be prepared to work with existing western powers, regional powers and China to ensure the security and stability of the region and of energy supplies from it.

While potential US-China and China-India rivalry in the Gulf cannot be ruled out, as Rajamohan (2009) suggests, it is not inevitable. Rajamohan (2009: 61) observes:

> China's own engagement with the region has gone beyond the supply of missiles and other advanced military technologies to select nations in the Gulf. The very same interests that drive Indian policy in the region—resource security and protection of sea-lanes—are encouraging China to raise its profile in the Gulf and the Indian Ocean. As it becomes the second largest economy in the world, China is determined to secure the supply of energy, and mineral and agricultural resources of the region. At the same time, the Gulf and Indian Ocean littoral states are beginning to see that the rise of Asia is offering a valuable alternative to their traditional dependence on the West for economic assistance and military support. This has created an entirely new context for thinking about the balance of power throughout the entire region. Implied in the rise of Asia is also a rivalry between India and China for political and economic influence in the region.

The changing shares of the trans-Atlantic industrial economies and the newly industrialising economies of Asia in world output and energy consumption, and the consequent 'power shift' from the West to the East, need not destabilise the Gulf region as long as all concerned—traditional powers, regional powers and rising powers—seek to ensure the stability and security of energy supplies. A cooperative security framework for the region can serve the interests of all, given everyone's stake in energy security. Equally, both the trans-Atlantic powers and Asia's rising powers have a shared stake in the political stability of the Gulf region and the growth of a liberal and plural social and political order in the region as a whole. The countries of the Gulf region and Western and Asian powers also have a shared stake in winning the war against extremism and terrorism.

Hence, the security implications of the strategic shift underway and the geo-political implications of the geo-economic changes in Asia need not be dramatic or unexpected. It is possible for the Gulf region to be stable and secure as long as the West (US) and Asia (China and India) are able to work together in the region and ensure that the Gulf remains a reliable source of energy, a growing and open economy, and a stable and plural polity that can manage the rise of political Islam.

References

Anderon, Kym and Anna Strutt (2011). "Asia's Changing Role in World Trade: Prospects for South-South Trade Growth to 2030", *Working Paper* No. 264, July. Asian Development Bank. Accessed at: *http://www.adb.org/Documents/Working-Papers/2011/Economics-WP264.pdf*

Alterman, Jon B. and John W. Garver (2008). *The Eternal Triangle: China, The United States and the Middle East*. Washington DC: Center for Strategic and International Studies.

Arasaratnam, Sinnappah (1994). *Maritime India in the Seventeenth Century*. New Delhi: Oxford University Press.

Asian Development Bank (2011). *ASIA 2050: Realizing the Asian Century*. Manila.

Baru, Sanjaya (2009). "India: Rising Through The Slowdown" in Ashley Tellis, Andrew Marble, Travis Tanner (ed.), *Strategic Asia 2009-10: Economic Meltdown and Geopolitical Stability*.Washington DC: National Bureau of Asian Research.

Braudel, Fernand (1984). *Civilisation and Capitalism, 15th- 18th Century. Volume 3: The Perspective of the World*. Collins/Fontana.

Bingbing, Wu (2011) "Strategy and Politics in the Gulf as seen from China", in Bruce Wakefield and Susan L. Levenstein, *China and the Persian Gulf: Implications for the United States*. Washington DC: Woodrow Wilson International Centre for Scholars.

Chakravarti, Ranabir (2001). *Trade in Early India*. New Delhi: Oxford University Press.

Cordesmann, Anthony (2002). *Geopolitics and Energy: Key Trends 2000-2020*. Washington DC: Centre for Strategic and International Studies. July.

Economist Intelligence Unit (EIU) (2011). *GCC Trade and Investment Flows: The Emerging-Market Surge*. London.

———. (2009). *The GCC in 2020: Outlook for the Gulf and the Global Economy*. Accessed at: *http://graphics.eiu.com/marketing/pdf/Gulf2020.pdf*

Furber, Holden (2004). *Rival Empires of Trade in the Orient, 1600-1800*. New Delhi: Oxford University Press.

Government of India (2011). *Economic Survey 2010-11*. New Delhi: Ministry of Finance.

Hokayem, Emile (2011). "Looking East: A Gulf Vision of Reality" in Bruce Wakefield and Susan L. Levenstein (ed.), *China and the Persian Gulf: Implications for the United States*. Washington DC: Woodrow Wilson International Centre for Scholars. p.41

International Monetary Fund (2011). *World Economic Outlook*. September.

King, Stephen (2011). *The Southern Silk Road. London: HSBC*. June. Accessed at: *http://www.research.hsbc.com/midas/Res/RDV?p=pdf&key=WZnyWSIf38&n=299714.PDF*

Maddison, Angus (2007). *The World Economy* (Vols 1 & 2). Paris: OECD (2006) and New Delhi: Academic Foundation.

Martin, Philip (2008). "Another Miracle? Managing Labour Migration in Asia", *Monograph* UN/POP/EGM-MIG/2008/1. United Nations Economic and Social Commission for Asia and the Pacific. September.

McPherson, Kenneth (1993). *The Indian Ocean: A History of People and the Sea*. New Delhi: Oxford University Press.

Molavi, Afshan (2011). "The New Silk Road, "CHINDIA," and the Geo-economic ties that bind the Middle East and Asia", in Bruce Wakefield and Susan L. Levenstein (ed.), *China and the Persian Gulf: Implications for the United States*. Washington DC: Woodrow Wilson International Centre for Scholars. p53.

Pradhan, Samir (2010). *Gulf-South Asia Economic Relations: Realities and Prospects*. Dubai: Gulf Research Centre.

Rajamohan (2009). "India's Strategic Challenges in the Indian Ocean and the Gulf", in Abdulaziz Sager and Geoffrey Kemp (ed.), *India's Growing Role in the Gulf: Implications for the Region and the United States*. Dubai: Gulf Research Centre & Washington DC: The Nixon Centre. p.61.

Reserve Bank of India (n.d.).*Remittances from Overseas Indians: Modes of Transfer, Transaction Cost and Time Taken*. Accessed at: *http://www.rbi.org.in/scripts/BS_ViewBulletin.aspx?Id= 11116*

Sager, Abdulazizand Geoffrey Kemp (ed.) (2009).*India's Growing Role in the Gulf: Implications for the Region and the United States*. Dubai: Gulf Research Centre& Washington DC: The Nixon Centre.

Subramaniam, Arvind (2011). *Eclipse: Living in the Shadow of China's Economic Dominance*. Washington DC: Peterson Institute of International Economics.

Tellis, Ashley, Andrew Marble, Travis Tanner (ed.) (2009). *Strategic Asia 2009-10: Economic Meltdown and Geopolitical Stability*. Washington DC: National Bureau of Asian Research.

Tellis, A., T. Tanner and J. Keough (ed.) (2011). *Strategic Asia 2011-12: Asia Responds to its Rising Powers*. Washington DC: National Bureau of Asian Research.

UNCTAD (2011). *Trade and Development Report 2011*. Geneva. p.2

Wakefield, Bruce and Susan L. Levenstein (ed.) (2011). *China and the Persian Gulf: Implications for the United States*. Washington DC: Woodrow Wilson International Centre for Scholars.